# Unpaid

# Unpaid

## *The Past, Present, and Future of Wage Theft*

Matthew Cole

London • New York

First published by Verso 2026




The manufacturer's authorized representative in the EU for product safety (GPSR)
is LOGOS EUROPE, 9 rue Nicolas Poussin, 17000, La Rochelle, France
contact@logoseurope.eu



1 3 5 7 9 10 8 6 4 2

**Verso**
UK: 6 Meard Street, London W1F 0EG
US: 207 East 32nd Street, New York, NY 10016
versobooks.com

Verso is the imprint of New Left Books

ISBN-13: 978-1-80429-566-3
ISBN-13: 978-1-80429-567-0 (UK EBK)
ISBN-13: 978-1-80429-568-7 (US EBK)

**British Library Cataloguing in Publication Data**
A catalogue record for this book is available from the British Library

**Library of Congress Cataloging-in-Publication Data**
A catalog record for this book is available from the Library of Congress

Typeset in Fournier by MJ & N Gavan, Truro, Cornwall
Printed in the UK by CPI Group (UK) Ltd, Croydon CR0 4YY

*For Salome*

# Contents

*Do they owe us a living? Of course they fucking do!*

– Crass, 1979

# Preface

This book was born from experience. Like many people, I have worked all kinds of jobs – freezing my fingers off delivering newspapers at twelve years old, washing dishes and cooking in restaurants, planting flowers as a gardener, tossing trash in the truck as a bin collector, topping cans in a grease factory, bussing tables, taking my life in my hands as a cycle courier in New York City, pouring cocktails at a bar, and making pretentious coffee in cafés throughout my twenties. In all these low-wage jobs, I experienced some form of wage theft. Even while finishing my PhD, I worked in a café that didn't pay me for months after they 'unhired' (their term) me.

I wrote this book for my younger self and for anyone else like me, who wants to understand how the origins of capitalist waged-labour structure the present and future of work. The book shows, with theoretical rigour and empirical detail, how workers are compelled to produce more than they receive and why this is unjust. From these insights, it also builds the case for our collective right to expropriate private property from the expropriators. This book is not simply about wage theft; it is about the nature of property itself.

There is obviously a political imperative to writing such a book; how you theorize the problem will impact what the possible solutions could be. And the solutions that are out there right now are clouded by liberal mythologies of labour and capitalism. It would be easy to simply dismiss these solutions as naïve, and many are. Yet, the liberal tradition is a modern one, born of the Enlightenment, which cast aside the old ways of doing things. We must understand how it developed as a justification for a certain set of power relations: to defend property and the interests of its individual owners. Understanding this system enables us to upend it, to stand the tradition on its head.

A critical interrogation of capitalism will reveal that capital tends to follow the path of least resistance. Concerning labour, this path generally leads first to the people who are the most exploitable – migrants, the poor, and racialized outsiders – and second to the places in which there are the weakest regulations. If there is ever a way to extract just a little bit of extra labour, by legal means or otherwise, capitalism will find it. This is not the exception but the rule. Yet this is not a grand conspiracy against humanity, conjured by some malevolent cabal secretly controlling the world. It is simply, as my friend Søren Mau puts it, the mute compulsion of capitalist competition, which prioritizes private profit over social need. This inversion of values undermines our collective right to the products of our labour, a right that we must enforce in order to live a dignified and free life. In the face of the growing existential threat from a technologically driven climate dystopia, it's socialism or extinction.

# Introduction: A Fair Day's Wage

There are as many ways to steal wages as there are to earn them. Sometimes it is a few minutes a day or a few hours a week of unpaid labour-time. Other times it is months of work amounting to thousands of pounds, dollars, or yuan, perhaps under conditions that look like modern slavery. Wage theft typically refers to a formal legal category covering unlawful deductions from wages, pay below the minimum wage, and other labour market violations. Yet if employers would just follow the law, then surely fairness would prevail? It is not that simple. Juridical institutions obscure fundamental injustices at the heart of capitalism – that the rules of the game are rigged in favour of employers. 'This is a very peculiar sort of fairness,' as Friedrich Engels wrote in 1881 for *The Labour Standard*, a union newspaper:

> the workman gives to the Capitalist his full day's working power; that is, so much of it as he can give without rendering impossible the continuous repetition of the transaction. In exchange he receives just as much, and no more, of the necessaries of life as is required to keep up the repetition of the same bargain every day. The workman gives as much, the Capitalist gives as little, as the nature of the bargain will admit.[1]

What is a fair day's wage and what is a fair day's work? If, according to market logic, wages and work are fixed by competition, fairness would require that both labour and capital meet on equal terms. But that was not the case in the nineteenth century and it is certainly not the case today. Bargaining power drastically favours capital over labour, with the former wielding threats to the state and international trade agreements as weapons to ensure its domination. To understand how and why the wage and its theft are foundational to capitalism's injustices requires zooming in to the microeconomics of the firm.

At a Marriott hotel in Luton, UK, a room-attendant is supposed to earn the minimum wage. Low wages ensure low liabilities, a strategy to protect shareholder returns rather than cover the cost of workers' food, rent, and transport, let alone childcare. The division of labour linking front-desk clerks, maintenance staff, night auditors, and housekeeping staff ensures that guests are checked in, hundreds of rooms are cleaned, room service is delivered, and pipes are clear. After costs, the UK branch of Marriot Hotels Limited made £8.2 million in gross profit in 2019, profit that simply flows upwards from the labour of these workers to management and shareholders. That year the multinational parent company Marriot International Inc. took $3.8 billion in gross fee revenue and returned a total of $2.9 billion to shareholders during the year.[2]

This surplus is not a magic mark-up, buying cheap and selling dear; it is the difference between what the staff produce and what they are paid. Were that surplus accumulated as investment for workers, the hotel company could trim shifts, lift hourly pay, or even distribute equity shares without changing room rates. But Marriott competes with Hilton, Accor, and others for market share and profit. In 2018 a UK government audit found that Marriot Hotels underpaid 279 workers £71,722 through unlawful deductions that lowered wages below the statutory minimum.[3] Capitalist imperatives incentivize the opposite of fair wages for fair work. Competition continually drives employers to gain an 'extra cut' of unpaid labour, as Karl Marx first pointed out nearly two centuries ago.[4] This is why wage theft is not a bug, but a feature of the capitalist system.

In the UK, over 5 million workers put in a total of 2 billion unpaid hours: £35 billion of free labour annually.[5] From 2017 to 2024, 45,781 claims were lodged with HM Courts and Tribunals Service for 'unauthorised deductions from wages' and 29,886 additional claims were made under the Working Time Regulations, mostly around unpaid holiday.[6] The success of these claims depends on the strength of the legal resources deployed by the representatives of labour versus capital. Yet out of more than 4,800 firms fined by the government since 2016, just 109 have actually paid. The state has recovered only £95,000 out of £9.6 million in fines or less than 1 per cent.[7] Prevention is also a non-starter. A UK employer can expect an inspection from His Majesty's Revenue and Customs (HMRC) once every 250 years and a prosecution once in a million years. Compared with thirty-three other OECD countries, the UK ranks twenty-seventh in terms of labour protections. There are a meagre 0.29 labour market inspectors per 10,000 workers. This number would need to more than triple just to meet the International Labour Organization (ILO) minimum standard.[8]

The situation is, if anything, worse in the United States. For example, from 2010 to 2012, a federal review indicated that nearly 84 per cent of approximately 9,000 full-service restaurants had committed wage and hour violations.[9] A report by the Economic Policy Institute estimates the total amount of wage theft across the economy to be as much as $50 billion a year.[10] It is impossible to arrive at a definitive figure, since most wage theft is not tracked and goes unreported. Such estimates also don't include the 1.9 million people held in state and federal prisons, two-thirds of whom are coerced to work under threat of solitary confinement or other violent punishments.[11] These incarcerated workers produce over $2 billion annually in goods for private companies and $9 billion in services for prison upkeep. Most earn literally pennies per hour, while seven states pay nothing at all. Even the most dangerous carceral jobs, such as firefighting in California, pay just $1 per hour.[12]

Meanwhile, despite its Marxist–Leninist origins, the Communist Party of China has seen a resurgence of wage theft in the country since the end of the Maoist era. In 2023 alone, the Ministry of Justice logged 480,000 legal-aid cases for migrant workers (more than 1,300 a day) recovering 6.8 billion yuan in back pay for 540,000 people.[13] While the scale of recovery is laudable, it is also an admission that wage theft is endemic. Subcontractors in industries from construction to logistics and delivery exploit legal loopholes, such as changing their business name and filings, to evade wage theft claims; they pay workers in cash without proper records; they misclassify workers; and sometimes, they simply refuse to pay. Even in a so-called 'workers' state, a fair day's wage for a fair day's work proves elusive.

The emergence of strong trade unions and collective bargaining during the twentieth century was a necessary counter-power to capital that limited wage theft. Union members are three times more likely to pursue a case to recover lost wages.[14] Yet, since the late 1970s, labour protections and trade union power have been undermined through successive waves of neoliberal reforms across the West, particularly in the US and UK. Penalties for labour violations are so low they effectively incentivize wage theft as a cost of doing business. Most workers have seen the unpaid portion of the working day rise and the paid portion fall. From 1975 to 2012, labour share of income consistently fell in most OECD countries, including the US, Japan, China, and Germany.[15] It has continued to fall into the 2020s, as wage theft and other attacks on workers' rights have increased.

In most countries, labour laws typically contain a range of provisions that specify what activities are counted as paid working time, the minimum pay floor, what conditions are deemed safe for work, and other rights and protections workers have vis-à-vis their employers. In the UK, things such as travel time between jobs, waiting time, overtime, and so on are part of the working day and must be paid at the normal wage rate. Workers have statutory entitlements to paid sick leave, annual leave for holidays, and maternity leave. Not paying workers for these activities constitutes 'unlawful deductions' or 'wage theft' in common parlance. Yet, from the birth of industrial capitalism itself, employers have attempted to avoid paying workers their due, calculating 'upon the chance of not being found out' and finding 'that if they should be detected there will still be a considerable balance of gain'.[16] After all, if something is punishable by a fine, that means it is legal for a price.

Still, evading labour obligations through legal loopholes remains preferable for most firms compared to the risks of litigation. A popular method of evasion entails classifying workers as 'independent' or 'self-employed', which exempts them from employment protections and places liability on them for risks and expenses. Digital labour platforms have normalized such practices. They require workers to use their own means of production – their car when working for Uber, bicycle when working for Deliveroo, computer when working for cloud companies – and shoulder the associated costs. Some platforms have litigated that self-employed workers attempting to unionize constituted a 'cartel', even though this is at odds with United Nations and ILO conventions. In Global South countries, platform promissory notes trap workers in a form of debt-bonded servitude, since they are legally transferable from one employer to the next. In Egypt, for example, food delivery platform workers are made liable for both the price of the order and the delivery fee (up to 25 per cent of the total) when they accept the job. It doesn't matter if a customer disappears or a driver has an accident; if the order is not delivered, workers must pay for it. When workers lack rights, abuse of power comes as no surprise.

Global capitalism has evolved such that it is utterly dependent on datafied digital infrastructures and artificial intelligence (AI). These technologies are not politically neutral. AI taps human knowledge to train its models, transforming intellectual labour into so many 'intangible assets', which are then deployed in ways that deskill society while withering democratic control. Initial research and development for such technologies requires colossal investments, yet reproduction costs are minimal pushing profits from monopoly rents rather than new production.[17] In this new era, if something can be datafied, then it will be. Platforms mine virtually all available activity, making private property out of what was once human knowledge. This is wage theft evolving.

This book argues that wage theft sits within a broader continuum of unpaid labour. In *Capital*, Marx contends that the wage under capitalism accounts for only a part of the total working day. As we shall see later in the book, the wage represents what Marx calls the value of labour-power, which is equivalent to all the direct costs of its reproduction: food, water, and housing as well as education and technical training that provide the skills levels necessary for the work. Marx's key insight was that capitalism compels workers to work longer than is necessary to simply meet these costs of reproduction. This extra labour-time produces surplus-value, enabling capitalist enterprises to turn a profit. For

Marx, 'there is not one single atom' of surplus-value 'that does not owe its existence to unpaid labour'.[18] Workers' unpaid contribution is an exchange without equivalent.

In light of Marx's insight, wage theft should be thought of less as a violation of a particular legal standard and more as part of the unpaid labour-time central to the capitalist system and the private property that underpins it. While the boundary between paid and unpaid labour-time is typically codified in contract and legislation, it is not static. Maximum profits are 'limited by the physical minimum of wages and the physical maximum of the working day', as Marx observed. Yet within these two limits, an immense scale of variations is possible. For example, Thomas Rotta, a Marxist professor of economics, estimated that the rate of surplus-value in the US rose from a low point of 125 per cent in 1974 to 200 per cent in 2011, meaning that workers laboured about a third of their time for themselves and two-thirds for capital.[19] Shifts such as this depend on the struggle between capital and labour. Classed (re)distribution is a 'question of the respective powers of the combatants'.[20]

Capital nearly always has the advantage in this battle, through its greater financial and legal resources, but also through liberal ideology, which pushes the idea that both the buyer and seller meet in the marketplace as equals. However, if a worker can't earn enough to live, they risk destitution. Equality is an illusion since workers and capitalists do not have equal power. Capitalism makes unpaid labour appear as paid, since the 'money-relation conceals the uncompensated labour of the wage labourer'.[21] Profit therefore appears as the alchemy of labour and capital.

From tilling the soil to mining ore; from laying cables and railway tracks to building homes and skyscrapers; from weaving fabric to programming computers; and from educating students to nursing patients: human labour transforms the world, producing great wealth hoarded by the few. What can we do to stop it? To abolish wage theft in the legal sense, that is, under the existing property regime, would require radical industrial justice and economic democracy. Strong sectoral collective bargaining protections, criminal liability for employers, the redistribution of resources through taxing wealth, the expansion of publicly owned infrastructure and services, capital controls and price setting for necessities such as food, housing, and care would all be essential. However, these reforms would still be vulnerable to the kinds of economic shocks that barraged social-democratic welfare states in the late twentieth century. And capitalism would still exist.

To fully abolish wage theft, we must rethink what is owed and what is owned. The accumulation of capital requires the transformation of unpaid labour-time into products and property that workers are denied a claim to. Denial of property is theft by law.[22] If workers have a rightful claim to the full products of their collective labour, then the slogan of 'a fair day's wage for a fair day's work' must be replaced with Marx and Engel's call for 'abolition of the wages system!'[23] As Engels puts it in his follow-up to the editorial quoted earlier:

> But it is not the highness or lowness of wages which constitutes the economical degradation of the working class: this degradation is comprised in the fact that, instead of receiving for its labour the full produce of this labour, the working class has to be satisfied

> with a portion of its own produce called wages. The capitalist pockets the whole produce (paying the labourer out of it) because he is the owner of the means of labour. And, therefore, there is no real redemption for the working class until it becomes owner of all the means of work – land, raw material, machinery, etc. – and thereby also the owner of THE WHOLE OF THE PRODUCE OF ITS OWN LABOUR.[24]

The notion that we all have a claim over that with which we mix our labour is not a new idea. In fact, it is very old, stretching from Thomas Moore and John Locke through to Karl Marx and Pierre Joseph Proudhon. It is an idea fundamental to a just society. The seventeenth-century English Revolutionary Thomas Rainsborough said: 'Either poverty must use democracy to destroy the power of property, or property in fear of poverty will destroy democracy.'[25] In other words, the collective right of every worker to share in the products of their labour is the only right to property that is compatible with democracy. Throughout the rest of the book, this notion is explored in different contexts from its genesis in classical conceptions of private property to the emergent forms of digital assets and AI driving the cloud empires of platform capitalism.

# 1
# The State of Wage Theft

In New York City, Jose Martinez worked on a construction site for six months before pay problems began. Martinez said the contractor, Star Builders, first blamed the building owner for delays, yet more excuses followed. Like many New Yorkers, these skilled workers lived from pay cheque to pay cheque. After weeks of unpaid work, Martinez and several others walked out, cutting their losses.[1] Fed up with wage theft, Martinez filed a claim for assistance from Make the Road New York, joining an ever growing number of cases. In New York State alone, over 2 million workers lose more than $3 billion a year to wage theft, more than all street crime combined.[2]

Across the Atlantic in London, bartenders, waitstaff, and porters unfolded placards demanding their unpaid wages outside Beach Blanket Babylon, an upscale Shoreditch eatery. Six workers had already taken the restaurant to court, claiming they were owed over £8,600. Staff described a pattern of delay and obfuscation by management over pay.[3] One supervisor who was owed nearly £2,000 said:

> We heard from the beginning of when we got hired that there were payment issues. We were always lacking money, cash-flows and staff ... At the end of the day they still drive Range Rovers and wear designer clothes, but I still haven't been paid and I get credit card charges daily.[4]

Some workers held out hope for justice, while others could not afford to and simply left. Anyone who has worked in UK hospitality long enough will have a similar story.

In China, Liu, a graphic designer at a gaming company, said he worked a '996' schedule (9 a.m. to 9 p.m., six days a week) but was denied regular employee status. Instead, he had his probation extended for another month with 20 per cent less pay than his promised salary. When he quit and filed a case against the company to claim back wages, the court ruled in the company's favour, saying Liu should have applied for overtime, and that the extension of probation merited a payment to him of only 500 yuan.[5]

These vignettes point to a much broader problem in a world where the capitalist mode of production reigns. While research has shown that wage theft is sometimes the result of an employer's ignorance of the law, it also shows that employers use wage theft as a calculated strategy to reduce labour costs.[6] While the quality and quantity of wage theft varies, workers in every industry, from higher education to software engineering, and in every country from China to Chile, experience it. Formal violations that constitute wage theft range from unpaid overtime to stealing tips, piece-rate manipulation to charging workers for uniforms, tools, fuel, and so on. Wage theft is reportedly most prominent in industries such as construction, agriculture, beauty and wellness, care/domestic work, logistics, and hospitality. These are industries associated with low wages and low unionization, reflecting low collective bargaining power. Yet better-paid professional jobs also are subject to significant unpaid labour, from higher education to finance.

The pervasiveness of wage theft is not merely down to a few rogue operators. It is a consequence of regulatory failures catalysed by inequality. This chapter examines the technics of wage theft in three different countries: the US, the UK, and China. These cases usually represent different labour market regimes. The US has a complex matrix of federal and state labour laws, which means there are significant variations for workers from state to state. The UK has a unified national system, with safeguards against wage theft and other violations that are mostly consistent with EU regulations (for now). And a more liberalized China has, alongside its market reforms, instituted new laws that provide workers with more protections from employers – whether state or private. Yet, despite a wide gulf between these three different national economies and their divergent legal protections and penalties, wage theft abounds. Beyond the rich world, meanwhile, the legacies of colonial domination and underdevelopment have left many workers exposed to forced labour and modern slavery. This chapter closes with a discussion of them.

## The US

With few exceptions over the past half century, successive US governments have enacted policies that bolster the power of capital over labour. From Reagan to Trump, we've seen social protections for workers, collective bargaining, real wages, and living standards decimated for nearly everyone. Upward mobility is near impossible. Maintaining a secure, middle-class lifestyle is challenging even for historically advantaged groups of people, while downward mobility is normalized. The costs of basic necessities such as food and housing have risen astronomically, while anti-labour legislation such as 'right-to-work' and 'at will' laws prohibit unions from recruiting workers and allow employers to fire on a whim. This situation has drastically undermined worker bargaining power while making very few people very rich. In the battle of capitalism against democracy, the former has been winning for far too long.

How much wage theft occurs in the US? Nobody really knows. In 2022, the US Department of Labor (DOL) Wage and Hour Division recovered $114.7 million in back wages on behalf of nearly 100,000 workers. A decade before this, $177.7 million was recovered on behalf of 196,600 workers.[7] Given the working-age population of the US topped 200 million in 2012, wage theft appears to be a very marginal issue based on DOL recovery statistics, impacting less than 1 per cent of the population. However, if private wage-and-hour lawsuits and administrative rulings are included, the amount recovered jumps to $933 million. And if we consider the fact that the number of successful cases is dwarfed by the total number of disputes, which in turn is a small portion of the true number of violations (since most go unreported), wage theft is revealed as a significant, structural problem.[8]

A study by the Economic Policy Institute estimates that US minimum wage violations alone surpass $15 billion annually. This amount exceeds the combined estimated annual total of all other kinds of theft, from burglary and bank robbery to grand theft auto, by over $2 billion. Young workers, women, people of colour, and immigrant workers are more likely to experience minimum wage violations, since they comprise a greater share of low-wage jobs. Wage theft from this group of the lowest waged and most vulnerable workers added $8 billion annually to employers' pockets. Eradicating these violations alone would reduce the poverty rate from over 21 per cent to below 15 per cent.[9] Yet workers' time is not considered their own property, so wage theft continues to be treated as a minor issue, which is rather galling considering the vast federal, state, and local resources spent on protecting private property.

Beyond minimum wage violations, there is limited data on wage theft in the US, especially at the federal level. Academics, journalists, and activists have made valiant strides to highlight the pervasiveness of the problem, but research is still persistently lacking.[10] The largest study on wage violations is the 2008 Unregulated Work Survey, which analysed responses from 4,387 low-wage workers in New York, Los Angeles, and Chicago and distilled eight categories of wage theft and other violations. The first category concerned minimum wage violations, which 26 per cent of workers experienced weekly. Next were overtime violations, which impacted 76 per cent of workers. Third, off-the-clock violations (extra hours worked before or after scheduled shifts) affected nearly a quarter of workers. Meal breaks were the fourth category and one of the most widespread violations. Fifth were unlawful deductions from wages such as for uniforms or other costs. The sixth category concerned tipped workers, 30 per cent of whom were paid less than the minimum wage, while 12 per cent had their tips stolen by their employers. Workers' compensation violations, as the seventh category, were pervasive, with half of workers who reported injuries facing illegal retaliation such as termination, calls to immigration authorities, and pressure to not file claims. Finally, due to exemptions or contractual manipulation, many workers were denied employment protections.[11]

These different types of violations manifest across a wide range of sectors, but certain industries are particularly notorious. Industrial food production is one egregious case. In 2014, National Beef agreed to pay up to $350,000 to settle 480 claims for unpaid wages and overtime in Kansas, without acknowledging any wrongdoing. The dispute was over systematic underpayment for time spent putting on essential safety gear, taking meal breaks, walking to another station, waiting, and cleaning equipment.[12] This practice is common in meat processing, as evidenced by a $3.1 million judgment against an IBP meat-packing plant won by Teamsters Local 556 for unpaid time dealing with safety equipment.[13] Recently, the DOL ordered a California poultry chain to pay $4.8 million in back wages and damages to 476 workers, disgorge another $1 million in profits, and absorb $222,000 in civil penalties in 2024. This was after investigators found workers as young as fourteen deboning chickens while adults were denied overtime through falsified payrolls. Even after being subpoenaed, supervisors retaliated, telling workers they'd 'put the noose around their own necks' for talking to the Department of Labor.[14]

Some of the largest corporations, with plenty of financial capacity to pay well above a living wage, are routinely brought to court for wage theft. Walmart workers won roughly $1 billion in damages in six disputes from 2005 to 2012 due to being forced to work off the clock, being denied breaks, and having their time records reduced by management.[15] Apple was ordered to pay $30.5 million in damages to nearly 15,000 retail staff in a nine-year class action lawsuit over unpaid time waiting for bag checks after shifts.[16] In 2014, attorneys filed a lawsuit on behalf of McDonald's workers such as Guadalupe Salazar, who earned about $480 for each fifteen-day pay period. McDonald's was accused of shaving hours off worker time cards, refusing to pay overtime, and forcing employees to work off the clock and pay for their own uniforms. The court, however, ruled that McDonald's was not an employer, as the company did not exert the requisite control under California common law and was therefore not liable.[17] Legal loopholes like this are too common.

Despite regular high-profile cases, the dice are loaded in favour of employers, who are unlikely to face an investigation. The odds that a penalty will be issued are even lower. In 2012, the probability of an investigation by the US Wage and Hours Division was just 0.5 per cent, even in the most heavily targeted industries.[18] In 2015 the Wage and Hour Division of the DOL employed fewer than 1,000 investigators, similar to levels from seventy years earlier despite a sixfold increase in the national workforce. In 1948 one investigator covered 22,600 workers, while it's now roughly one for every 135,000. The decline in the investigator-to-worker ratio has led to a 63 per cent drop in federal cases investigated between 1980 and 2015. In fourteen US states (mostly in the South) there is no wage and hour office at all, which means workers are solely reliant on federal enforcement or private litigation.[19]

In the wake of the Great Depression, the Franklin D. Roosevelt administration enacted the Fair Labor Standards Act (FLSA), which established federal minimum wage and overtime pay regulations, creating a 'wage floor' and an 'hour ceiling'. At the time, European workers didn't yet have such provisions, although eventually they won stronger protections. Subsequent amendments to the FSLA, such as the 1966 expansion to service and hospitality sectors and the 2016 extension to home care workers, broadened coverage. Yet overall, the story of the FLSA is one of consistently in adequate, even declining standards. Central to this decline is a failure to increase the federal minimum wage in line with the rising cost of living. In 2024, the federal minimum wage was $7.25 per hour, 25 per cent lower than fifty years ago when adjusted for inflation. Tipped employees remained exempt from this meagre floor; they are only entitled to a mere $2.13 per hour. The law takes it for granted that tips will increase workers' total earnings to meet the federal minimum wage, yet there is no guarantee that this occurs.[20] State minimum wages on the coasts and in cities tend to be higher, but so are the costs of living.

The federal minimum wage is a poverty wage, forcing people to take on multiple jobs in what some have called 'polyworking' or 'side hustles' in order to simply survive. Over 8.9 million Americans were working multiple jobs as of March 2025. This is the highest share since the Bureau of Labor Statistics began tracking such data in 1994.[21] Among them are a disproportionate number of university-educated millennials and Gen Z workers, stuck in dead-end jobs. According to a 2024 Deloitte report, 45 per cent of Gen Z and 36 per cent of millennials maintain side gigs simply because their primary jobs don't pay enough.[22] A hostile economy forces them into moonlight hustles.

Furthermore, only 88 per cent of workers are protected by minimum wage laws, due to the FLSA's many built-in exemptions.[23] For example, workers in newspaper delivery, seasonal farming, fisheries, canneries, private investigation, and telephone switchboard operation are all exempt. These exclusions stem from when the act was first proposed and the Roosevelt administration struck a 'grand compromise' with conservative congressional wings of both the Republican and Democratic parties who opposed FDR's New Deal legislation. The compromise meant the FLSA excluded farm and domestic workers, who also happened to be largely Black. So-called independent contractors (many of whom are misclassified as such) are also exempt from protections. Salaried workers with executive, administrative, or professional roles above a certain pay threshold are also excluded. Finally, businesses with total revenues under $500,000 that partake in 'interstate commerce' also don't fall under the FLSA's wage and hour provisions.

In addition to this cascading series of exemptions, the FLSA does not even guarantee workers a regular rate of pay. This means that if a worker's weekly hours don't exceed forty and their pay rate meets the minimum, they cannot claim a violation. You could be contracted to earn $50 an hour at thirty hours a week but work ten additional hours unpaid and not be able to claim wage theft under the FLSA (though you could make an independent claim). Additionally, FLSA's claim process is restricted to collective actions that workers must opt into, rather than out of, which favours employers. Limited participation can leave most affected employees without redress.

The FLSA also fails to protect workers against technological means of wage theft. In a 2018 study of 330 wage theft cases, Elizabeth Tippett, an associate professor at the University of Oregon, found that the FLSA fails to prevent time-shaving, rounding, and automatic break deductions.[24] Time shaving is when managers alter timesheets to shortchange employees. For example, at Walmart, some managers reportedly altered records in such a way that workers who forgot to clock back in after lunch were clocked out for the day one minute after their lunch breaks began. According to the *New York Times*, 'five former Wal-Mart managers acknowledged erasing time to cut costs'.[25]

A decades-old DOL regulation allows industries using hourly wages to round up or down start and end times. This affordance was originally intended to ensure full compensation for actual work time, but is often taken advantage of by employers to do the opposite, since the legal burden is on workers to prove systematic disadvantage. Fractional deductions can amount to huge surpluses at scale, and courts rarely rule rounding policies illegal. Strict timings and penalties on breaks, meanwhile, lead to automated deductions and a 'no-win' scenario for workers. Supervisors may discourage missed breaks, but at the same time offer few opportunities to take them. For example, in one case brought against a children's hospital, a worker estimated that she missed 60 per cent of her breaks. In a different hospital case, the lead plaintiff claimed he worked through between 80 per cent and 90 per cent of his scheduled meal breaks. There are often no records of actual break times, making collective action claims difficult, especially when legal challenges hinge on documenting the frequency and consistency of deductions.[26]

The uneven matrix of labour laws at federal and state levels means geography is often destiny with wage theft. Mississippi lacks wage and hour laws entirely. Alabama only regulates child labour, and weakly at that. In Iowa the complaint process contains procedural obstacles that disadvantage workers, such as banning third-party assistance (including a lawyer, union representative, and pastor), while employers are free to use legal resources.[27] States such as Florida abolished its Department of Labor and Employment Security in 2002. However, other states such as New York, California, and Massachusetts have robust wage theft protections, with civil and criminal penalties, statutes of limitations lasting at least three years, and an opt-out (rather than opt-in) approach for class action lawsuits.

Over the past few decades, workplaces have also been subjected to what David Weil, who ran the Wage and Hour Division of the DOL during Obama's presidency, has called 'fissuring'. Fissuring refers to the cracks that open in a workplace where different parts of the labour process are subcontracted and outsourced, often misclassifying workers as 'independent contractors' to evade FLSA rules, tax obligations, and employer liability.[28] Up to 20 per cent of employers have been shown to engage in these practices.[29]

Misclassification of workers as supervisors is also a method of wage theft, allowing the denial of overtime payments. A 2020 Harvard Business School study found that employers avoided paying $4 billion annually in sectors from retail and hospitality to tech and financial services. Their data shows that from 2010 to 2021 the number of employees in all occupations excluding management increased 9 per cent, while the number of managers increased by over 47 per cent. Many of these new managers held completely bogus titles such as 'director of first impressions', a baroquely elevated name for a front-desk assistant. These jobs came with salaries just above the federal overtime threshold of $455 per week (at the time), exempting them from overtime pay, even though working overtime was the rule. In 2019, there were an estimated 2.65 million workers with jobs with management titles who earned less than $50,000 annually. Approximately one-third of these roles were not genuine, which means employers stole 151 million hours of overtime in a single year. States with more stringent overtime regulations saw no comparable surge in fake management roles.[30]

Summing up, wage theft in the US assumes many forms of sub-minimum-wage pay, unpaid overtime, off-the-clock work without compensation, the denial of meal breaks, automated deduction, and more. Corporate giants and small enterprises alike take advantage of labour laws that aren't fit for purpose. Loopholes exempt whole occupations, while penalties are the exception, written off as a business expense. The world is going badly for American workers, but they aren't alone.

## The UK

In the UK, the bargain struck between capital and labour is scarcely more in labour's favour than in the US. And for those workers balanced precariously on the edge of the wage floor, the safety net is meagre. A cost-of-living crisis has amplified existing class polarization post-pandemic, with food prices increasing up to 20 per cent alongside rising energy bills and rents. Real wages remain stagnant or are falling across sectors. Yet companies still seek their 'extra cut' from farm to factory.

Almost one-third of workers with minimum wage contracts are actually paid below this threshold. Yet, as in the US, wage theft extends far beyond violations of the minimum wage. The legal right to paid holidays is denied to roughly 900,000 individuals; 1.8 million workers never even receive a payslip, stripping them of a basic mechanism to verify their earnings and protect against wage theft. The brunt of this injustice is borne most acutely by the low-paid.[31]

Fast-fashion factories in Leicester, a mid-sized British city, channel the spirit of nineteenth-century satanic mills. In one, an undercover reporter was told to expect to earn between £3.50 and £4.00 per hour, around £5 less than the statutory minimum for workers over twenty five years of age at the time.[32] According to estimates by the groups Labour Behind the Label and ShareAction, factories supplying the fast-fashion giant Boohoo owed workers up to £125 million in unpaid wages.[33] Warehouse workers seem to fare no better. One worker named Rowan Chalmers said he was hired by an agency, PMP Recruitment, to work at the Boohoo-owned Pretty Little Thing. Agencies supply nearly one in ten warehouse and storage workers. Not long after he started, he was missing two entire shifts' pay and holiday pay. Chalmers won his employment tribunal, but a year later he had still not been paid: 'I did the hours, the time, the shifts and I didn't get paid for it ... agencies just see employees as disposable.'[34]

These examples are symptomatic of the UK's dysfunctional enforcement regime, with its vast gap between recovered wages and the estimated total stolen. Statistics are sparse because there is no comprehensive database of wage theft. But in 2017, research from the Low Pay Commission estimated that between 300,000 and 580,000 workers were paid below the National Minimum Wage (NMW).[35] When multiplied by the average 'arrears' of £177, as identified by HMRC, this meant that workers were owed between £53 million and £103 million in unpaid wages – roughly how much the royal family cost taxpayers annually.[36] Minimum wage violations are just one of many unlawful deductions, such as making workers pay for uniforms, omitting pension contributions, not paying annual leave, theft of tips, and more. Some of these violations are picked up by employment tribunals, but most aren't.

The contemporary state of wage theft in the UK contrasts starkly with the history of workers' power struggles. From

1909 until 1993, wage rates, safety standards, and other conditions were negotiated through a combination of collective bargaining agreements with trade unions, Joint Industrial Councils (one for each industry) and Wages Councils (from 1945).[37] These councils roughly consisted of both employer and employee representatives, serving as a form of collective bargaining and negotiation for different industries from garment manufacturing to retail and hospitality. Regulations established by the Wages Councils were legally binding, and social support for the system was strong. It protected millions of lower-waged workers. Employers found it beneficial for avoiding complex wage bargaining and protecting against unfair competition. Trade unions supported its expansion alongside a statutory minimum wage.

All of this changed after the 1979 general election victory that secured a new Conservative government driven by the ideology of free market fundamentalism. They viewed regulation of employment conditions and collective bargaining as distorting and inflationary. The reforms were swift and brutally upended whole communities, most notably the miners, whose initial strikes were successful but then summarily crushed in 1985. The Thatcher government also launched a series of attacks on the Wages Councils. This period gave no heed to the costs of social reproduction or potential failure of the market to allocate resources. Setting wage rates was anathema to this ideology, which held that labour markets should function competitively without state intervention, based purely on supply and demand (see Chapter 5).

This neoliberal government also re-engineered the family income supplement, which was a means-tested benefit for a parent working at least twenty-four hours a week, into what was called the Family Credit system in 1988. This credit was expanded to those working sixteen hours a week and payable for six months at a flat rate regardless of changes in circumstances.[38] This new system might have seemed generous, but it effectively provided a wage subsidy to employers, enabling them to pay workers less than they needed to live while increasing their margins. The Thatcher era closed with the full abolition of the Wages Councils system in 1993. In its place was an employer-friendly tax-credit system with no minimum wage for workers (save for agriculture).

By the mid-1990s, the political mood was shifting. The notion of monopsony in labour markets – the idea that employers have disproportionate power to set wages – became increasingly mainstream. In a monopsonistic labour market, minimum wage regulations can both boost wages and consumption, rather than reduce profits and labour demand. This can then drive employers to increase their labour supply as aggregate demand increases.[39] In what Tony Blair's 1997 New Labour government hailed as 'the most lightly regulated labour market of any leading economy in the world', the Minimum Wage Act set a floor of £3.60 per hour for adult workers over the age of twenty-two. The act also prevented employers from reducing wages in response to expanded Working Tax Credits and Child Tax Credits. These were, in effect, social wages – that is, socially necessary services provided in lieu of the money wages otherwise used to purchase services on the market.[40]

While today there is a contractual wage floor for employees, it is a paltry one. As of 1 April 2025, the UK's minimum wage was £7.55 per hour for under-eighteens and apprentices, £10.00 per hour for eighteen- to twenty-year-olds, and £12.21 per hour for adults aged twenty-one and over. The minimum wage for over-twenty-ones was rebranded by David Cameron's Conservative government as the National Living Wage, despite the fact that the real living wage as calculated by the Living Wage Foundation was £12.60 nationally and £13.85 in London.

Beyond the wage floor, other rights are meant to limit unpaid labour. For example, the right to 5.6 weeks of paid leave was established by the EU-derived Working Time Regulations. The Employment Rights Act 1996 also explicitly protects against deduction of 'any sums payable to the worker in connection with his/her employment'. If there is a dispute over pay or other protected aspects of employment, a worker can file a formal grievance, which can escalate to an employment tribunal claim, through the UK government's Advisory, Conciliation and Arbitration Service.

The UK's system of statutory protections provides workers with more legal protections than the US. However, it's a disorganised patchwork of protections and enforcement powers compared with many of the UK's OECD peers. This could change with Labour's proposed Fair Work Agency, although, as of the time of writing, there are six different core enforcement bodies, plus local authorities, overseen by seven separate government departments. For example, HMRC deals with the NMW and theft of statutory entitlements such as Statutory Sick Pay and Statutory Maternity Pay; the Gangmasters and Labour Abuse Authority deals with labour agencies and vulnerable migrant workers; and the Employment Agency Standards Inspectorate oversees the private recruitment sector.

The law around wage theft is also opaque. The Theft Act 1968 defines theft as dishonestly appropriating another person's property with the intention of permanently depriving them of it. 'Property' here includes money as well as tangible and intangible assets. In court, it is difficult to establish whether wages owed are in fact a worker's property and therefore subject to 'dishonest appropriation' by the employer. Theft law is concerned with situations where victims lose rights over assets they previously possessed. Even if wages can be recognized as the subject of property rights, in British law, it must be established that property rights were held by the worker before any employer action that could be deemed appropriation. To apply the Theft Act to wages, the property status of the claimed monies and the temporal order of events must be proven. Workers' unpaid wages will often not legally count as 'property belonging to another' at the time when an employer is engaging in wage theft. Because of this difficultly, legal cases of wage theft are usually pursued as 'unlawful deductions' or 'damages'.[41] The liberal foundations of the legal concept of property (see Chapter 2) ensure employers are protected from criminal claims of theft.

As we saw in the US, the law is only as good as the power of its enforcement. This also gives employers an advantage in the UK. HMRC has the power to force employers to repay workers and impose fines of up to twice the total amount owed, though it tends to reduce fines if back wages are paid promptly. Documented wage theft and penalties are significant. In 2019, HMRC identified over £20.8 million in arrears for more than 263,000 workers and fined non-compliant employers an additional £18.5 million with nearly 1,000 penalties.[42]

But enforcement agencies still often operate with a presumption that firms act in good faith. In 2021–22, HMRC's NMW unit failed to issue penalties in 41 per cent of cases where underpayment was uncovered. Serious penalties are deployed exceedingly sparingly, almost symbolically. Since their introduction in 2017, just eighty-four Labour Market Enforcement Undertakings and four Enforcement Orders have been issued. As for criminal prosecutions of employers for underpaying the minimum wage, there have been just eighteen (fewer than one per year) since 2007.[43] Only six firms were prosecuted for paying employees less than the minimum wage from 2016 to 2022, despite HMRC finding over 6,500 violations.[44]

According to one study, employers essentially play a 'numbers game' to underpay without displacing their entire workforce or attracting regulatory scrutiny. Wage theft through non-payment of accrued annual leave upon a worker's departure is one tactic; 'losing' a few hours per week but fixing this if a worker notices is another tactic, with the benefit of plausible deniability.[45] Even when caught by regulators, the consequences are often so minimal that even when taken to a tribunal, many employers simply don't bother defending themselves. Some pay the ordered compensation while others sometimes just ignore the judgments entirely, closing the company if payment demands persist. Employers may also simply dissolve a company despite owing wages (known as 'knocking' in the construction industry), or close one company only to start another one (known as 'phoenixing'). When employers vanish into thin air without paying wages, the taxpayer picks up the bill. The UK government's Insolvency Service paid out more than £490 million in redundancy payments to 85,592 people during 2023–24.[46]

Like their US counterparts, UK employers take advantage of their legal power to carve out exemptions from regulators. A common tactic is to misclassify workers as self-employed contractors, or to use agency workers, limiting tax and wage obligations while curtaining workers' statutory rights.[47] Self-employment in the UK has grown rapidly over the past twenty years, from 3.2 million in 2000 to a peak of over 5 million in 2020. After a steep, pandemic-induced drop to 4.1 million, it slowly increased again to nearly 4.5 million in 2025.[48] The prevalence of such contracts cuts across sectors including construction, administrators, cleaners and gardeners, transport, design, and retail. Yet, legal challenges tend to only target the worst offenders. A 2015 study by Citizens Advice found that at least 10 per cent of those identified as self-employed should have been legally classified as workers or employees.[49]

Britain's employment tribunals reveal a gap between contractual rhetoric and workplace reality. Contracts often do not clarify the employment relationship but obscure it instead, often in ways that deny workers their rights. The construction industry is a notorious violator. Take the 2011 case of *Guiri v. East of England Building Services Ltd (EEBS) and Howe Construction*. The judge determined that attempts to portray the claimant as a subcontractor were 'a sham' and that paperwork relating to EEBS and its contract with the claimant 'bore no relation whatsoever to the actual contractual terms and legal obligations'. The claimant was awarded £1,764 in unpaid holiday pay. Notably, the contract had apparently included a clause stating that the services provided were not subject to the NMW or Working Time Regulations.[50]

The predatory use of such contracts to engage in wage theft is nowhere starker than in seasonal farm work. In 2022, nearly 35,000 migrants arrived to legally work in the UK on six-month visas, most on British farms. An investigation of over twenty UK farms, nurseries, and packhouses revealed that workers had weeks of wages withheld, were charged extortionate fees and interest, and were forced to perform tasks off the clock.[51] Miljana Istokovic, a Serbian migrant, said she arrived in September to work at a fruit farm in Lancashire that supplies Tesco and Lidl. Istokovic said that just three weeks later, she was dismissed and stranded at the farm for two weeks waiting for her recruiter, Concordia, to transfer her to another farm. She could not apply for another job herself because the visa programme tied workers to specific companies. Eventually her electricity supply was cut, and she had to go into £500 debt to fund her return journey home.[52]

The Conservative government deflected blame onto recruiters. The Independent Chief Inspector of Borders and Immigration reported that 'no allegations were investigated by the Home Office, by scheme operators, or by other government organisations'. Compounding the damage, the government announced that farms had to guarantee thirty-two hours of work per week, but they no longer were required to pay seasonal workers above the minimum wage. This policy shift also came with no enforcement mechanisms. Workers were essentially bonded to farms with no wage floor or left without work for weeks after being dismissed.[53] The Conservatives, self-styled champions of farm owners, had recreated a quasi-feudal labour regime.

Abuse of self-employment contracts goes hand in hand with the abuse of piece-rate pay systems. In the UK, piece-rates should be calculated at 1.2 times the rate at which a worker of average speed can earn the NMW. The law requires documentation of this rate and how they calculated it; however, companies often ignore this. Many companies use piece-rate pay to redefine essential work tasks as peripheral and therefore unpaid labour-time. The more unpaid activities companies can force workers to perform, the more surplus-value they can capture.

Overall, wage theft in the UK at best reflects a crass lack of care by companies for their workers and at worst exposes calculated strategies of evasion enacted at workplaces across the country. The erosion of collective bargaining power combined with a flaccid enforcement regime means most workers end up simply absorbing violations.[54] Yet wage theft doesn't merely affect individuals. It puts downward pressure on wages across industries. UK employers watch one another and see what they can get away with, while working families must resort to side hustles and welfare programmes, straining threadbare safety nets. In nearly every sector, from hospitality to higher education, wage theft continues unabated.

This is a systemic failure to protect the dignity and rights of millions of workers.

As Westminster Lords pine for the unfettered capitalism of the nineteenth century, a more polarized British class system has emerged, catering for aspiring oligarchs. Is there any alternative? China is often used as a social, political, and ideological counterpoint to Western capitalism. Yet as the next section shows, when it comes to stolen wages, Chinese workers have far more in common with those of the West than Donald Trump or Xi Jinping might have us believe.

## China

Despite nominally being a 'workers' state', wage theft, dangerous conditions, and retaliatory violence are common experiences in China. In 2015, Zhou Xiuyun, a forty-seven-year-old migrant worker, was fatally beaten by police in Taiyuan City when he demanded his employer pay him what he was owed. Known as the '12/13 incident', Zhou's death sparked a veritable prairie fire over workers' rights in China.[55] And yet wage theft continues unabated. A particularly egregious case was in 2022 when the Lanzhou Public Transportation Group, a state-owned bus company in northwest China, asked its employees to take out personal loans to cover unpaid wages. The company's debt ratio had recently reached a critical 72 per cent, making it impossible to secure additional loans from banks.[56]

There appears to be a generational shift in attitudes to wage theft, with young workers increasingly speaking out. At a large book retailer, some workers reported being owed up to half a year's worth of pay: 'After five years of working conscientiously, I ended up here ... now I'm just an average, angry, former employee who is owed wages.'[57] This sentiment was echoed by many others who found themselves forced into complex arbitration processes. A student worker at a media company reported his wage theft case to the local labour inspectorate, who simply told him to find a lawyer. 'Bringing this case costs 5,000 yuan [US$785], which is more than my salary,' he said. 'If I could afford a lawyer, why would I still be working and studying?'[58] A gap between rhetoric and reality is structurally embedded in modern China.

The All-China Federation of Trade Unions (ACFTU) is the only legal trade union. With 300 million members and 1 million full-time officials, it is by far the world's largest national trade union. However, it often fails to represent workers effectively, acting more as a social welfare organization aligned with management and local government. Attempts to establish independent unions are suppressed since they are seen as political threats. Politics determine how labour regulations are enforced. So like their Western counterparts, employers frequently ignore laws, leaving workers to attempt to resolve issues themselves either through wildcat collective action or arbitration in court. Labour Dispute Arbitration Committees (LDACs) handle most disputes, with a high volume of cases settled through mediation rather than formal arbitration.[59]

Most wage theft disputes and strikes are not tracked by the state or reported in Chinese media. The China Labour Bulletin (CLB), a non-governmental organization (NGO) based in Hong Kong, took up this task until its closure in June

2025. The CLB was established in 1994 by Han Dongfang, a prominent activist. Dongfang was a key figure in the 1989 Tiananmen Square protests and has spent time imprisoned for labour activities. The CLB played a crucial role in advocating for labour rights, focusing on wage theft, collective bargaining, and occupational health and safety. It maintained an index of strikes, protests, and violations in China as well as established a network of lawyers who offered pro bono services to workers. This support was crucial in navigating the complex and employer-biased legal system.

As Figure 1.1 shows, the CLB's Strike Map recorded 1,509 incidents in 2024, a modest dip from the previous year, but still well above pre-pandemic levels. The numbers signal a new baseline of endemic wage theft in various forms, as employers shifted the burden of economic turbulence onto workers.

Figure 1.1 Number of CLB strike incidents collected annually, 2018–24

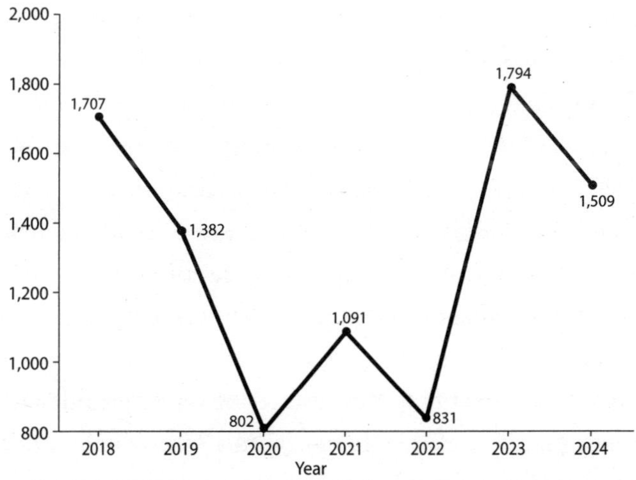


*Source:* 'China Labour Bulletin Strike Map Data Analysis: 2024 Year in Review for Workers' Rights', China Labour Bulletin, 29 January 2025.

Construction accounted for the largest share of protests: 733 incidents, or 48.6 per cent, mostly linked to unpaid wages on residential projects. Manufacturing followed with 452 incidents (30 per cent), marking a notable increase. Services saw 148 protests (9.8 per cent), then came transport and logistics (4.2 per cent), heavy industry (1.4 per cent), education (1 per cent), and mining (0.8 per cent). Unrest was concentrated in coastal provinces such as Guangdong, which reported 346 incidents. Yet inland regions also demonstrated resistance: Henan (80), Hebei (69), and Shaanxi (59) all recorded significant activity. Wage theft remained the dominant grievance, driving 88 per cent of all disputes. While President Xi Jinping has repeatedly promised labour market reform, the current system looks more like an employers' than a workers' state.[60]

By the metrics of the World Bank and the International Monetary Fund (IMF), China is a great economic success. It is arguably the largest economy in the world. In 2024, it had a population of 1.41 billion people, a larger GDP (at purchasing power parity) than the US, and 19 per cent of the world's total GDP.[61] China's electricity generation overtook the US in 2010 and was nearly double the terawatt hours (TWh) in 2023.[62] The state capitalism that enabled China's rise has increasingly come at the expense of workers in ways that are strikingly similar to that of its rivals. How did this happen? And what does this tell us about the nature of capitalism and wage theft?

After Mao's death in 1976, a series of reforms under Deng Xiaoping started to take effect from 1978, which aimed to transition China from a state-planned to a market-planned economy, transforming it into the 'world factory'. During the state-planned period, rural peasants were temporarily brought to cities to fulfil industrial labour demands, often resulting in seasonal employment with lower wages. This was enabled by the *hukou* or *huji* system, which restricted rural migrants' integration into urban areas, creating a state of 'permanent temporariness'.[63] The right to strike was removed from the constitution in 1982, though there is no explicit prohibition on strikes. The introduction of the labour contract system in 1986 marked another significant shift, as it aimed to replace lifelong employment with more of a contract-based system. These reforms aimed to improve efficiency and productivity, but they also led to the deregulation of labour markets and the rise of informal employment.[64]

The early 1990s saw cities in the Pearl River Delta such as Shenzen, Macau, and Guangzhou become the epicentre of this transformation, characterized by rapid industrialization and an influx of internal migrant and informal workers, which had profound social and economic consequences. The lack of formal contracts and social insurance for informal workers left them vulnerable to exploitation and abuse. While the China Labour Act (1994) introduced legislative measures aimed at protecting workers' rights and stabilizing labour relations, the state's regulatory attempts also faced employer resistance.[65]

The politics of the labour market shifted significantly in the new millennium. The Hu Jintao and Wen Jiabao administration, which took office in 2002, introduced socio-economic reforms aimed at building a 'harmonious society' and addressing the 'three rural problems' related to farmers, rural areas, and agriculture.[66] By 2003, China had surpassed the US as the largest recipient of foreign direct investment, yet China also faced labour shortages, which bolstered bargaining power during rising strike waves in the Pearl River Delta, pressuring the government to increase the minimum wage and introduce new labour laws.[67] The 2008 Labour Contract Law introduced provisions including: mandatory written contracts, severance pay for dismissals, and permanent contracts after two consecutive fixed-term contracts or ten years of continuous employment. These measures aimed to reduce informal employment and enhance job security for workers, although many employers still found ways to circumvent them.

Later that decade, the global financial crisis of 2008 economically decimated much of the West, which led to a 16 per cent decrease in China's total exports in 2009.[68] Labour bore the brunt of this, with companies downsizing their workforce, to the tune of 20 million migrant workers. The Communist Party of China (CPC)'s official urban unemployment rate reached 4.3 per cent by January 2009, but estimates from the Chinese Academy of Social Sciences suggested it was over double that figure at 9.4 per cent. Numerous factories shut down, especially in the South, while others scaled back operations. Workers at the Kaida factory in Dongguan were told that their contracts would be terminated, and they would receive an average of just one month's wages as compensation, sparking intense protest in November 2008. Factory owners pressured the government for assistance to weather the economic malaise, leading to waivers on social insurance contributions, tax reductions, and delays in implementing labour laws.

Workers were not happy with this retrenchment, resulting in a 30 per cent rise in labour disputes nationwide in the first half of 2009, with even higher increases in Guangdong, Jiangsu, and Zhejiang provinces. Additionally, labour protests surged, with a reported 94 per cent increase in the first ten months of 2008 compared with the previous year, and a dramatic 300 per cent rise in Beijing.[69] International pressure also mounted as labour NGOs worked to support worker rights. One NGO, the Clean Clothes campaign, accused major clothing retailers including H&M and Primark of tolerating wage theft by Chinese suppliers under the rubric of 'continuous improvement' towards legal compliance. One H&M supplier was quoted as saying, 'H&M buys cheap, they need us to sell cheap to them', while a Primark supplier noted, 'Primark wants us to give them minimum prices, why would they require us to pay overtime wages?'[70]

China's GDP growth rate fell from a high of 14.2 per cent in 2007 to 7.9 per cent in 2012.[71] By 2010, global political and economic instability was provoking further unrest in the Chinese labour market. The CPC responded differently this time, encouraging local government to provide concessions to workers. In Shenzhen, the government provided financial aid to employees of a factory whose owner disappeared. In Guangzhou, the government offered support to workers of a Taiwanese factory that just shut down. However, by Xi Jinping's rise to power in 2012, an increasing number of factories were relocating regionally or internationally with minimal or no compensation to workers. Unrest became increasingly radical. For example, in 2013 fifteen security guards staged a rooftop protest to demand unpaid wages and social insurance at the Guangzhou Chinese Medicine University Hospital.[72]

The number of strikes and protests in China doubled from 1,379 in 2014 to 2,774 in 2015.[73] One of the largest strikes began at Yue Yuen on 5 April 2014 and involved over 60,000 workers from a shoe factory in Dongguan operated by the Taiwanese Pou Chen Group. This factory had been underpaying workers' pension insurance for years while supplying global brands such as Adidas, Puma, Reebok, and Nike. Despite extending social insurance coverage to all workers after 2008, Yue Yuen's contributions were based on the minimum wage rather than actual salaries, drastically cutting pensions. Additionally, many workers were falsely classified as temporary, further reducing the employer's contributions.[74] Out of 802 total worker collective actions found in CLB's Strike Map in 2022, 87 per cent involved wage arrears.[75]

This prompts reflection on the limitations of a so-called workers' state that effectively treats workers like a capitalist nation does. Similar to the US and UK, while China's labour laws theoretically provide extensive rights to workers, enforcement is completely inadequate. Could this not be by design? China's Supreme People's Procuratorate officially prosecuted only 2,554 cases of wage theft from January to November 2023, recovering about RMB 325 million ($46.5 million).[76] When case numbers are set in context of the truly massive Chinese labour force, they appear miniscule. In 2023, China's National Bureau of Statistics reported the total active labour force to be around 733.5 million.[77]

In China, the future of wage theft and the struggle against

it remains contested. Conflict is inevitable in an increasingly marketized, capitalist system, just as it is in the West. Stealing wages will nearly always be more advantageous for a company in competitive markets. And no amount of NGO campaigning or bad press will make all companies pay workers more and raise standards. This is only achieved on a mass scale through stronger collective bargaining (sometimes by riot, if necessary), enforcement of regulation, and controls on capital. In the absence of such pressures, unpaid labour can become unfree labour, especially for international migrants.

## From Unpaid to Unfree

Labour conditions are usually worse for workers at the margins. Because of their precarious status, migrant workers often end up working in informal sectors, beyond the scope of labour market protection and enforcement. They are paid cash-in-hand via piece-rates, profit-sharing arrangements, or tips, exposing them to a higher risk of fraud and wage theft. Discriminatory wage setting is another concern, as employers might pay different wages to workers performing the same job due to personal characteristics such as nationality, race, gender, or sexual orientation, especially when laws don't exist to protect against this.

There are international policy benchmarks designed to militate these exploitative tendencies. The primary standard is the Protection of Wages Convention (N95), a 1949 international treaty ratified by ninety-nine states. The UK, which ratified it in 1951, later denounced and withdrew from it in 1983, while the US never ratified it at all. The convention consists of twenty-seven articles that state how wages should be paid and what protections workers should have from deductions.

More recent ILO conventions include the Protection of Workers' Claims (Employer's Insolvency) Convention (C173) and the Domestic Workers Convention (C189). The first of these responds to a common problem: when employers go under, workers are often the last to be paid. The convention offers two ways to fix this. First, through a privilege model, in which workers' unpaid wages, holiday pay, and severance are given priority over most other creditors, including the state. Second, through a guarantee fund (public or insured), which can step in to pay at least eight weeks' wages and claims if the employer cannot. Countries should adopt either approach, or both, so long as it meets a vaguely defined 'socially acceptable' minimum. C173 also reflects a shift in emphasis from winding up businesses to salvaging employment where possible. But its commitments are deliberately open to interpretation. As of 2023, the convention had been ratified by twenty-one states.

The Domestic Workers Convention (C189) attempts to push household labour into the realm of formal employment relations. It obliges ratifying states to treat maids, nannies, and cooks as workers proper: written contracts, the right to organize, minimum wage coverage, daily rest, and a full twenty-four-hour weekly break are mandatory. The convention also bans child domestic labour, protects from violence, and forbids passport confiscation or tethering live-in workers to the household when they have off time (common practices). Further clauses propose 'decent living conditions' for resident staff and demand that migrant workers receive full contract details before crossing borders.

These are reasonable regulations, but in reality they are rarely abided by. Again, the problem comes down to enforcement. As with many ILO conventions, they set out principles but leave the difficulty of implementation to national legislators, who struggle to deliver real protection.

One of the gravest risks for workers is when unpaid labour becomes unfree labour. The greater the cut of unpaid labour in the working day, the closer workers get to unfreedom, as economic coercion morphs into *force majeure*. Forced labour, or 'modern slavery' as it also termed, can be state-imposed or enacted by private sector companies or criminal organizations. It also includes forced sexual exploitation of adults and children. On average, one-third of forced labour victims are coerced through forms of wage theft.[78] In addition to the withholding of wages, victims experience threats, psychological abuse, physical violence, and threats or even violence against family members. Over half are held in debt bondage, often created through recruitment fees and agency charges. Migrant workers are most at risk, especially in Gulf States, where forced labour is widely reported.[79] In 2017, there were an estimated 24.9 million people in the world who were subject to forced labour. This was highest in Asia and the Pacific, where four out of every 1,000 people were victims, followed by Europe and Central Asia, and Africa. Children represented around 18 per cent of those subjected to forced labour exploitation; 7 per cent of people were forced to work by state authorities.[80]

According to available data, domestic work represents the greatest share of forced labourers, at 24 per cent. Globally, there are approximately 67 million domestic workers, including 11.5 million migrant domestic workers. The vast majority are women who are routinely subject to unpaid wages, lack of overtime pay, long hours, inadequate rest days, absence of healthcare and maternity leave, poor living conditions, lack of contracts, sexual coercion, and other forms of violent abuse. Recruitment is often fragmented through subcontractors evading enforcement meant to prevent brutal conditions, contract substitution, and passport confiscation. Excessive fees burden workers through direct payments, high-interest loans, or salary deductions. Visa arrangements can further trap migrant domestic workers with restrictions on movement, isolation, and no recourse against abuse.

In East and South East Asia, as well as the Gulf States, migrant women are recruited for household work under *kafala* systems that legally bind their residency to their employer. Wages are withheld or stolen; passports are confiscated; physical and sexual abuse are common. Many cannot leave without forfeiting everything. In Qatar and the United Arab Emirates (UAE), African and South Asian construction workers lured with promises of good wages end up as indentured labourers, working in fifty-degree heat, living in overcrowded slums or camps, building luxury hotels and sports stadiums they will never enter.

Across the world, wage theft is a gateway to forced labour. In South Asian garment factories, the boundary between employment and coercion blurs for the men, women, and children who sew for fast fashion retailers. In the cobalt and lithium mines of the Democratic Republic of Congo, children and their parents dig through toxic earth for Tesla to produce electric vehicles, their future mortgaged to feed fantasies of a green capitalism. In the agricultural fields and meat-packing plants of North America, undocumented migrant children work without contracts, under threat of Immigration and Customs Enforcement (ICE) raids and deportation to Salvadorean prisons. Even within European capitals, migrants are pushed into begging and unfree labour because of bare economic necessity, often in plain sight. These are not vestiges of premodern slavery but the structural result of a capitalist system buttressed by passport apartheid and a legal architecture that protects capital against democracy.

This chapter explored wage theft in three different states and the link between unpaid and unfree labour. Across different labour markets, policies, and worker protections, the common denominator is the persistence of an 'extra cut' despite regulation. The US and the UK stand out as examples of rich countries with liberal labour markets that resoundingly fail to protect workers from wage theft. China is, by contrast, a non-liberal state, yet capitalism with Chinese characteristics is still capitalism. Abuse of workers by state and non-state employers has led to strikes, riots, and protests, such as the Marxist 996 movement.

Theft in law speaks to a deeper problem with the concept of capitalist property. What claim can a worker make to the products of their own labour? When we work without distribution according to contribution, a rightful share of the product, why is this not considered theft? To answer these questions, we must delve into the history of capital and labour, the origins of unpaid labour, and the original sin of the capitalist mode of production.

# 2
# Lineages of Unpaid Labour

*The law locks up the man or woman*
*Who steals the goose from off the common*
*But leaves the greater villain loose*
*Who steals the common from off the goose.*
*The law demands that we atone*
*When we take things we do not own*
*But leaves the lords and ladies fine*
*Who take things that are yours and mine.*
*The poor and wretched don't escape*
*If they conspire the law to break;*
*This must be so but they endure*
*Those who conspire to make the law.*
*The law locks up the man or woman*
*Who steals the goose from off the common*
*And geese will still a common lack*
*Till they go and steal it back.*

– Anonymous eighteenth-century English poem

For centuries, England's manorial lords thrived off the backs of their serfs' toil and tribute. Peasants, bound by feudal law, worked their masters' demesne fields in exchange for the right to grow their own food on small plots of land. They enjoyed a degree of control over their labour as long as they produced enough surplus to provide grain to the manor's mill, eggs to the lord's pantry, and tithes to the parish. All the while, a spectre of additional taxes, such as the chevage or death tax, marriage tax, and so on, loomed over them. The Black Death, which decimated the population, somewhat improved the bargaining position of surviving peasants and artisans. However, this consolation was short-lived, as the aristocracy quickly countered with the Statute of Labourers, freezing wages and binding workers more tightly to their lords' manors.

When poll taxes, imposed to fund a distant war, began to drain what little the peasantry had amassed, discontent erupted into the Great Peasant Revolt, also known as the Insurrection of Wat Tyler, in 1381.[1] The peasants demanded emancipation from serfdom, a repeal of the poll and other taxes, the purge and punishment of corrupt ministers and judges, curbs on intrusive royal courts, village self-government, and a general amnesty for rebels. King Richard II briefly issued charters promising freedom, but when Wat Tyler met with him at Smithfield, in London, he was stabbed in the back by the mayor, Sir William Walworth, before being reduced to a severed head on a pike. The revolt left a deep impression on English society, appearing in Chaucer's *The Canterbury Tales*, and later becoming a symbol of working-class rebellion. William Morris's *A Dream of John Ball* portrayed it sympathetically and prophesied the eventual triumph of socialism. This is but one tale of many representing the violent and protracted transition from feudalism to capitalism, a transition which lays bare the role of unpaid labour in forming our modern world.

The development of the capitalist mode of production required a cosmological alignment of forces over centuries. Its imperatives of competition, profit-making, and productivity increases are coterminous with the vicissitudes of economic development and underdevelopment on a world scale. The question of how capital became capitalism has been subject to decades of debate, sometimes due to contending definitions of what capitalism itself is. The Latin *capitale* was used from around the twelfth or thirteenth centuries onwards to refer to sums of money, stocks of goods, and other assets.[2] But *capitale* is not the same as capitalism, which could be minimally defined as a system driven by the hegemonic imperative of competitive accumulation 'by formally peaceful means'.[3] Within this minimal criteria there are roughly three competing theories for capitalism's emergence.[4] Yet only one explains why capitalism is inextricably bound to unpaid labour and how labour's metamorphosis manifests the secret of exploitation.

The first theory is the 'commericalization thesis'. Broadly put, it approaches capitalism as any economic system organized principally around production for exchange and profit. Capital is simply any form of property that is expected to yield an income. This theory naturalises capitalism. It is inspired by Adam Smith, the Scottish 'father' of classical political economy, who wrote that humankind has an inherent propensity to 'truck, barter and exchange one thing for another'. Every individual 'lives by exchanging, or becomes in some measure a merchant, and the society itself grows to be what is a properly commercial society'.[5] This merchant mythos tells history as the story of *Homo economicus* mastering their destiny of commercial development.

The famous liberal economist John Maynard Keynes held a similar view. Capitalism, as the highest form of commercial society, required an ever-greater division of labour, degree of technological innovation, and scale of production. Yet, Keynes argued it was born in ancient Babylonia, before being incorporated into Greek and Roman civilizations and gradually adopted across Western Europe.[6] For Keynes, the move from ancient to modern capitalism began after Sir Francis Drake stole Spain's gold in 1580 (Spain had obviously stolen it from their South American colonies). It was only after this colossal theft that Queen Elizabeth could both pay off England's debts and kick-start commercial capitalism by investing in Levantine shipping.[7] Freed from political constraints, so the story goes, markets spread across the world due to their superior efficiency.

Others argue that the first time capitalism emerged was in the merchant economies of the Italian city-states between the eleventh and fifteenth centuries. It was Venice 'which nurtured the first capitalist society', Oliver Cromwell Cox contends, centuries before England.[8] Italian merchants dominated European economic life from the eleventh to fifteenth centuries, amassing a significant volume of money capital, according to the Marxist political economist Ernest Mandel.[9] Ferdinand Braudel, a contemporary of Mandel, also came to similar conclusions, noting that capitalism emerged as early as the thirteenth century, when Venice as well as Genoa were 'merchant and colonial powers'.[10]

While there may have been individual instances of capitalism in the Mediterranean, they failed to spread as capitalism did in England. The question of what spurred generalized development is central to this chapter. The economic historian Angus Maddison compares detailed statistical accounts of the past millennium or so of economic activity. Figure 2.1 shows GDP per capita, or the total value of everything produced annually, divided by the population of a given region in relation to average annual income. Looking closely at the graph we can see a clear and dramatic shift in Britain from around 1800, from relative economic stagnation to

Figure 2.1 History's hockey stick: worldwide historical real gross domestic product per capita, 1000 to 2018

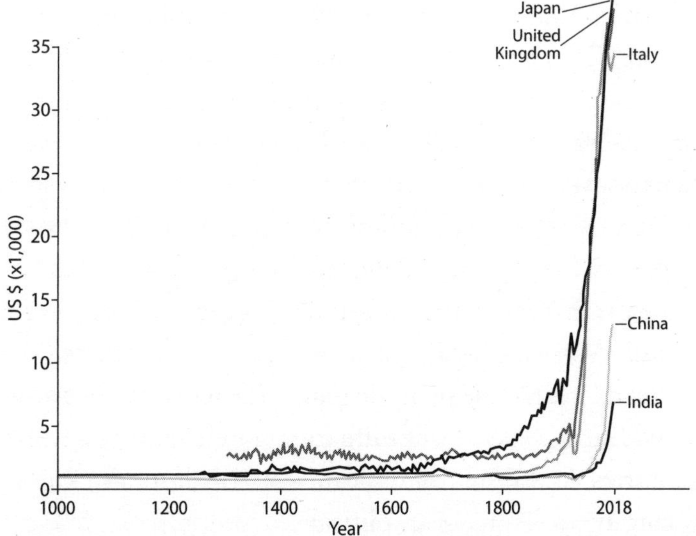


*Source:* Maddison Project Database, 2018, Our World in Data.

Note: The unit of measurement is 2011 US dollar, which is used to compare purchasing power parity and GDP across countries over time.

continuous productivity growth.[11] This suggests that capitalism as a hegemonic system of production is only a relatively recent phenomenon, rather than an inevitable result of human nature.[12] As the historian Ellen Meiksins Wood notes, in naturalizing capitalism, the 'commercialization thesis' ultimately de-historicizes it and forecloses a non-capitalist future.[13]

The second theory of capitalism focuses on the particular cultural norms and institutions that moved our collective 'animal spirits' towards a calculating frugality, a desire for 'improvement', and the profit-seeking 'capitalist mindset' of bourgeois society. This ideological narrative was first put forth by Werner Sombart in his 1902 treatise *Modern Capitalism*, which gave us our first introduction to the idea of the 'spirit of capitalism'.[14] Sombart actually said that his work was 'nothing other than a continuation and in a certain sense a completion of that of Marx'. Yet he believed society's prime mover was culture, not economics or nature. Max Weber, Sombart's more famous German contemporary, reformulated this culturalist approach into an enduring sociological paradigm. For Weber, capitalism emerged primarily from the Protestant moral spirit, particularly Calvinism, following the Reformation. The idea that propelled it was the Protestant work ethic conceived as a calling from God. Such a spirit of capitalism, for Weber, pervaded Western, Christian society before it spread throughout the world by the Christian and imperialist mission.[15] Protestant values, mixed with a drive towards rationalization, spurred the genesis of capitalism from the mid-1600s in Northern Europe, principally in Holland and England.

The Weberian account may seem plausible enough, but the Christian, and specifically Protestant cultural-ideological explanation, simply does not hold outside of Europe and its colonial territories. If capitalism is principally a values-driven system, then how did it also emerge in the Arab world and other regions where Christianity remained a minor religion? In Weber's later work, he moved away from the cultural-ideological argument towards a more techno-bureaucratic and economic justification that is closer to Karl Marx than John Calvin.[16] This drift indicates the importance of a historical materialist account of how capitalism became the dominant system through obscuring unpaid labour.

The third theory of capitalism is Marxist. It offers insights that the others do not through deconstructing the notion of capitalism as a natural order while interrogating its underlying forces and relations. The Marxist account holds that capitalism is an economic and social system in which the means of production (and social reproduction) are private property, owned by a distinct class of individuals. The vast majority of people must sell their capacity to work to this property-owning class in exchange for wages because they have no other way to acquire the things they need to live. In the three volumes of *Capital*, Marx tries to conceptualize the patterns of this system: its reliance on waged labour; the tendency towards the consolidation of property ownership; its imperatives of competition, efficiency, and control; the importance of finance and investment; the specifically capitalist legal form of state governance; and more. Marx's theory shows how unpaid labour has made the capitalist world. We elaborate this story below.

For Marx, capitalism stemmed from a 'historical process of divorcing the producer from the means of production' through violent expropriation, during the pre-history of capital and its mode of production. He calls this process primitive accumulation – the 'original sin' of political economy.[17] It entailed the privatization of land through the forceful eviction of rural and indigenous communities; the transformation of common property rights into exclusive private ownership; the violent colonial seizure of communal resources and human beings (as slaves) through imperial strategies; the taxation of land; usury; and the growth of the credit system. The dispossession of workers from their means of subsistence compelled them to become increasingly dependent on exchanging their labour for a wage to purchase necessities.

The development of capitalism, then, is coextensive with the development of a system of private property and the violent pillaging of the world. In England, where modern capitalism originated, the Enclosure Acts served as a 'Parliamentary form of robbery', which, as Marx argues, constituted the 'systematic theft of communal property'.[18] Between 1604 and 1914, some 5,200 enclosure bills were enacted, which amounted to the privatization of 6,800,000 acres of land – roughly one-fifth of the total area of England. As the historian Jairus Banaji shows, the 'collusion between commerce and state' facilitated the rise of merchant or 'commercial' capitalism, a protean precursor to the eighteenth century's industrial system.[19] Production for markets and the development of more codified property relations gradually spread across Northern Europe, spurring competition between lords and regions for resources.[20] In *Capital*, Marx noted that 'the treasures captured outside Europe by undisguised looting, enslavement and murder flowed back to the mother country' to be turned into capital. This violent 'series of thefts, outrages and popular misery' was combined, Marx wrote, with 'the forcible expropriation of the people from the last third of the fifteenth to the end of the eighteenth century'.[21] It is to the question of expropriation that we now turn.

## The Origins of Capitalism, a Shorter View

Twentieth-century Marxists generally agreed that capitalism as we know it today emerged in the English countryside during the late sixteenth and early seventeenth centuries. Feudal production transformed into capitalist production. But how exactly did capitalism leave feudal models of custom and culture behind? Why does this matter for our understanding of wage theft and unpaid labour? Because genesis is as important as structure in social relations. And the genesis of capitalism hinges on the question of whether it could have grown into the dominating force that it is today without the theft of land, natural resources, and labour to kick-start and sustain production at scale. Understanding how the original surpluses were accumulated through unpaid labour, whether through feudalism or slavery, connects the unwaged histories to the waged in capitalism. The origins of capitalist wage labour are also the origins of capitalist wage theft.

Paul Sweezy, an American Marxist economist, argues that the transition from feudalism to capitalism was primarily driven through external, quantitative dynamics. The provision of luxury items and weaponry through trade set off a degree of competition between lords to increase their incomes, leading to the quest for increasingly efficient forms of accumulation. A growing division of labour between urbanized villages and rural estates turned out to be more productive than the feudal manorial systems. It therefore came to dominate. This led to the development of systems of money rents and the use of capitalistically organized tenant labour rather than labour services by feudal serfs. As capitalistically organized systems of accumulation became more common, this quantitative shift gradually yielded a qualitative change in the mode of production.[22]

In contrast to Sweezy, Maurice Dobb, another Marxist, claims that internal, qualitative transformations in the forces (technology) and relations (class) of production provoked the quantitative changes in productive capacity characteristic of capitalism. An increasing division of labour, alienation of the worker from means of production, and technological innovations enabled the intensification of labour and productivity gains. The compulsion of competition and profitability incentivizes the extraction of an ever-greater amount of unpaid labour, and the reinvestment of surpluses in technology to produce and accumulate more efficiently. Dobb maintains that it was these internal, qualitative transformations that facilitated the transition from feudalism to capitalism rather than external transformations through trade and specialization of production.[23]

The core points of divergence between Sweezy's account (external, quantitative, trade-driven factors) and Dobb's (internal, qualitative, technologically driven factors) were sharpened in the debate that followed between the world-system theorist Immanuel Wallerstein and the historian Robert Brenner. Brenner builds on Dobb's account of internal, qualitative changes, noting that feudal lords had to dispossess labour from the means of production and increase productivity for the purpose of competitive accumulation. In other words, the lords had to develop a capitalist logic and imperatives of market competition for the first time.[24]

According to Brenner, the failure of English landlords to curb peasant mobility after the Black Death spelled the demise of serfdom; but landlords held on to the land if not to their serfs, blocking the kind of peasant proprietorship that became common in France. Lords consolidated their holdings and increasingly leased them out to tenants, who worked them as waged labourers. Agricultural land was thus increasingly subject to lease-holding conditions and responsive to price competition, which spurred specialization in production for efficiency gains and to maintain land access. Villeins were dispossessed from their direct means of subsistence and no longer shielded from the risks of price fluctuations. As Ellen Meiksins Wood points out, the compulsion of a competitive market is the 'operative principle' in Brenner's account that distinguishes it from others that emphasize 'opportunity'.[25]

The 'rules of reproduction' in England meant both direct producers and landlords became dependent on the market for subsistence, marking a rupture with ancient forms of social reproduction not mediated by the market. England thus incubated the agrarian precursor to Marx's industrial capitalism in one country. Brenner's argument is predicated on the Marxist distinction between pre-capitalist societies that relied on 'extra-economic' means of political, juridical, and military power to coerce the extraction of a surplus product or labour from producers; and capitalist societies, in which that coercion occurred principally through market mechanisms.[26] Those who support this perspective are often referred to as 'political Marxists' because they maintain that under capitalism, surplus extraction must be 'purely economic'.

Many people find this account convincing. Yet, while it may explain the emergence of agrarian capitalism in England, it fails to convincingly explain how its growth was sustained and this model spread across the world. As André Gunder Frank asks, how is it possible that the internal mode of production in the colonies can solely account for its dependence on the relations of exchange 'between the colony and its metropolis'?[27] Or, as the historian Albert Bergesen probes, 'How can the autonomous evolution of Aztec and Inca class relations have created Spanish Latin America?'[28]

In contrast to the political Marxists, Wallerstein contends that the transition to capitalism must look beyond the bounds of a single country. For Wallerstein the key to understanding capitalist development lies in the economic peripheralization of Eastern Europe. Feudalism encountered a crisis in the fourteenth century that drove the nobles' need for gold to ease their liquidity problems, new sources of essential commodities such as fuel and food, along with a desire for heightened accumulation of reserves. Western European states sought external trade overseas. In Eastern Europe, however, overseas expansion was not a viable solution. Therefore, they supplied grain to the West and re-feudalized in the 1500s to meet increased trade demands. The transfer of surplus product, extracted by unpaid labour from Eastern Europe to the West, enabled Western countries to develop a capitalist system and industrialize.[29] Wallerstein essentially says that the situation in any given country can only be fully explained by its relation to development and resource allocation on a world scale.[30]

Legitimacy in resource extraction, whether through legal or extra-legal force, ultimately hinges on who holds political power. In classical political theory, the state is the sovereign arbiter of legality. Perry Anderson offers a Marxist account of how modern power was forged. In Western Europe, the erosion of feudal relations forced landholders to accept a centralized legal authority in exchange for stabilizing a restless peasantry. This trade-off birthed the absolutist state, which compensated landlords for the loss of serfdom with institutional guarantees of property, order, and wage discipline. By contrast, in Eastern Europe, absolutism served not to dismantle serfdom but to entrench it, using state power to reassert feudal control over a mobile labour force.[31]

The rise of state capacity in Western Europe produced military, economic, and ideological pressures that rippled eastward, compelling parallel and competitive institution-building. Anderson argues that state formation was not merely a backdrop to capitalism's rise but its necessary precondition: it enabled the enforcement of labour contracts, the defence of property, and the expansion of markets. He lends credence to why England was the birthplace of capitalism, but also why colonial conquest was necessary to sustain and amplify its growth. Development is not fully intelligible when confined within national borders.[32] From Iraq in the ninth century and Islamic Spain in the twelfth century, to northern Italy in the thirteenth to sixteenth centuries and Bengal in the sixteenth to eighteenth, there are many historical examples of advanced merchant societies. Yet none of them sustained the transition to capitalism at scale.[33]

In this context, it is unlikely that agrarian capitalism alone could have generated the resources necessary for continued development and industrial evolution without European tributaries, the consolidation of state power, and the vast spoils of colonial theft and conquest. In his path-breaking 1944 book, *Capitalism and Slavery*, Eric Williams makes the argument that slavery was not an archaic hold-over but a central motor of capitalist accumulation. The Atlantic slave trade, colonial plantations, and the market monopolies they fed constituted a global supply chain of expropriation.[34] Without sugar, cotton, and other commodities produced by brutal unpaid slave labour, British capitalism would likely have faltered. In other worlds, the capitalist 'core' cannot be separated from the 'periphery'.

In *The Making of New World Slavery*, the historian Robin Blackburn shows that while slave systems did not produce capitalism, slave labour on plantations 'helped British capitalism to make a breakthrough to industrialism and global hegemony ahead of its rivals'.[35] The British slave trade emerged in the 1560s and expanded significantly after 1640. As industrial capitalism ramped up, British ships transported over 2.5 million enslaved persons, mostly to the Americas, out of an estimated 6 million total from 1701 to 1807.[36] However, it was not slave *trading* but rather slave *holding* that enabled this acceleration, contributing up to 5 per cent of GDP in the late eighteenth century.[37] Growth increased with Atlantic plantation production from the 1640s.[38] Britain exported manufactured goods such as textiles to its colonies, whose plantations shipped back sugar, tobacco, coffee, cotton, and other commodities. As John Stuart Mill remarks, it was 'hardly to be considered external trade, but more resembles the traffic between town and country'.[39] Marx, too, notes that the 'veiled slavery of the wage-earners in Europe needed, for its pedestal, slavery pure and simple in the New World'.[40]

Summing up, this section argues that the transformations driving the rise of agrarian capitalism in the English countryside could only be materially sustained and expanded through extra-national tributaries, including unpaid slave labour. In other words, quantitative increases sublated into a qualitative change. However, the plantation economies of the New World, rooted in slave labour and extraction, served not only to finance industrial capitalism in the core, but also to refine its techniques of domination. The factories of Manchester and the sugar fields of Barbados were linked not only by trade routes but also by shared methods of control: time discipline, productivity quotas, to ensure surplus extraction. The capitalist labour process, with its formal freedom and a contractual wage, was built from technologies of coercion drawn from feudalism and slavery. It is to these systems that we now turn.

## Feudal and Slave Labour Processes

While modern capitalist labour management techniques such as time-control discipline, technical divisions of labour, and so on emerged during the Industrial Revolution, these methods did not arrive on the scene fully formed. They evolved over decades and centuries from patriarchal and racial divisions of labour, which we explore below.

At the core of feudalism were peasant family units who worked the land and raised animals, along with limited artisanal work such as weaving or making clothing. Feudal patterns like this recur in civilizations as distinct in time and space as Han China, the Roman Gauls, and much of Sub-Saharan Africa. Peasant families had, of course, highly gendered divisions of labour, with men often doing tasks that required greater brawn while women tended towards child rearing and domestic tasks.[41] From Neolithic times to the twentieth century, peasants made up the majority of humans in the world. They lived lives of subsistence in the shadow of scarcity, but they also at least largely controlled their own time and production processes.

Peasants' main responsibility, however, was to their lord, who under the implicit or explicit threat of violence demanded a surplus (whether in bags of grain, weeks of unpaid labour, or coins) as rent in exchange for continued access to land. Sometimes this surplus led to exchange relations in a market, but pure cash cropping (producing only for sale and not subsistence) was rare until the emergence of industrial capitalism. Under feudalism, the expropriation of the surplus product through rents or tithes was literally separate in time and space from the work that serfs did to reproduce their lives. Under capitalism, waged labour obscured this separation.

In fourteenth-century England, roughly half of peasant land was freehold, with the remainder on villein tenure. Villeins were effectively 'part of the landlord's agricultural equipment'.[42] They were required to work on the lord's land for a variable number of unpaid days in addition to the time they worked on their own rented land. Only once the villein had paid the lord could they keep the products of their own labour. Feudal surpluses (see Table 2.1) took a wide-ranging mixture of forms, all of which could be estimated in unpaid labour.[43]

Table 2.1: Feudal surpluses

| | |
|---|---|
| *merchet* | a fine levied as permission for villeins' daughters to marry |
| *leyrwite* | a charge upon unmarried female serfs for fornication |
| *childwite* | a charge for birth |
| *chevage* | a payment (literally meaning 'head money') due to any serf who did not hold land or property on his home manor – like a charge on immigrants; it could also be a charge to live away from a manor, since serfs had no right to move away permanently |
| *licences* | a charge for education and apprenticeships |
| *tallage* | a land tenure tax or rent charged at the will and frequency of the lord |
| *heriot* | a payment to the lord from the estate of a deceased villein tenant, often in the form of the most valuable chattel of the deceased tenant or sometimes as a cash sum equivalent to one-third the value of their chattels |
| *entry fine* | a sum payable upon succession to, or acquisition of, customary land that was circa the thirteenth-century equivalent to a year's (or sometimes two years') rent |
| *millsuit* | a toll for the use of the lord's mill that usually consisted of a percentage – between 3 per cent and 8 per cent of the ground grain or 'multure' |

This was not an equal exchange, or a free market. Villeins were neither compensated if crops failed, nor did they have legal protection from eviction or abuse. They were legally bonded to lords and the manor. Absconding risked imprisonment for vagrancy or death. Forced dependency meant entire families served as a reserve of labour.

Unpaid labour under feudalism had been established as early as the eleventh century. There were essentially two types. The first were works such as agricultural labour that were performed for a fixed number of days each week throughout the year, excluding the harvest period. The second type were seasonal harvests, or 'boon works' such as ploughing, reaping, and so on. Labour services ranged from 10 per cent (across parts of the Midlands, North, and South West England) to 30 per cent (in East Anglia, Sussex, Oxfordshire, and others) of the value of all customary rents on lay manors. Manors kept track of these works in the annual 'works account'. Those works not performed for a permissible reason (such as holy days), or those works that the landlord chose not to utilize, were 'sold' back to the tenant as a standard cash sum in lieu of the service, a process known as commutation (like a prison sentence).[44]

Serfdom was never officially abolished in England.[45] Rather, it withered away through increasing commutation of labour services and taxes from 1350 to 1580. Direct exploitation gave way to lords leasing their demesnes (land) for money rents. At Merton College, Oxford in 1262, for instance, the rent package on the half virgate (a measure of land roughly equivalent to 30 acres) primarily consisted of two days a week unpaid labour (a cash equivalent of 20 shillings) plus payments in kind through grain and poultry, an entry fine, heriot, millsuit, and money rent. Before the Black Death, each villein owed around a hundred labour services per annum, which by the early 1420s was reduced to thirty days of labour service from all the tenanted lands as money rents came to form the dominant share of fees. Serfdom had mostly disappeared in England by the time that the early modern slave mode of production was developed.[46]

In the colonial Americas, Caribbean, and antebellum United States, slaves were treated as fixed capital investments, bought and sold as human machinery to increase plantation productivity.[47] The market price of a slave was roughly equivalent to ten to twelve years of a free worker's wages with a similar skill set.[48] In 2025, if the median full-time British salary was £39,039, the price of a slave would be roughly £390,000 to £469,000 for a lifetime of unpaid labour. Collateralized investments in slave labour stimulated significantly higher economic growth for slave owners in port cities such as Bristol and Liverpool.[49]

Britain's 'slave' mode of production could be said to have been kick-started by William Courten and Associates, in 1627, as their company started cultivating tobacco, cotton, indigo, and sugar cane on Barbados, establishing a roaring trade by 1643. By 1690, 80 per cent of the island's arable land, 90 per cent of its labour force, and 90 per cent of its export earnings were from sugar cane. From the 1650s the British started importing African slaves to the Caribbean and by 1690 all labour other than supervisory roles was performed by slaves.[50] As the Dutch labour historian Marcel van der Linden shows, the labour discipline developed during the

'Sugar Revolution' would serve as a prototype for the organization of industrial factories in the late eighteenth century.[51]

Plantations were on average around 200 acres in size with around 100 slaves. Field labourers only had three tools – an axe, a hoe, and bill. They performed a wide range of tasks, including those that animals did in England or North America, such as pulling ploughs and harrows. Tasks were assigned often purely to keep slaves busy at all times. The systems that overseers and plantation owners developed transformed work into a brutal, unhuman, machinic process. In 1861, the social critic Frederick Olmsted observed a US hoe gang moving in trace-like synchronicity. '[Slaves] are constantly and steadily driven up to their work,' he wrote, 'and the stupid, plodding, machine-like manner in which they labour is painful to witness.'[52] Such uniform gang labour became the backbone of the agricultural labour process under slavery, in both the British Caribbean and the Southern United States. This despotic discipline and control yielded chilling results. Economic historians have shown that labour productivity growth exhibited on cotton plantations was significantly higher (2.1–2.4 per cent annually between 1800 and 1860) than Britain's textile labour productivity growth (1.8 per cent per year during the same period).[53]

It was in these circumstances that the origins of our contemporary regime of unpaid labour are found. To manage and control large numbers of people completing mechanistic, repetitive, and monotonous work, a minute division of labour known as the gang system was developed. This system relied on overseeing the *effort*, in contrast to overseeing the *result*. Overseeing the result is referred to as the task system and entails assigning a particular job to a worker for a day. When the task is finished, so is the workday. However, when tasks are interdependent, it becomes harder for overseers to judge the individual effort as part of the result. When overseeing the effort, the overseer constantly monitors the intensity and quality of work. Overseeing the effort and compelling workers to work harder are both easier the simpler the tasks are. The gang system focused on overseeing effort, which was innovative from a capitalist perspective, since it stole nearly all autonomy from workers. As Van der Linden notes: 'totalizing control and unfree labour went historically hand in hand'.[54]

The close relationship between Caribbean planters and the British bourgeoisie meant the plantation labour techniques boomeranged back into the metropole.[55] Wealthy landlords sent their privileged children born in the West Indies to England to be educated, bringing methods of agricultural 'plant' management to the industrial factory and transferring disciplinary knowledge.[56] The English poet Robert Southey criticized Robert Owen's New Lanark Cotton Mills (a famous attempt to create a utopian community in Scotland) for treating workers as 'human machines', reflecting the spread of wage slavery.[57] Many plantation techniques, like a detailed division of labour, eventually found their way into Frederick Taylor's 1911 bible of factory discipline, *Scientific Management*.

However, change was uneven. As the Marxist maritime historian Marcus Rediker notes, the capitalist labour process 'arrived in some parts of the production process much earlier than in others'.[58] After slavery was formally abolished in most of the British Empire from 1834, former slaves aged six and older were still made to work for their former owners for several extra years. In exchange for labour, the owners were obliged to provide them with food, clothing, lodging, medicine, and other necessities. The bondage of ex-slaves was called 'apprenticeship', directly referencing the European guild system, and required forty-five hours of unpaid labour per week.

The decline of West Indian sugar plantations from the 1830s and 1840s also spurred the migration of planters to other parts of the colonial world, particularly South Asia. The coffee plantations of British Ceylon, later Sri Lanka, for example, were modelled directly on the slave plantations of the British West Indies. Extracts from a handbook for the management of coffee plantations in the Caribbean were published in British Ceylon in 1842, 'without even changing the word "Negro"'.[59]

Citizens of the European metropole continued to benefit from unfree, unpaid slave labour after abolition. As detailed in the Legacies of British Slavery (LBS) database, the Crown via parliament granted £20 million (or £17 billion today) in compensation from 1835 to 1843 to over 10,000 former slave-owners, indirectly financially benefiting over 47,000 British people.[60] Similarly, the corvée system of unpaid labour persisted in the French colonies well into the twentieth century, with conscripts in the Ivory Coast being forced to work unpaid at least one day a week on cacao plantations. France's blockade of Haiti, after the latter overthrew colonial slavery, enforced a financial penalty on the country equivalent to 2 per cent of French national income at the time or €40 billion euros today.[61] There is a direct line from the unpaid labour of workers – whether free or unfree – to the wealth of nations.

In conventional Marxist accounts of capitalism, a key distinguishing feature is the emergence of 'doubly free' labour – that is, labour that is both freed from the means of production and free to sell labour-power in an open market. This freedom, however, was partial for a very long time. This chapter explored how the origins of capitalism are bound up with the brutal unfreedom that enslaved people endured at the hands of white colonial masters. It shows how modern waged labour was forged with blood and fire from the laboratory and wealth of the plantation system. But the violence of this system raises deeper philosophical questions about ownership.

The right to property is the foundation of the wealth of nations. The question of who has the right to property has provoked intense debate among thinkers from John Locke and Adam Smith to Pierre Joseph Proudhon and Karl Marx. On what grounds do those who own the wealth produced by labour lay claim to it? The next chapter takes aim at the concepts of property and ownership, interrogating the historical construction of these ideas to better understand the means by which the products of our labour are stolen.

# 3
# Property Is Theft?

*There is nothing which so generally strikes the imagination, and engages the affections of mankind, as the right of property or that sole and despotic dominion which one man claims and exercises over the external things of the world, in total exclusion of the right of any other individual in the universe. And yet there are very few, that will give themselves the trouble to consider the original and foundation of this right.*

– William Blackstone, *Commentaries on the Laws of England*

During the bleak midwinter of 1795, Jean Valjean breaks a bakery window and snatches a loaf of bread. He is swiftly caught and then sentenced to five years' hard labour at Bagne of Toulon prison. This scene in *Les Misérables* makes the boy a thief because the law deemed the bread 'property'. In early bourgeois France, titles, deeds, contracts, and wages were the material base for the moral order of society, an order enforced by the state through discipline and punishment. Yet we can also see how the law makes a crime from necessity because property is not a natural but a juridical construction. The laws that secure private property rights negate social need, seeding class conflict over necessary resources. However, history shows that laws shift over time with conquests, enclosures, mortgage crises, and revolutions. Definitions of ownership are politically determined. In this light, Pierre-Joseph Proudhon's anarchist slogan 'property is theft' is more than a rhetorical flourish. To grasp theft, we must first interrogate the notion of property itself.

As discussed in the previous chapter, in early modern Europe, property took both private and communal forms, reflecting feudal legacies and norms of social land use. Yet the old regime was upended starting from the seventeenth century, as the nobility in cahoots with a rising bourgeoisie began to restrict collective rights to land and resources.[1]

As an editor of the *Rheinische Zeitung* from 1842 to 1843, Marx penned an eviscerating critique of a new set of Prussian laws characteristic of the new bourgeois property regime. For a long time, collection of fallen timber from forests was a customary right among peasants. A new set of Prussian laws, however, authorized the seizure of common property (the timber) and criminalized those who relied on it (peasant gleaners). For Marx, the law was rife with problems: it failed to differentiate between the theft of fallen wood and timber; gave excessive power to forest wardens and owners; imposed forced labour on violators; made thieves of both gleaner and receiver; and placed the burden of proof on the accused.[2] Peasants were made into thieves because wealthy burghers (merchants and craftspeople) had already stolen the wood themselves by changing the letter of the law!

When the law is manipulated to serve the exclusive advantage of particular groups, it loses its moral legitimacy, contravenes the natural order, undermines its universality, and erodes the state's authority. Writing in *Rheinische Zeitung*, Marx says:

> If every violation of property without distinction, without a more exact definition, is termed theft, will not all private property be theft? By my private ownership do I not exclude every other person from this ownership? Do I not thereby violate his right of ownership? If you deny the difference between essentially different kinds of the same crime, you are denying that crime itself is different from right, you are abolishing right itself, for every crime has an aspect in common with right.[3]

The contradictions inherent in bourgeois law reveal its political function as a tool of the capitalist state, which only *appears* to offer an equal right to property alongside an equal threat of criminalization.[4] While every citizen may appear to have *de jure* equality, they *de facto* lack it due to the unequal distribution of property ownership and resources it bestows upon the owners. Ignoring the extra-legal and coercive origins of property rights reproduces the asymmetrical domination of owners over producers, of the few over the many. As this chapter shows, without a critical interrogation of the notion of property itself, we risk missing the forest for the trees.

## The Liberal Trap

The liberal tradition birthed the idea of private property as the inviolable right of 'man', and the pinnacle of civilization. Yet this same tradition also sows the seeds of its own destruction. In what follows, we examine how liberal accounts of property and theft are dissonant with our contemporary ideas of private ownership. We begin with John Locke and trace his political theories through those of Marx himself.

The second of John Locke's *Two Treatises of Government* is central to both contemporary Western political philosophy and the liberal theory of property.[5] It begins with the Christian notion that 'God … Has given the Earth to the Children of Men; given it to Mankind in common'.[6] By common, Locke means the absence of private ownership. But, if land and all its products are given to humanity, how can one person deny another's claim to that common property? Locke answers:

> The Labour of his Body, and the Work of his Hands, we may say, are properly his. Whatsoever then he removes out of the State that Nature hath provided, and left it in, he hath mixed his Labour with, and joined to it something that is his own, and thereby makes it his Property.[7]

In other words, since labour indisputably belongs to the worker, the adding of labour to nature yields a product that becomes the worker's property. For Locke, then, the primary value of land comes from labour: 'For 'tis labour indeed that puts the difference of value on everything.'[8] Adding labour to nature (land held in common by all) establishes a right to claim ownership over what is produced.

Locke establishes two conditions for the right to claim ownership over the products of one's labour. First, this right only extends as far as 'there is enough, and as good left in common for others'.[9] Second, claims to property are only legitimate insofar as an individual uses it. This counters against hording and spoilage. 'Whatever is beyond this,' Locke states, 'is more than his Share, and belongs to others.' While Locke argues that 'As much Land as a Man Tills, Plants, Improves, Cultivates, and can use the Product of, so much is his Property', he also qualifies that 'he cannot appropriate, he cannot inclose [*sic*], without the Consent of all his Fellow-Commoners, all Mankind'.[10] Locke's 'rule of property' is that 'that every Man should have as much as he could make use of'. This is the 'original' state of things.[11]

With the introduction of money, 'and the tacit Agreement of Men to put a value on it', things get more complicated. Money, as an abstract quantification of value, enables hording and 'larger possessions'.[12] Locke tries to bypass his own moral restrictions on property ownership by equating a servant's labour (cutting turfs) with the master's act of digging ore, suggesting that the master's appropriation of his servant's labour is equivalent to the master's own labouring activity. This implies that the landlord, who uses a servant to enhance their land, is labouring by proxy. This logic not only legitimizes the master's claim over the fruits of the servant's labour but also perversely elevates the landlord to producer rather than extractor. Readers might find this resonates with the CEO-worship that festers among entrepreneurial types today.

There is a still darker side to Locke's logic, highlighted by Ellen Meiksins Wood. It justified the enclosure of 'unprofitable' common land in England and the violent conquest of 'unproductive' indigenous territories.[13] For Locke, the notion of 'improvement' was essential to claim the right to property; free commons are essentially wasteful. Only those who labour to improve land can lay claim to it. What constitutes 'improvement' also conveniently reflects specifically European bourgeois values. Locke's own actions lend weight to Wood's criticism. He was employed as secretary to the Earl of Shaftesbury, one of the eight original Lord Proprietors of Carolina, profiting through stock ownership in numerous slave-trading companies.[14]

Given the morally and politically objectionable logic of Locke's theory, some might think it would be best to simply dispose of it. However, Locke's ideas are pervasive in Western liberal societies, underpinning our cultural and legal systems. Better, then, to provide an immanent critique.

The political philosopher C.B. Macpherson offers a starting point for this task. Known for his critique of 'possessive individualism', Macpherson argues that Locke can only provide a justification for the accumulation of property prior to the establishment of civil society and the consent of its members. When Locke asserts that the 'labour thus sold becomes the property of the buyer, who is then entitled to appropriate the produce of that labour', he projects an individuated conception of labour and the wage back onto the state of nature.[15] Yet, individuated labour existed neither in

Locke's time nor in his imagined state of nature. The individuated wage system arose from historically contingent social relations as outlined above. Macpherson also points out that Locke's theory lacks a quantifiable threshold for the amount of labour required to claim property rights. How much labour is enough to claim an acre of the woods? To claim a room in a house? To claim a share of Tesla?

Locke's reasoning fails to fully justify why labour alone should determine right. However, if read against the grain, there is also a radical kernel to Locke's theory. As political theorist James Tully argues, Locke defines labour as the actions determined by an individual's will, which means there is no inherent right for the master to appropriate a servant's property without equivalent compensation.[16] For Locke, '[the] Freeman makes himself a Servant to another, by selling him for a certain time, the Service he undertakes to do, in exchange for Wages he is to receive'.[17] A freeman's service must be exchanged for an agreed monetary equivalent as compensation for giving up their right to the products of their labour. There is no right to appropriate based on improvement, if it violates another individual's right to use that property or violates another individual's compensation for their labour. Appropriation without equivalent of property and appropriation without equivalent of labour are equally unjustifiable. This is key to the theory of wage theft developed in this book.

Finally, given the idea of individuated labour was a historical illusion (as Macpherson points out), we instead must apply Locke's theory to collective labour. Logically, this would mean that the quantity of labour expended upon any given common object, upon any element of nature, must become the shared property of all who contributed to the transformation of said object. In this way, Locke unwittingly laid the groundwork for the abolition of private property. History shows that this isn't merely speculative theorizing; it is praxis. Nineteenth-century radicals used Locke's labour theory of property (and value) to justify various revolts against industrial alienation and the emerging domination of private property.[18] Classical political economists such as John Stuart Mill and Adam Smith were also influenced by this radical interpretation, to which we now turn.

In Mill's *Principles of Political Economy*, he maintains that the right to property is something gained through labour. For Mill, the institution of property essentially consists in the mutual recognition 'of a right to the exclusive disposal' of what each person has 'produced by their own exertions' or of what each person has received without coercion from the producer. Mill is unequivocal that the entire 'foundation of the whole is the right of producers to what they themselves have produced'. Against Locke, however, Mill maintains that this principle finds its limit in land, since 'no man made the land'.[19] Mill recognized that land, if held in common, could never wholly be appropriated, since it produced a common bounty.

Adam Smith, another founding father of political economy, was also influenced by Locke. In the 'original' state of nature, Smith argues, 'the whole produce of labour belongs to the labourer' with 'neither landlord nor master' entitled to take it from the worker. This 'original foundation of all other property', he says, is the 'most sacred and inviolable right to property derived from one's own labour'.[20] 'The real price of everything,' Smiths writes, 'is the toil and trouble of acquiring it.' He continues:

> Labour was the first price, the original purchase-money that was paid for all things. It was not by gold or silver, but by labour, that all the wealth of the world was originally purchased; and its value, to those who possess it, and who want to exchange it for some new productions, is precisely equal to the quantity of labour which it can enable them to purchase or command.[21]

Smith holds that the value of any product is determined by the amount of labour it can command in exchange for other goods, rather than the labour required to produce it. This means that for Smith, one can exchange a lesser amount of labour for a greater amount of labour. There is no equal exchange in this system.[22]

Unlike Mil, Smith then proceeds to justify the right to private property and accumulation of wealth from labour. Once land becomes private property, and property owners begin to accumulate stock, labourers become wage-labourers, who must (that is, are compelled by force, violating one of Locke's principles) share the products of labour with the owners of land and stock. Once private property is acquired, Smith argues, it is only *natural* to expect greater returns from the sale of produce, exceeding what is necessary to replace one's initial investment. Without this incentive, Smith contends, there would be no reason to employ a large stock instead of a small one.

Ultimately, the transformation of nature into capital hinges on the justification for hoarding. Smith argues that landlords have a rightful claim to profits derived from a portion of the labour's produce as this is the sole factor that adds fresh value to goods. However, in *The Theory of Moral Sentiments*, Smith also argues that landlords are 'led by an invisible hand to make nearly the same distribution of the necessaries of life, which would have been made, had the earth been divided into equal portions among all its inhabitants'.[23] The invisible hand of the market is supposed to mimic equal distribution of the necessities of life, as if in the original state of nature. This idealized projection of market distribution and fairness has been used as a cudgel against labour for centuries (see Chapter 4).

In contrast to Smith, Marx radically challenges Locke's ideas. Marx holds that there is a natural right to collective property based on one's labour. But this is an individual claim to collective property, rather than an individual claim to private (bourgeois) property. For Marx, Locke shows that 'in spite of the common property in nature, individual property could be created by individual labour'.[24] Like Mill, Marx believed that there is no legitimate claim to land itself. Locke's theory in fact upended the foundation of landlords' claims to rents as well as the claims on interest by the usurer. The right to property must therefore be limited by labour and use, even when money is introduced. The means of collective production should be held common, like 'nature' in the original state of things. Workers have a natural right to the products of their labour, as collective property. This would be what Marx refers to as the 'individual property system'. The labourer would receive the value of his contribution to the collective product, and any action that deprived him of it would be deemed 'unjust'.[25]

Through a Marxist lens, one can observe that capitalism does a strange thing to the right to property; it transforms it from a claim based on one's own labour into a claim over the appropriation of the products of another's labour. Capitalism spurs specialization, replacing individual craft labour by a collective and detailed division of labour. In factories, no single worker produces the final product; instead, each worker contributes to specific parts of a collective whole. The means of production are controlled by one class, while the other simply controls their ability to work.

Against Locke's theory, Marx shows that the capital exchanged against labour-power is actually already the result of the appropriation of unpaid labour: 'The ownership of past unpaid labour is thenceforth the sole condition for the appropriation of living unpaid labour on a constantly increasing scale.'[26] The capital exchanged for labour-power is already dead labour, alienated from the worker and 'appropriated *without equivalent*'; in exchange, that capital will again be replenished 'with a surplus by living labour capacity'; the relation between capital and labour only appears as 'a mere semblance' of equivalents.[27]

In summary, the history of private property is the history of its separation from those who mixed their labour with the land. The property regime arose from a moral law that should have preserved collective rights to land. If modern laws are designed to protect property rights, then true equality before the law is impossible without equal and collective ownership of property. Treating unequal individuals as if they are equal does not eliminate the material fact of inequality. In actuality, this is tried and tested strategy of subordination. Thus, the concept of equal rights within this framework serves to uphold inequality. Our modern idea of property simply affirms the right of the few to steal and hoard the unpaid labour of the many. Liberal political theory casts a historically contingent conception of property as a universal law to naturalize the norms of bourgeois society.[28]

The historical nature of the system of private property and its relationship to the theft of labour is illustrated in a lesser-known debate between Marx and Proudhon. Their disagreement reveals more about their common philosophy and critique of bourgeois property than either of them would admit during their own lifetime. And it directly addresses the relationships between property, labour, and theft in a way that illustrates their co-constitution.

## Marx Versus Proudhon

In the cafés and smoke-filled bars of the Rue Coquillière in mid-1840s Paris, Karl Marx and Pierre-Joseph Proudhon could often be found arguing over Hegel, history, and the nature of exploitation. Proudhon, a printer by trade and anarchist by instinct, had just published *Qu'est-ce que la propriété?* [*What Is Property?*]. His answer, 'Property is theft', resonated throughout the French working classes. Marx, who arrived in 1843 to work as an editor at the short-lived *Annales Franco-Allemandes*, called Proudhon's work 'epoch-making' for its 'audacity'.[29] At the time, he praised Proudhon's legalistic concept of exploitation as the personification of proletarian thought, a bold and uncompromising theory that overlapped with his own concept of surplus-value.[30] Their early friendship was intense, bound by shared commitments and overlapping critiques. But by 1844, the alliance began to fracture. The core of their disagreement concerned the concepts of property, value, and labour. Understanding this rupture sheds light on the deeper nature of the wage and its theft.

The sociologist Georges Gurvitch thinks that the mutual antipathy between Marx and Proudhon 'was based more on purely personal feelings than on their ideas'.[31] Of course, Marx never shied from controversy, and he begins his treatment of Proudhon's 1846 work *The System of Economic Contradictions or The Philosophy of Poverty* in his characteristically unforgiving fashion:

> M. Proudhon's work is not just a treatise on political economy, an ordinary book; it is a bible. 'Mysteries', 'Secrets Wrested from the Bosom of God', 'Revelations' – it lacks nothing. But as prophets are discussed nowadays more conscientiously than profane writers, the reader must resign himself to going with us through the arid and gloomy erudition of 'Genesis', in order to ascend later, with M. Proudhon, into the ethereal and fertile realm of super-socialism.[32]

Marx derides Proudhon's political theory as the 'code of socialism of the petit bourgeois [shopkeepers and so on]'.[33] Never one to shy from conflict, Proudhon returned fire, lambasting Marx's essay as 'a tissue of crudities, slanders, falsifications and plagiarism', claiming that Marx 'regrets that I have thought like him everywhere and that I was the first to say it'.[34] Reflecting on their hostile exchange, Marx admits that it 'ended [their] friendship forever'.[35]

Was there political or theoretical substance to this conflict? Marx argues that Proudhon, in maintaining that 'property is theft', establishes property as the transhistorical foundation of profit. Yet Marx counters that the production of surplus-value only occurs in the capitalist mode of production, not across all time and all modes of production. He points out that since theft is 'a forcible violation of property', this 'presupposes the existence of property'.[36] A *hysteron proteron*, this puts the cart before the horse. In *The Ego and Its Own*, the anarchist philosopher Max Stirner agrees, asserting that 'property is not theft, but a theft becomes possible only through property'.[37]

Proudhon's work has its deficiencies, placing too much trust in scientific progress yet also indulging in mysticism, transcendental appeals, and unfinished dialectics. Yet he was on to something important, which could explain why Marx attacked him so vigorously, fashioning a bitter rivalry to obscure a fundamental commonality. Both Marx and Proudhon put forward the idea that there is an unpaid, uncompensated contribution of the worker to the social whole that is hoarded to build wealth. The criticism that 'theft becomes possible only through property' is *precisely the point*.

Indeed, Proudhon argues via Locke that the 'labourer retains, even after receiving his wages, a natural right of property in the thing which he has produced', and that humanity has a universal right to freely and mutually access vital resources to sustain life.[38] Like Marx, Proudhon maintains that capitalism dispossesses workers from their own means of subsistence, which compels them to work for a wage. He also, like Marx, defines the wage as the cost of the reproduction of the labourers' means of existence. The employer takes advantage of this by extracting a surplus or excess of value from collective labour, which cannot be reduced to the sum of each individual labourer's efforts. Thus, workers have a legitimate collective claim, a 'natural property right', to this surplus of value.

> If the farm was originally worth 100,000 francs, and if by the labour of the tenant it increases its value to 150,000 francs, the tenant, who produced this surplus value, is the legitimate proprietor of a third of the farm.[39]

It is important to emphasize that Proudhon does not believe that any single payment could make waged labour equitable, unless it represents a complete redistribution of the product among all the producers: 'For when you have paid all the individual forces, you have still not paid the collective force.'[40] A right of collective property remains, which has no individual justification. Proudhon and Marx align here again.

Proudhon's theory is more tenuous where he diverges from Marx. For example, he claims that 'all capital, whether material or mental, is the result of collective labour and so is collective property'. In a moral sense, Proudhon is right – everything transformed into capital on this earth has involved labour at some stage. Private property, as the exclusive appropriation of what should be held in common, casts its owner as 'either a parasite or a thief'. This is sharp political sloganeering, but too blunt for political economy. As Marx observes, Proudhon's theory lacks crucial distinctions between capitalist and rentier, between exploitation and expropriation, between different forms of profit and between different historical modes of production.[41] Proudhon 'garbles them into pre-existing eternal ideas'.[42]

As shown above, Marx conceives of property historically. The shift from communal property to modern private property was a wholesale change in its very nature. Communal rights to land use enabled a subsistence way of life with collective norms quite alien to our world of individuated consumption. But these rights and norms were upended by the bourgeois regime. Thus, the concepts of property and theft should not be treated as fixed and unchanging abstractions. Yet private property does have its origins in a kind of theft. Violent acts of colonial looting and robbery from the East Indies to West Africa and beyond claimed land, raw materials, and human beings as property. Waged and unwaged slaveries relied on both the 'man-stealers' of the slave trade and 'child-stealers' of the English workhouse.[43] These thefts facilitated the sustained expansion of capitalist production in Europe and its global tributaries.

While Marx maintains that it is impossible to attempt to separate the individual contribution of each labourer in a social system of collective exploitation, he still claims that private property 'rests on the labour of the individual himself'.[44] We can say, then, that individual deductions from wages are an attack on the labour share of the product, which takes the form of a commodity or money before becoming property. While the notion of equivalent exchange between wages and labour-power is a ruse, capitalism would collapse without it. Equivalent exchange is what obscures the extraction of unpaid labour in the working day. Surplus-value is not produced *simply* by stealing the wages of individual workers. Yet, the entire history of the labour movement and socialist politics revolves around bargaining over workers' share of the collective products of labour – from higher wages to equity shares. Equal exchange reifies the exploitation of labour as a natural right, as if 'it is an inherent quality of human labour to furnish a surplus product'.[45]

We might conclude this chapter, then, by turning to Soviet legal theorist Evgeny Pashukanis's insight that the cardinal principle of capitalist societies is the equal chance of achieving inequality. In his *General Theory of Law and Marxism*, Pashukanis argues that law, including the notion of private property, is rooted in the relations of exchange: individuals are legally constructed as 'owners' of commodities, and the legal system codifies the parameters of what can (and cannot) be taken or transferred. Theft thus becomes a breach of the sanctified exchange relation that upholds the primacy of private property under capitalism. Ownership itself rests upon the social appropriation of surplus-value generated by workers. The formal legal protections over property serve to entrench the class divide.[46]

If ownership is a historical construction rather than a natural fact, then so too is the wage system. Understanding this system is essential to overcome it. The next chapter presents a brief genealogy of labour-power as the conceptual key to unlocking this knowledge. It explores how the capacity to work became a commodity, the only property of the dispossessed, and how this abstraction (which is central to Marx's critique) was forged in a crucible of violent industrial discipline.

# 4
# The Commodification of Labour and Its Limits

In 2013, a Reddit user known as 'Doreen' created r/Anti Work as a space for those disillusioned with the demands of American work culture. Initially, the subreddit was a modest forum hosting discussions about shit bosses, boring jobs, and various problems with our contemporary work environment. Yet this airing of grievances evolved into a communal consciousness-raising activity about dehumanization, alienation, and a lack of free time under capitalism. In 2020, as hundreds of millions of people found themselves unemployed, furloughed, or struggling with the demands of remote work during the COVID-19 pandemic, r/AntiWork grew exponentially and people re-evaluated their relationship with work. The subreddit grew from a few thousand to millions of members in just a few months.

The pandemic highlighted some hitherto obscured vulnerabilities and inequities in the labour market. While essential workers were lauded as heroes, most continued to endure poor working conditions, low wages, and job insecurity. Those working from home faced their own challenges, such as burnout, isolation, and the erosion of the boundary between work and personal life. r/AntiWork became a refuge for these individuals, a place where they could share their stories and find a community that understood their struggles.

As the subreddit grew, it became a repository of personal narratives about workplace exploitation, toxic environments, and unfair treatment. The community was no longer just a place to vent; it evolved into a political resource. Members shared advice about how to win in disputes, offered support, and even helped each other find alternative employment or income. Terms such as 'quiet quitting' (reducing effort to the minimum) and 'The Great Resignation' (the mass churn of the labour market) were largely popularized due to the forum. More significant acts of protest, including workplace walkouts and unionization drives, were bolstered by it.

The rejection of work is not new. Like the r/AntiWork subredditors, the ancient Greeks of the patrician class viewed work as largely a distraction and burden, best suited for plebs and slaves. Plato and Aristotle both thought of work negatively, as activity focused on necessary bodily needs, hindering contemplation and community participation. As Hannah Arendt notes, the etymology of the word 'labour' in European languages reflects an association with pain, effort, and poverty. The Latin *labore* means 'to stumble under a burden', while the Greek *ponos* and German *Arbeit* share an etymological root with 'poverty' (*penia* in Greek and *armut* in German). And we must not forget the relationship between the labour of work and the labour of birth. Biblical referents underscore this negative connotation: God cursed Adam, declaring all work a source of toil and pain.

Many classical political economists also conceived of work negatively. Adam Smith thought labour was primarily suffering and sacrifice. While labour produces wealth, Smith believed that the actual activity lacks any inherent worth: work is merely a means of self-denial required for survival. In his *Economic and Philosophic Manuscripts of 1844*, Marx outlines a contrasting view. Drawing on the German philosopher G.W.F. Hegel's recognition of labour as a human essence, Marx conceives of labour as a free and conscious activity, with emancipatory potential.[1] Labour 'in this universal form', Marx writes, is 'as old as the hills'.[2] Yet this emancipatory potential is eclipsed by class domination: the serf by the lord, slave by the master, and worker by the capitalist. The capacity to labour becomes the only thing of value that workers can sell to earn a living.

During the English Civil War (1642–49), a proto-socialist political movement known as the Levellers had already anticipated Marx's critique. For these craftspeople, the capacity to labour was literally considered a form of property. The movement held that people who sold their labour-power for a wage instantly abdicated their right to this property and the associated claim to freedom, as if they had sold their only plot of land.[3] Their alienation meant they lost the power to exclude others from the use of their labour-power. As C.B. Macpherson notes, the politics of the Levellers movement reflects their experiences as craftspeople who lacked property ownership in land or membership of a trading corporation.

They could only protect themselves from the anarchy of the market by protecting their autonomy over their capacity to work.[4] Gerrard Winstanley, leader of the Diggers, a more revolutionary section of the Levellers, rejected waged labour altogether, declaring, 'We can as well live under a foreign enemy working for day wages as under our own brethren.'[5]

How was human labour transformed into labour-power? How did the drive towards the profit imperative and the 'valorization of value' supplant the drive towards satisfying social needs? Juridical, technological, and patriarchal institutions frame what counts as value under capitalism. The histories of these forces are integral to the story of wage theft.

## The Making of Labour-Power

Capitalism operates according to the 'law of value', defined as the regulative principle that compels the equalization of exchange-values (prices) in the economy and an average profit rate in competitive markets. In this system, commodities are produced by labour-power, an individual's productive capacity, which is exchanged as if it is like any other commodity. Yet labour-power is not like any other commodity, because it generates more value than it costs. While workers receive wages that sustain their ability to reproduce their labour-power, these wages represent only a fraction of the total value produced – the rest is surplus-value 'in its pure form'.[6]

To fabricate labour-power, capitalists needed to take control over the production process through the violent discipline of the factory system. European craftsmen's customary power was upended and peasant ways of life destroyed to make way for satanic mills and coke ovens. This long and arduous period of transition was juridically facilitated by laws that bolstered class domination by criminalizing mobility, unions, and protest while also denying suffrage to prevent democratic change. However, despite the efforts of a burgeoning bourgeoisie, pre-industrial class culture persisted well into the late eighteenth century.[7] In the 1760s, for example, the relationship between employer and employee was still based primarily on class status rather than contract.[8] Any man or woman who was not already employed, apprenticed, or bound to an agricultural holding could be forced to work for any farmer or tradesman who needed them.[9] While customary work hours existed, employers had the authority to make demands of their workers at any time, day or night. Only independent producers could treat their labour as freely transferable property.[10] Access to a workforce of 'permanent' servants meant the rich ontologized subservience, making working-class subordination seem natural and inevitable, as if it were fundamental to worker identity rather than a product of economic and social forces.

As Richard Biernacki notes in his magisterial study *The Fabrication of Labor*, the newly proletarianized workers of the eighteenth century were legally an inferior class of individuals all the way up until 1867. While local justices could fix wage rates and order employers to pay workers their wages, most workers lacked access to the legal means to enforce this. Just like today, employers exploited the system to steal wages. Some employers forced their workers to accept promissory notes (a promise to pay in the future) instead of immediate payment. Labour was still, at least partially, unfree.[11]

If employers accused workers of neglecting their duties or leaving their jobs, the courts treated it as a criminal rather than civil offence, which meant workers were sometimes incarcerated for months, merely for quitting. Both male and female domestic workers could face prosecution if production deadlines weren't met. A similar fate awaited artisans who did not meet delivery quotas.[12] Time discipline in production (the quantification of effort and output) was already part of the legislative apparatus before new machinery, such as the power loom, could be used to set the pace of work.[13] This punitive legal regime was meant to break resistance to new industrial processes, and ensure that the balance of power between labour and capital lay firmly on the side of the latter. Furthermore, protests against wage theft or to demand fair wages were illegal. This explicit, punitive legal compulsion was needed to ensure the capitalist law of value took hold.

These laws were necessary because of the particular nature of labour-power, or what Marx termed *Arbeitskraft*. The worker sells their labour-power, but as soon as the labour begins, it is alienated from the worker, who must then wait for remuneration from their employer. There is a bargain over labour quality alongside quantity, including the portion of the working day that will be paid and how much that pay should be. The commodification of labour-power obscures this indeterminacy.

Biernacki, in his analysis of nineteenth-century work

in German and British textile mills, shows how workers' perception of labour-power shaped its commodification and their labour processes. German employers and workers regarded employment as the purchase of labour *effort* and control over the *activity*. British employers, by contrast, regarded employment as the purchase of the final *result* and control over the *product*. This difference is slight, but it is key to the social construction of labour-power.[14]

In Germany, a worker's 'statement of wages' represented compensation for labouring activity and its products in a *metaphorical* way. Pay scales classified the product as a mirror of the concrete labour performed, as a surrogate for workers' action without accepting the product as the actual object of payment itself. Germans took the activity itself (the use of labour-power) as the basis for deriving the value of different fabrics. Visible output was distinct from the actual labour the worker was remunerated for.

In Britain, by contrast, the dynamic between labouring activity and its products was understood *metonymically*. The product itself was the medium through which labour was transferred. British pay scales classified the product as the result of concrete labour but did not calculate the value of the product specifically in terms of the performance of the work. Labour was quantified by the dimensions of the complete piece of cloth. Materialized labour in the commodity form was what 'comprised the object of remuneration'. As such, surplus-labour was easily obscured. Marx's concept of labour-power combines both *metaphorical* and *metonymic* representations.[15]

These distinctions in the representation of labour-power were also reflected in the legal determinations of the wage and its theft. Court records from 1891 show that English factory inspectors prosecuted mill owners in cases where overseers added extra length to the loom 'weft threads' without extra payment or the knowledge of weavers. While this was a violation in Britain, it was not in German mills, which measured labour-time in broader intervals aligned with pay tables. The British focused on fine distinctions in the product, lacking categories for labour-time, while Germans consistently measured labour-time but were less precise about output measures.[16]

Time-discipline on the factory floor followed a similar pattern. In Britain, labour discipline was enacted to ensure goods were produced on time (with fines for damages). As a Leicester factory owner named John Baines testified in 1855, instead of fining workers for tardiness or absence, they were charged a weekly fee for use of the machinery. If workers failed to turn up and earn piece-rates, they would waste their machinery 'rent'. Delay fines were based on the exchange value of products. This reinforced the belief that workers transferred a quantity of labour embodied in finished commodities. Furthermore, adjustments in piece-rate lists in Britain were implemented based on when the product entered the market, not when labour-power was expended. In Germany, by contrast, fines disciplined workers for careless expenditure of labour-power at the point of production. This reflected the belief that workers sold their capacity to work as a specific quality and quantity. German managers had emphasized efficiency ratios, assuming time was transferable. They compared labour-time utilization across different days and years to gauge progress, unlike the English who focused on material output.[17]

Wrapping up, Biernacki shows that German and British cultural processes of labour commodification are fused together in Marx's concept of labour-power. These norms form the historical and material foundations for the way in which modern industry treated labour contributions, costs, and wage distribution. As the forces of production developed, large-scale industry continued an extensive growth pattern commodifying an ever-greater share of the social reproduction of society. The following section interrogates how the mode of production overdetermines the politics of technology. The question is not 'Does technology have a politics?' but rather 'How is technology political?'

## Technology Is Not Neutral

The façade of AI-optimism spread by oligarchs such as Elon Musk has largely crumbled as most people have realized that tech mainly serves the interests of its owners. Workers' living standards are eroding as their knowledge, skills, and control are sacrificed to the moloch of techno-capital. And yet the idea that technology itself is neutral still endures. While technological systems have progressive potential, their design and use under capitalist social relations ensures exploitation trumps liberation. Capitalist technologies are primarily designed to increase efficiency at the expense of labour-time, which typically manifests in increased labour discipline, deskilling, and intensity. This is not unlike the way the legal regimes discussed above were used to force control over labour from custom to market.[18]

During the first Industrial Revolution (roughly 1771 to 1830), real wages in England stagnated as productivity rose. Known as 'Engels's Pause', this long lag provoked a radical workers' movement against the forced introduction of new machinery.[19] In the textile sector, new machines could produce much faster and more cheaply than skilled human artisans, reducing demand for skilled labour and undermining workers' control. The Luddites saw the machines for what they were: a technological vanguard meant to enrich factory owners while devaluing craft skill. Under the mantra 'No King but Ludd', workers targeted and destroyed automatic stocking frames and power looms across Nottinghamshire, Lancashire, and Yorkshire. Despite the Frame Breaking Act of 1812, which enabled those who resisted to be sentenced to death (up to seventy were executed), the movement continued with military precision until 1817. Yet this was not the end.

Spurred by a combination of economic desperation, fear of unemployment, and a deep-seated belief that the machines represented an unjust and dehumanizing future, thousands rioted across Lancashire in 1826. In Blackburn, wages had plunged from about 23 shillings (1802–06) to under 8 shillings for handloom weavers. Diets were reduced to porridge. As factories cut shifts this mounting distress bred resistance escalating from stoning coaches and windows of the wealthy to mass loom-breaking at the Jubilee Mill.[20]

Other industries faced similar threats over mechanization. In 1810, printworkers at *The Times* went on strike (illegally at the time) over wages, working conditions, and the threat of new steam-powered presses. At the time, printing was a skilled manual trade relying on many workers. The new owner, John Walter II, who had taken over from his father, wanted to introduce the Koenig press, which could produce up to 1,100 sheets per hour, compared with the manual press's output of about 200 sheets per hour. Walter II responded with a legal attack, prosecuting twenty-one of the striking printers for conspiracy to damage property. All were imprisoned and one was murdered in custody. The owner then offered a bargain: continued employment if workers remained peaceful.[21] However, Walter II then arranged for the parts of the new press to be shipped and assembled in secret before he covertly printed the 29 November 1814 edition of the paper. The workers were forced to accept the new machines only to have their jobs and share of the product stolen from them.

In the 1830s, steam-powered threshing machines spread throughout England like an iron contagion. These agricultural machines were capable of processing grain much faster than humans, threatening rural culture and the livelihoods of skilled farmers. Landlords used the influx of desperate Irish workers willing to accept lower wages as leverage to sow resentment between the native and migrant working classes.[22] Farm workers sent letters to landlords, threatening violent retribution, which were signed 'Captain Swing' (this was a thinly veiled threat of insurrection and an allusion to the action of the flail, a fieldworker's tool). And they made good on their threats, smashing their way through machinery and barns. While the eponymous Swing Riots were subsequently crushed and the organizers hanged, imprisoned, or deported, they were yet another expression of resistance to capitalist technological discipline.[23]

Workers across continental Europe also knew they would only see the benefits of new technologies if they could bargain for a greater share of the product. And so they led their own waves of protests, riots, and revolts. The violent revolutions of 1848 gave way to a growing trade union movement and new statutory rights for workers (see Chapter 7). As Gavin Mueller notes: 'The struggles against machines *were* the struggles against the society that utilised them.'[24]

Marx analysed this new technological subordination of work, drawing on insights from Charles Babbage's *On the Economy of Machinery and Manufactures* (1832) and Andrew Ure's *The Philosophy of Manufactures* (1835), in *Capital*. These works showed how the disaggregation of the production process into precise components allowed for both a more efficient use of labour and the exercise of power over workers. Emergent ideas at the turn of the century drew on this intellectual momentum. For example, Frederick Taylor's notion of scientific management was developed by analysing human movement and the organization of the factory in order to rationalize it down to the second, with no wasted cost or effort. Frank and Lillian Gilbreth, who invented the Therblig Chart, brought micromotion study to the forefront, often filming workers with slow-motion cameras to make every motion count. As Harry Braverman later argued in *Labour and Monopoly Capital*, scientific management was used in factories to re-engineer workers as if they were machines.[25]

In the 1910s, Henry Ford aggressively standardized and deskilled the labour process as a strategy to achieve low-cost, machine-driven, continuous assembly-line production for the mass market. However, he had a problem with retaining labour. Some factories saw nearly 400 per cent annual attrition, as workers quit in droves, unable or unwilling to endure the repetitive, dehumanizing pace of assembly-line work. Ford effectively bribed workers to stay by introducing the 'Five Dollar Day', doubling the average wage in 1914. This was an unprecedented move, paired with a brutal campaign against unionization that involved hiring spies, private police, and violent enforcers under the Ford Service Department to intimidate and suppress union organizers. Higher wages came at the price of submission.[26]

Ford didn't stop at the Model-T. The mass-produced Fordson tractor rolled onto American farms in 1917, dragging with it a revolution in agricultural production. What once took teams of men and horses days could now be done by a single operator in hours. Mechanized efficiency came at a human cost, kick-starting the Great Migration. Displaced by machines, Black sharecroppers and white tenant farmers alike streamed into northern cities. The farmland workers left behind was often consolidated into large-scale agribusiness, while overcultivation with Fordson tractors stripped the plains of their topsoil, sowing the Depression-era dust storms.[27]

Marx recognized how machinery can be weaponized against workers and integrated this critique into his theory of capital. As we know, to produce surplus-value, firms require workers to work longer than the time required to simply reproduce their labour-power. This surplus labour-time is unpaid. Machines, as means of production, produced and sold under capitalist conditions, become stores of surplus-value (pure unpaid labour, alienated from workers). A machine creates no new value but instead bestows its 'value to the product it serves to beget', increasing the value of the product 'in proportion to the value of the machine'. This value transfer depends on the total value of the machinery employed and the rate of transfer. Paradoxically, the 'less value it gives up' over the long term, the more productive a machine is for capital, giving it comparative advantage over less durable machinery.[28]

Machine substitution for labour tends to reduce the cost of labour's products, since such machinery needs less labour to produce the same amount of products compared with less technologically advanced competitors. The availability of cheaper products overall leads to lower costs of social reproduction, therefore lowering the value of labour-power. New machinery increases both fixed capital (through machinery itself), but also the overall constant capital by allowing a greater quantity of raw materials to be transformed by labour-power into commodities. This can exponentially increase the productivity of labour and the efficiency of the use of raw materials.

However, there are countervailing forces to these productivity effects. Competition tends to drive down profit rates within industries and in adjacent industries along the value-chain. Technology also tends to degrade over time. The value a machine contributes involves physical deterioration, but also a 'moral depreciation', which occurs when cheaper or more efficient machines enter into competition with existing machines. When a machine becomes technologically obsolete, Marx argues, the value of the machine is 'no longer determined by the necessary labour-time actually objectified in it, but by the labour-time necessary to reproduce either it or the better machine'.[29] With each technological revolution, labour and capital become more productive, but also cheapened. The value of labour-power is always in flux, in and against the machine.

The value contribution of machinery is multiplied in a complex system where the entire machine framework is 'consumed in common by its numerous working parts' including the energy source, transmitting mechanisms, and so on by all the other operating machines in the network. The more productive a machine is, according to Marx, the 'more its services approach those rendered by natural forces'.[30] That is, they move towards a system of enclosure, extraction, and rent – themes that we will address in Chapter 6. While some technologies have limited, specific applications, others such as electricity or information and communication technologies (ICTs) are general-purpose, diffusing across entire socio-economic systems.

Like the juridical structures discussed previously, we can see that technologies shape not just what we do but how we do it. They mediate how power is distributed between labour and capital. Technology is never politically neutral. Every tool, every system, and every machine is imbued with intention, whether explicit or implicit in its design. Intention is political and will have consequences, both anticipated and unforeseen. For example, the users of early steam engines aimed to use them to pump water out of mines. That was its intended effect. Yet as these engines allowed deeper mines to be worked, they also introduced new challenges such as poor ventilation, which workers bore the cost of, which also spurred further technological developments. The steam engine set the stage for solutions, shaping the conditions under which innovation unfolded. Take a more contemporary example: an AI system designed to streamline financial management. On the surface, its role seems to be to improve efficiency and accuracy. But financial datafication of the globe means that the technology embeds financial discipline into every aspect of existence.

While some consequences of technology design are immediate and direct, many emerge indirectly. Consider the manufacturing of arms in the US. An army equipped with rifles enables soldiers to be directed or act independently. Now introduce artillery such as a heavy machine gun that requires a team of three to operate. A reorganization of labour is required, since the three soldiers will be grouped into a unit with a hierarchy. The same logic plays out in factories. The Fordist assembly line was meant to organize the immediate process of production, but its influence extended beyond it to the social fabric. Workers in supporting roles from logistics to quality control and administration had their work reshaped through pace and coordination mechanisms. Technology itself often necessitates certain forms of social organization.[31]

In the next section, we consider the third element in our triad of labour-power fabrication: the gendered divisions that determine the context of commodification. The forces of production reproduce the relations of production, but in the context of social reproduction. Historical patriarchal domination meant men tended to control technical knowledge outside the domestic sphere and thus retain control over industrial systems. These dynamics have subordinated women based on a gendered division of labour within and beyond production.[32] For example, during the early industrial era, women performed various tasks in the hosiery industry, including knitting and operating the stocking frame. However, they were excluded from repairing and adjusting the frame, which were considered male tasks. In the twentieth century, the first 'computers' were actually women mathematicians, who also became pioneers in programming – before being pushed out.[33] The education gap has since shifted, but the legacies remain.

## Social Reproduction and Domestic Labour

No study of unpaid labour would be complete without a discussion of the particularly gendered nature of social reproduction and the work it requires.[34] The concept of social reproduction encompasses a broad range of activities: housework, child-rearing, schooling, healthcare, emotional support, in vitro fertilization, surrogacy, and more. Social reproduction, notes Nancy Fraser, 'is an indispensable background condition for the possibility of economic production in a capitalist society'. Today, most socially reproductive activities have been commodified – that is, they are produced and consumed via a market and therefore subsumed into capitalist labour processes. Fraser classes these activities as 're-externalised' or 'commodified for those who can pay for it and privatised for those who cannot'. Such conditions are the relatively recent consequence of the dismantling of many social welfare services alongside the erosion of single-earner households and household subsistence production.[35]

What does the re-externalization or re-commodification of many of these activities mean for the theory of unpaid labour and wage theft? The boundary between commodified and non-commodified activities is important because it determines what counts as labour-power and thus enters into the circuit of capital. This boundary is contested and shifts throughout history. Where the boundary is set impacts our understanding of what claim workers can make on the share of the collective products of their labour, and what that means for economic justice.

To understand this boundary, we might begin in 1884, with Engels's pioneering materialist theory of the family, *The Origin of the Family, Private Property and the State*.[36] Drawing on Lewis H. Morgan's anthropological work and Marx's political economy, Engels argues that early communal societies were more egalitarian, with matrilineal kinship and collective ownership. The rise of private property catalysed patriarchal structures alongside class relations, with the state as an enforcer of this order. For Engels, the production of surplus-value is mediated by the costs of reproduction of the labour force, which were largely shouldered by the nuclear family or household unit. Production is not the same as reproduction, but the resources they use are similar.

Alexandra Kollontai, a Bolshevik revolutionary, took up Marx's insight that 'the conditions of production are at the same time the conditions of reproduction' in her 1920 essay 'Communism and the Family'.[37] She conceives of the bourgeois family as a product of capitalist property relations that economically subordinates women and reinforces domestic servitude through patriarchy. One of her key insights was understanding the transformation in the family from a site of subsistence production to a consumption unit: 'All that was formerly produced in the bosom of the family is now being manufactured on a mass scale in workshops and factories. The machine has superseded the wife … The family no longer produces; it only consumes.'[38] This change marks a shift in the boundary between private and social reproduction. Kollontai's critique of the domestic division of labour led her to develop programmes to replace the bourgeois family's private functions with social institutions. After the Bolshevik Revolution, Kollontai put theory into practice, establishing communal kitchens, laundries, childcare centres, literacy programmes, and workshops to liberate women from domestic servitude and socialize the private drudgery of housework.[39]

Western socialist thinkers also aimed to break down the boundary between private and social reproduction. Some went further, transposing the capitalist class antagonism into the household. Mary Inman's 1940 book *In Women's Defence* defined 'housewives' as a distinct class, oppressed by the patriarchal male breadwinner. Christine Delphy and Simone de Beauvoir co-founded the journal *Nouvelles Questions Féministes* to develop a theory of materialist feminism. Delphy argued in her 1970 essay 'The Main Enemy' that the household is where the family mode of production operates, where women are exploited by men. It is similar, yet separate, from the capitalist mode of production in the workplace.[40]

Drawing on and dovetailing with these ideas, Mariarosa Dalla Costa, Silvia Federici, Brigitte Galtier, and Selma James founded the International Wages for Housework Campaign (IWFHC) in 1972. Through a strategic demand, this now-famous movement sought to make visible the unpaid labour that women perform in the household, arguing that this work is essential for the reproduction of the labour force and, by extension, productive for capitalism itself.[41] For Dalla Costa and James, the notion that housework is private is a fallacy. The housewife's role in capitalist production was 'invisible, because only the product of her labour, the labourer, was visible'.[42] During a 1974 demo in Italy, an organizer declared: 'Half the world's population is unpaid – this is the biggest class contradiction of all! And this is our struggle for wages for housework.'[43]

A wave of critical debate among materialist and Marxist feminists such as Angela Davis, Lise Vogel, Wally Seccombe, Juliet Mitchell, and others developed throughout the 1970s and beyond.[44] Much of the debate revolved around Delphy's 'dual systems theory' versus a more unitary approach. It also foregrounded the question of whether housework produces labour-power as a commodity and therefore is part of the value-productive circuit of capital. Seccombe takes up the latter position against other Marxist feminist critics.[45] For Seccombe, housework produces value because Marx subsumes the family's means of subsistence under the wage of the male breadwinner, yet it should actually be broken down into its component parts. The housewife, argues Seccombe, 'creates value, embodied in the labour-power sold to capital, equal to the value she consumes in her own upkeep'.[46] Seccombe's theory is based on the assumption that the value of labour-power is expressed in a wage that is equal to the reproduction of the entire household. But this isn't the case. By this logic, children must also produce value for factories by cleaning their rooms. Seccombe's interpretation could, in effect, be applied to virtually any non-waged contribution to the social reproduction of labour-power, from grandparents to priests. Wages, as the price (not necessarily the value) of labour-power, are set by worker bargaining power. The value of labour-power corresponds to the total social costs required to reproduce it within and beyond the household – not only food and housing but education and training as well. Thus, neither the wage nor the value of labour-power can be determined by household subsistence alone in Marx's system.

Another problem with the argument that domestic labour 'produces' labour-power as a commodity like any other is that it conflates the reproduction of human labour-power with the reproduction of human beings themselves. As shown in the previous two sections, the production of labour-power as a commodity is a historical and social process, mediated by law and technology. Domestic labour alone cannot privately produce labour-power as a commodity since labour-power 'is not produced by labour but by the individual consumption of the labourer'.[47] The household is a site of consumption of resources by human beings, not the production of labour-power. Employers' needs dictate the reproduction of labour-power as a commodity. In other words, demand for labour-power creates the supply.

From child-rearing to toilet cleaning, housework is socially reproductive, but not directly subject to market imperatives of competition or the standardization and control of tasks in the same way as the commodification of labour-power. If real wages fall below subsistence, labour contributions do not fall with them; people instead find side hustles or ask favours of friends and family to survive. Capital is disinterested in domestic productivity and ultimately lacks control over it. The use-values reproduced in the household are indispensable background conditions but do not have exchange-value unless they are put on the market and sold. Without the commodification of labour-power, work activities remain outside the value-circuit.

Does the demand to pay 'wages for housework' strategically address this issue? Perhaps it did, given the limits to women's reproductive and economic autonomy in the latter half of the twentieth century. It certainly still resonates in patriarchal societies. For Davis, however, demanding wages for housework fails to provide 'a long-range solution to the problem of women's oppression' or 'substantively address the profound discontent of contemporary housewives'.[48] Why? Because housework is a prerequisite for the production of labour-power, but does not itself produce it.

Capitalism needs a labour force of skilled and unskilled workers, which the state, schools, and other social infrastructures ensure. However, the rest is safely left to 'the workers' drives for self-preservation and propagation'.[49] Davis uses the example of apartheid-era South Africa, where Black men were valued for their labour, but Black women and families were deemed 'superfluous', banned from living in white areas, and subjected to policies that eroded domestic life. The government actually viewed stable Black families as a threat, fearing that they could become a base for resistance. Paying women for domestic labour in this context would reinforce their domestic invisibility. In countries of racial apartheid, domestic workers have spent decades resisting subordination to the role of the surrogate housewife for families. Davis argues that securing paid jobs outside the home would better enable women to pursue economic equality and power through the labour movement. Ultimately, as Davis says, the 'abolition of housework as the private responsibility of individual women' is essential for women's liberation, but this requires an end to the capitalist profit-motive through 'the socialization of housework – including meal preparation and child care' rather than an hourly wage.[50]

Defining clear conceptual boundaries and classifications in our analysis of capitalism does not diminish the importance of domestic, reproductive, and feminized labour. Rather, without a consistent and coherent boundary between what is productive and what is not, the political critique of unpaid labour simply becomes vague moralism. This is why Marx distinguishes between productive labour in general and productive labour for capital.[51] Productive labour in general is a 'unique activity', which when applied to nature, provides society with the 'indispensable material elements of its reproduction'.[52] This labour includes all the necessary subsistence tasks for the reproduction of human society, but also the subset of productive labour for capital.

Understanding why this matters for wage theft and unpaid labour requires zooming out a bit. At the abstract level of any given economy, four types of social reproductive economic activity become apparent: production, distribution, social maintenance, and personal consumption. Production occurs when constant and variable capital are consumed in the process of creating new objects or services of use and exchange-value. This includes most areas of our modern economy: from agriculture to manufacturing, logistics to hospitality. Distribution involves the deployment of use-values to transfer these new objects or services from their producers to those who will consume them. This covers a more narrow set of activities such as sales, marketing, banking, and so on. Social maintenance comprises processes that sustain the social order in public and private administrative capacities, including the government, the legal system, security apparatuses, education, health, and public infrastructure such as roads, rail, and communications. Personal consumption involves an individual using the object or service for private purposes: buying groceries, clothing, concert tickets, books, food delivery, mobile phone apps, and so on all fall into this category. These categories are networked and responsive to one another.[53]

As Figure 3.1 makes clear, only three of these four activities qualify as labour and only one set of activities constitutes productive labour for capital. Distribution and social maintenance are productive in a general social sense but not for capital, and consumption activities are not subject to direct control by capitalist production nor feed back directly into the circuit. Productive labour for capital depends on its capacity to produce surplus-value – that is, directly valorize capital.[54] This labour is productive because it produces *more*

Figure 3.1 Social reproductive economic activities

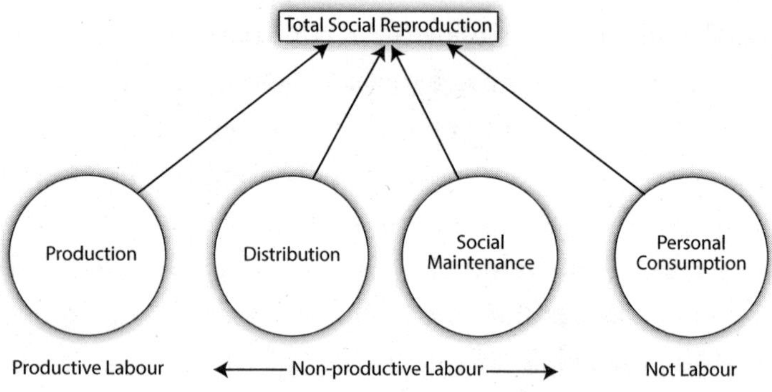


*Source:* Anwar Shaikh and Ertuğrul A. Tonak, *Measuring the Wealth of Nations: The Political Economy of National Accounts*, Cambridge: Cambridge University Press, 1994, pp. 21–2.

*than is necessary* for total social reproduction. Simply being paid to perform labour does not mean that labour is productive of surplus-value. Some labour, whether 'of a prostitute or of the Pope', as Marx notes, 'can only be paid for out of the wages of productive labourers, or out of the profits of their employers'.[55] For example, in the 1860s there were over a million domestic servants in England alone, greatly outnumbering factory workers.[56] Yet these services were privately consumed. Servants were paid from the rentier income of landed gentry and the emergent bourgeois without producing a surplus. The production boundary means that while labour might be socially useful, it is not value-productive for capital unless it produces a surplus. This is why housework is not value-productive for capital.

There is a broader issue at stake here. Human beings, in all their chaotic, creative, loving, and intellectual brilliance, are resistant to the homogenizing and mechanizing forces of capitalist relations. The activities that reproduce labour-power are socially valuable. But human culture is far too heterogeneous to subordinate all activities into quantified relations of equivalence, as capital requires. A conceptual and material boundary between waged life and unwaged life is necessary to protect our humanity and the potential for alternatives outside capitalism. Love takes effort, but effort is not the same as labour (in the Marxist sense or otherwise) and we should object to unwittingly surrendering the cultivation of emotional bonds to capital. If all housework, family activities, or even emotional support for friendships and partners are considered 'labour' that serves capital, then the possibilities for prefigurative alternatives, resistance, and so on are foreclosed. This is why it is important to parse the limits to the commodification of labour-power. At the very least, it helps to avoid the fatalism of total subsumption.

This chapter aimed to show how labour-power was forged as a commodity under duress, through legal, quasi-legal, and technological means. The limits to this power are also the boundary between capitalist and non-capitalist life. The wage form is the very foundation and essential prerequisite of the capitalist relationship. Capitalism actually has an interest in fully commodifying all activities, including domestic labour. If workers must fend for themselves for subsistence in a feudal fashion, then this could take time away from their waged and therefore potentially productive labour. This is also why some of the most intensive tech jobs have social reproductive necessities on site, including meals, coffees, showers, sleep pods, and so on. Workers with no revenue to purchase commodities would slow down the system; indeed, there are modern economic terms for the benefits of greater wage distribution, such as affective demand and wage-led growth. By providing a monetary wage, the employer absolves themselves of personal responsibility for the workers' social reproduction, while also ensuring the smooth circulation and realization of profit. And it is to this wage form that we now turn.

# 5
# Rethinking Wage Theft

*All labour appears as paid labour.*

– Karl Marx, *Capital*, vol. 1

In the gospel of Luke, first-century Judaean preacher John the Baptist scolds the 'brood of vipers' crowding around him eager to be baptized: 'Whoever has two coats must share with anyone who has none; and whoever has food must do likewise.' To the tax collector he says 'Collect no more than the amount prescribed for you'; and to the soldiers, 'Do not extort money from anyone by threats or false accusation, and be satisfied with your wages.'[1] The moral principles are clear here: share resources, don't be greedy, and don't exploit a position of power.

Moral tensions over the wage and its theft have existed for millennia. What did not exist, however, was a scientific theory of the wage. Historically, wages were mainly set by custom, tradition, and occasionally a bargain. What *is* a wage in the modern sense? The International Labour Organization (ILO) defines wages or 'earnings' as 'remuneration in cash and in kind paid to employees, as a rule at regular intervals, for time worked or work done together with remuneration for time not worked'.[2] So wages are money for work. Yet, money is simply a measure of price, and price is a measure of value and value represents abstract labour or the total average labour-time needed to reproduce something. But price also diverges from value according to supply, demand, and market power in situations like monopoly (one seller) or monopsony (one buyer). Furthermore, not all wages are paid with money. Thus, the question 'what is a wage?' is more complicated and political than it first appears. Indeed, a significant thread in the history of economic thought concerns the debate over how to determine wages. More recently, those on the side of capital have attempted to erase this debate from history altogether.

In economic theory, there are essentially two contrasting conceptions of the wage. The neoclassical view, institutionally dominant today, is based on a few assumptions: the notion that all humans are utility-maximizing individuals with perfect information, all firms aim to maximize profits, and that markets tend towards equilibrium between supply and demand. Neoclassicals see wages as merely the price of labour, determined by the laws of supply and demand in the labour market. They believe that a wage floor – that is, a minimum wage – should only exist as a tool to correct market imbalances and restore equilibrium.

Classical political economists, by contrast, ground their theories of the wage in the assumption that wage setting is based on the social resources required to reproduce labour-power. The wage is not simply the price for labour. Rather, this theory holds that there is a 'natural' wage rate that should meet the customary living costs of workers. This rate can vary depending on worker bargaining power. Classical political economists also recognize the inherent potential for conflict between the market-determined price for labour and the socially determined costs of reproducing it. For example, the recent spike in the costs of living in the US and the UK was driven by price inflation for essentials such as food, energy, and housing, yet increased costs have not been met with proportional increases in wages. Workers engaged in militant strikes to attempt to win back what they lost.

Neoclassical economists tend to overlook the conflict between social need and capitalist market imperatives. Instead, the allocation of social resources is supposed to follow Adam Smith's abstract ideal of market redistribution, one that largely sidelines the role of the state and other institutions in shaping those markets. Neoclassicals also tend to minimize concerns of distribution and fairness within the scope of the wage.[3] In fact, the term 'unpaid' does not even appear in their theories of labour and the wage. Instead, they use phrases such as 'deferred compensation', 'human capital accumulation', or 'Pareto improvement', neutralizing negative moral or political connotations that might reveal conflicting interests between labour and capital. These theories claim that workers are rewarded in other ways such as through 'experience' or 'networks' (unpaid internships), as if one can buy bread with knowledge alone.[4]

We cannot understand unpaid labour without understanding paid labour; we cannot understand wage theft without understanding the wage itself. The history of class struggle is also the history of the struggle over the ratio between paid and unpaid labour-time. This chapter tells the story of classical wage theory and why demands of a 'fair' or 'living' wage ultimately fail to address the underlying problems of waged life under capitalism.

## What's in a Wage?

One of the most influential wage theories was developed by the English political economist and demographer Thomas Malthus, who was made famous by his 1798 publication, *An Essay on the Principle of Population*. What is now known as the Malthusian 'Law of Population' stated that an increase in population leads to growth in the supply of labour, which in turn lowers wages and eventually leads to poverty. As he wrote in an 1817 letter to fellow political economist David Ricardo, 'The land in Ireland is infinitely more peopled than in England; and to give full effect to the natural resources of the country, a great part of the population should be swept from the soil.'[5] This argument is still used today, often by right-wingers to justify the introduction of racist population-control measures in the face of resource scarcity.

Malthus's theory was based on the so-called wage-fund doctrine, which refers to the idea that there is a fixed and finite sum of capital (the hoard of money and property owned by elites) available at any given time for the payment of wages. Both wages and employment are, for Malthus, arithmetically determined by the quantity of workers in relation to the magnitude of this fund. This wage-fund doctrine was no mere academic exercise; it became public consensus. In the middle of the nineteenth century, politicians tried to persuade workers that their demands for higher wages would precipitate economic crises. Aristocrats told workers that the only way they could improve their position in society was by forgoing children or emigrating to reduce their number. Any action that might discourage capital from expanding and boosting the size of the wage fund must be avoided at all costs.[6] These sorts of arguments might sound familiar because they are still trotted out by politicians and media commentators alike.

Two centuries of pointed criticisms ranging from 'pessimistic sophistry' (Thomas Carlyle) to 'school-boyish, superficial plagiary' (Karl Marx) followed the publication of Malthus's *Essay*.[7] Critics generally agree that the main problem with the wage-fund doctrine is that it fails to account for the uneven distribution of resources in society and the productivity-enhancing effects of new technologies. Advocating population control as the first measure to control scarcity is idiotic, unless of course your aim is merely to preserve class hierarchy and hoarding.

Against Malthus and his followers, Marx developed a wage theory that drew on the classical political economy of Adam Smith, David Ricardo, and others, but also went beyond it. Understanding Marx's influences illuminates his break with them. Smith is generally credited with developing the first systematic theory of wages and labour. He starts with the assumption that every society has 'an ordinary or average rate both of wages and profit in every different employment of labour and stock'. He calls these the 'natural rates of wages, profit, and rent'. The natural rate serves as a gravitational centre around which the real or market rate of wages revolves. For workers, the wage, as the 'money price for labour' is regulated by 'demand for labour', alongside the price of those 'necessaries' that enable social reproduction.[8]

If demand for labour increases, then employers tend to increase wages to attract and retain workers. The price of necessities for social reproduction can also influence wage setting, since workers will try to avoid taking jobs that don't pay enough to cover their means of subsistence. Smith's natural rate of wages is ultimately determined by the unequal power that employers wield over employees, reinforced by the law. Smith anticipates Marx when he says: 'Whenever the legislature attempts to regulate the differences between masters and their workmen, its counsellors are always the masters.'[9]

Ricardo's wage theory built on insights from Smith and others. For Ricardo, political economy required analysing total social reproduction, as discussed in the previous chapter. Wage theory thus needed a conception of the relations between production, consumption, distribution, and exchange within the institutions of politics, the law, and culture.[10] He recognized that price and social value could diverge: 'The value of a commodity depends on the relative quantity of labour which is necessary for its production, and not on the greater or less compensation which is paid for that labour.'[11]

Ricardo's 'natural wage' was established by custom and reinforced by institutions that insulated it from volatile market fluctuations in supply and demand. The natural wage was a benchmark for market wages, though they often deviated from one another due to factors such as worker agency that could push the natural wage higher or technological changes that increased productivity. As we know, labour is a unique input that is socially determined, influenced by institutions such as the family, culture, material need, and mobility (often tied to border regimes). To align the 'market wage', which is set by the needs of employers, with the 'natural wage', which is set by the customary needs of workers, the latter need to maintain a degree of bargaining power.

Marx's wage theory went beyond Ricardo thanks to the concept of labour-power, which we explored in the previous chapter.[12] The value of labour-power is represented by the wage, which equals the social cost of its reproduction. The inputs to the cost of its reproduction can be calculated according to their exchange-value or equivalent pure use-values. Marx's labour theory of value holds that surplus-value is produced by extracting more labour-time from workers than is socially necessary to produce a given use-value under average conditions, skill, and efficiency of labour.[13] This labour-time, as we know, is unpaid. The rate of surplus-value is the average 'excess of the total amount of labour contained in the commodity over the quantity of paid labour contained in it'.[14]

> the value of 3 shillings, which represents the paid portion of the working day, i.e. 6 hours of labour, appears as the value or price of the whole working day of 12 hours, which thus includes 6 hours which have not been paid for.[15]

The money form of the wage itself erases any distinction between socially necessary labour-time and surplus labour-time, and thus between paid and unpaid labour.

Marx shows how profit is 'the excess of the value of the commodity over its cost price'.[16] Cost price refers to the price of the necessary inputs to produce a given thing. If the cost price of the commodity were equal to its value, capital could not be valorized; there could be no surplus-value produced. For capitalism to function it 'must wring every drop of unpaid labour-time from the workers it can'. The value of the commodity is equivalent to the value of constant capital consumed (machinery, raw materials, and so on), *plus* the value of the wages of the labour consumed, *plus* the value of the unpaid labour consumed and realized through the commodity's sale. Unpaid labour-time is not part of this cost-price. Marx is very clear that the 'capitalist has paid no value in return for this unpaid labour, no equivalent, and it therefore costs him nothing'.[17] This *exchange without equivalent* is the secret of the wage and of profit-making.

From this insight it follows that, all other factors being equal, when workers win higher wages for the same work, this decreases the quantity of unpaid labour-time they contribute.[18] While companies that expand and profit can share gains with workers, they can also expand and profit while they decrease wages, reaping the rewards of workers' additional unpaid labour contributions. What makes the difference in this distribution is balance of power between labour and capital.

Before the factory system took hold, the average

labour-time for a set of commodities was usually fixed by custom, which meant pay rates were standardized and controlled by craftsmen. For instance, in London tailors' workshops, they would call a waistcoat an hour, because that is how long a waistcoat took to make – the hour was valued at six pennies or half a shilling. It is understandable, then, why when it came to pay, workers fought to keep customary rates. For example, in 1802, a woollen weaver hailing from England's West Country noted that the rate for a particular fabric had remained static, not only for his entire life, but also that of his father. Stocking makers claimed during a strike in 1814 that rates had changed only twice in two centuries.[19] Such stability could mask the sway of the fluctuating market, but it could also provide protection from it; during labour scarcities, employers could increase rates with perquisites such as a share in produce or work materials.

There are many forms of payment: time-wages, piece-wages, monthly stipends, annual salaries, seasonal bonuses, commissions, tips, and so on. Different forms of remuneration can facilitate different degrees of control.[20] Time-wages may be calculated per hour, day, week, month, or year. Yet time is always connected to a certain amount of expected output – fifteen dollars to sort a hundred parcels per hour in an Amazon warehouse, for example. Time-wages enable more flexibility for workers since, despite output targets, workers in the same role who produce less than the target, as well as those who exceed the target, tend to receive the same compensation. Teams of workers usually receive relatively similar compensation but also can be pitted against one another. Piece-wages are paid by output unit, but units also take time to produce or deliver. Workers have limited time during the day to earn enough to meet their costs of living. In a piece-wage system, employers might benchmark an average compensation level, yet each worker's actual wages will fluctuate in accordance with their output. This encourages competition between workers based on ability and effort.

Marx observes that piece-wages were 'the most fruitful source of reductions in wages, and of frauds committed by the capitalists'.[21] During the Industrial Revolution, from 1797 to 1815, piece-wages acted as a tool to extend work hours and consistently decrease the price of labour-power.[22] Later in the nineteenth century, a series of investigations known as the Reports of the Inspectors of Factories (1859 to 1860) found that employers were using different wage rates for the same tasks to steal wages undetected.[23] Their method was simple. Say a firm employed 200 people, half of whom were paid by the piece and therefore have an incentive to continue working longer hours, while the other half are paid by the day and get no extra pay for overtime. If a boss can pit these workers against one another and get a hundred people to work just an extra fifteen minutes, they pocket an extra twenty-five hours of labour output for free.

Piece-wages also enable the proliferation of middlemen since cost and output are more directly determinable. Middlemen profit from the 'sub-letting' or 'sweating' of labour, buying labour-power cheap and selling dear. These 'parasites', Marx wrote, 'interpose themselves' between the worker and the capitalist; even foremen who lead a team of assistants also participated in exploiting their fellow workers.[24] Such practices are still prevalent today.

The power dynamics of payment systems illuminate problems with the slogan discussed at the outset of this book: 'a fair day's wages for a fair day's work'. The demand of 'fair wages for fair work' addresses payment, time, and output abstractly, but fails to consider what would be fair for each individual. A related slogan, 'equal pay for equal work', was partially an attempt to remedy this and aimed at securing women and racial minorities the same compensation as white men. However, this slogan can also be interpreted to mean 'equal pay for an equal amount of work done', implying equal output. Consequently, if women produced less than men during a given time, they could receive a lower pay rate.[25]

Summing up, wage theory is more complicated than it first appears. Classical political economists knew that wages should be determined by more than supply and demand. Today, laws that protect workers' right to collective bargaining and laws that regulate capitalist accumulation limit market volatility. Workers lose out from volatility because of the asymmetrical power dynamics: if workers cannot earn a wage, then they cannot reproduce their lives. Capitalists have more resources available to them to leverage over others. No amount of utility-maximizing behaviour can ensure that workers earn adequate wages if there are no employers willing to pay them.

## Wage Floors and Ceilings

In our contemporary capitalist world, labour market policy can make or break bargaining power. In the US and the UK, neoclassical theory still reigns. As noted above, neoclassicals believe that that the most efficient allocation of scarce resources is achieved through decentralized pricing mechanisms within competitive markets. Labour regulations are seen as largely detrimental to the magic self-regulation of the market, leading to 'misallocation' of resources. Only 'market failures' require regulation to restore equilibrium between supply and demand.[26] Neoclassical theory, however, relies on a fantasy of perfect information, ignoring the messy reality of asymmetrical power dynamics and that workers have material needs that coerce them to work longer if wages fall. Workers' expected standards of living, working hours, family dynamics, bargaining power, and the broader institutional environment are not automatically reflected in wage rates because equilibrium pricing is not designed around human needs.

Laws to protect human rights, to support collective bargaining, to enforce a wage floor, and so on are necessary to reduce the risks to individual workers' livelihoods by sharing them across society. The idea that there should be a minimum wage floor to prevent people falling into destitution would seem like an obvious social good, even from a capitalist perspective. Without an adequate minimum wage, for example, social welfare programmes can end up subsidizing exploitative or inefficient firms that don't pay their workers enough (as shown by the Family Credit system introduced by the

Thatcher government in the UK).[27] Most UN member states today have a minimum wage. However, this norm took a long time to become established.

When the American Federation of Labor (AFL) was founded in 1886, they championed the idea of a general living wage that would ensure all workers, unionized or not, could support their family, participate in public life, and uphold a 'standard of living' *higher* than their European counterparts. The idea also gained traction across the Atlantic. In 1894, Mark Oldroyd, a Liberal MP and Yorkshire textile factory owner, penned the first comprehensive defence of a living wage. Addressing the Dewsbury Pioneers Industrial Society, he argued that '[a] living wage must be sufficient to maintain the worker in the highest state of industrial efficiency, with decent surroundings and sufficient leisure'.[28]

One of the first legislative measures to protect wages was the British Trade Boards Act in 1909, which provided a wage floor for 'sweated' trades. This referred to work done in the home that paid exceptionally low wages, since it was not subject to factory regulations and had not been unionized. The act gave wage boards the power to set minimum rates in accordance with organized sectors. That said, the justification for the act was not to provide a liveable means of subsistence for workers and their families, but to correct a market distortion that enabled some employers to gain a competitive advantage by paying below the market rate for labour. It raised 'the price paid by the bad employer to the level of that paid by the good employer'.[29] At the time, wage rates were still largely set according to established practices, rather than an evaluation of the cost of living or an ethics.

While it fell short of the 'social' wage floor advocated by Fabian socialist reformers Sydney and Beatrice Webb, the Trade Boards Act did help reform in labour protections. Just before the act passed, the Liberals had won a landslide victory in the 1906 general election and conceded measures sponsored by Labour trade union MPs to legalize strikes with the Trade Disputes Act. Now industrial action 'in contemplation or furtherance of a trade dispute' was immune from civil law sanctions.[30]

Around the same time, Benjamin Seebohm Rowntree, son of the famed Quaker philanthropist and industrial chocolatier Joseph Rowntree, also advocated for a living wage. He created one of the first methodologies for determining the living wage based on extensive research in York, England (home of the Rowntree Cocoa Works). Rowntree evaluated wages in the city in relation to the costs of essential items such as food, rent, clothing, and fuel, for a family with three children.[31] He pushed for the Trade Boards' remit to be spread across industries and to be able to set wages based on his new standard (thirty-five shillings and three pence weekly at 1914 rates for adult men).

Broader support for a living wage started to gain traction as the Independent Labour Party, a socialist caucus, made it official policy in 1925. James Maxton MP proposed a living wage bill in 1931. He believed that stable consumption could help in combating economic crises, unemployment, and stagnation, spurring growth through mass redistribution. While the 1931 bill garnered substantial support, it was too radical a measure for the Labour front bench (months later, Prime Minister Ramsay MacDonald defected to a Conservative-dominated National Government). The interwar and post-war rise of trade union power made the living wage redundant, as sectoral collective bargaining was established. It was not until 2001 that the idea of a living wage was revived in the UK by the London Citizens' campaign, in response to falling real wages and diminished trade union power.

Yet, the idea that labour should be more than just another 'commodity or an article of commerce' endured throughout the twentieth century.[32] Born from the Versailles Treaty, the ILO enshrined in its 1919 Constitution the demand for 'adequate living wages' and better working conditions as prerequisites for lasting peace. The ILO's 1944 Declaration of Philadelphia reiterated this with renewed force, calling for wages to reflect not just productivity but a 'just share of progress' anchored in living costs, economic development, and social security. More recently, their 2019 Centenary Declaration reaffirmed this commitment in the language of contemporary labour crises, asserting the principle of living wages as 'the wage level that is necessary to afford a decent standard of living for workers and their families ... during the normal hours of work'.[33] Parallel efforts emerged in post-war Europe. The 1961 European Social Charter articulated the right to 'fair remuneration', and by the 1970s the European Committee of Social Rights set a living wage floor at 68 per cent of national average gross earnings, later revised to 60 per cent of net earnings.

More recently, non-governmental organizations (NGOs) have stepped up to put pressure on global capital. For example, the Global Living Wage Coalition (GLWC) developed standardized metrics for wage floors in global supply chains. Fairtrade and Rainforest Alliance certifications attempt to anchor living wages in the moral economies of consumer choice. Action, Collaboration, Transformation, a formal Memorandum of Understanding between nineteen global brands and the IndustriALL Global Union, advocates for living wages in garment and textile industries. The UN's Guiding Principles on Business and Human Rights and the UN Global Compact's Think Lab have also framed living wages as not just ethical necessities but corporate obligations.[34] These initiatives are examples of the transnational recognition that wages should be determined politically and socially, rather than simply by the alchemy of supply and demand.

And yet the calculation of living wage is itself contested and contingent on what data and models are used to determine the costs of social reproduction. To calculate living wages, most NGOs begin with the essentials: food, housing, transport, utilities, education, and healthcare. Indexing wages to local prices determines the minimum income needed for a decent life for a given family size in a given location. These calculations must be adjusted over time for inflation, but also development trajectories as societies shift from measuring poverty in absolute terms to assessing it relative to median income. Benchmarking methodologies can vary, sometimes producing divergent outcomes, and access to reliable data in remote regions can be fraught. While living wage benchmarks are indispensable tools, they cannot supplant collective bargaining.

In a more just world, states and corporations would follow living wage principles. Yet the world is not just. No countries enforce an official, real living wage. Statutory minimum wages rarely, if at all, meet the basic needs of workers. And out of 193 UN member states and eight former members, thirty have no minimum wage at all. But the absence of a floor means different things in different contexts. Sweden, for instance, has no statutory minimum, but it does have strong trade unions, sectoral collective bargaining, and social protections. Brunei, Rwanda, and Saudi Arabia also lack minimum wage laws, but there, the absence of labour standards translates directly into some of the worst conditions of unpaid and unfree labour, especially for migrant workers.

Living wages typically diverge from minimum wages. They also vary by country, or even different regions within the same country, because costs of living and social welfare provisions vary.[35] Cambodia's living wage, for example, was approximately US$588 in 2019, while the minimum wage was set at only US$194, only a third of what was necessary. In India, the living wage was approximately 29,323 rupees, while the minimum wage was only 42 per cent of that, at 12,250 rupees. In Romania, the living wage was estimated at €1,448, while the minimum wage was set at €249, only 17 per cent of what was necessary. Across the world, statutory wage floors fail to keep pace with actual living costs, thereby exposing vast disparities in worker protections and pay.

Disparities among the lowest paid, however, are dwarfed by the disparities between the lowest and highest earners in society. The foregoing discussion focuses on a floor to stabilize the volatility of capitalist economy. Yet the image of a floor also conjures the notion of a ceiling. If a society deems certain forms of poverty unconscionable, then the upper limits of income should also be targeted. Wage discourse must transcend minimal decency to bound economic avarice. If a living wage is the base of a just, liberal society, then a maximum wage becomes its apex.

The notion of a maximum wage is actually an ancient idea that spans back to Plato. In the *Laws*, he argued that the richest class should be limited to acquiring no more than quadruple the poverty line, determined by the necessary land, tools, and animals for subsistence.[36] In Plato's ideal republic, anyone who accumulates more than the limit would both have to forfeit the surplus to the state and be fined an amount equal to that surplus.[37] Such a limit is far more egalitarian than anything those in mainstream policy circles today would dare to propose. Contemporary economic realities are far worse than the ancients could have imagined. In the US, the median chief executive pay ratio for 2018 was 254:1, which dwarfs other nations. Elon Musk was paid 40,668 times more than the median Tesla worker. Of the hundred largest companies by revenue, eleven CEOs were paid more than 1,000 times that of the average employee. These pay ratios varied widely between industries and do not correlate to performance.[38] In the UK, FTSE 100 CEOs were paid 117 times more than the average worker in 2018. On average, executives made £901.30 an hour, compared with the average full-time worker on £14.37 an hour.[39]

More in the Platonic spirit, some policies have been proposed that would establish a pay ceiling or maximum wage ratio. During the Second World War, Franklin D. Roosevelt proposed a maximum income of $25,000 in 1942 (adjusted for inflation, this would be $481,309 in 2024), accompanied by a 100 per cent tax on all income above this. More recently, an ordinance was passed in Portland, Oregon, that mandated companies pay a 10 per cent surcharge if their CEO pay is 100–250 times more than the median employee and a 25 per cent surcharge if executives make more than 250 times median pay. Research has shown that workers value not only their pay but also how it compares with that of CEOs. Capping executives' pay obviously benefits workers through capacity for redistribution, but it also is shown to improve motivation. Maximum wage rules reduce high-skill workers' incentives to reduce effort and mimic lower earners. Enforcing a maximum wage ensures there is an upper limit to the inequitable distribution of the gains from enterprise at firm level.[40]

In closing, the central thread running through this chapter is that we must understand the wage in economic theory and policy to fully comprehend wage theft under capitalism. The wage is a social phenomenon, dictated by the power of labour to bargain for a share of what is produced. A minimum wage should at least be a fair share of this produce, but it often isn't. Throughout history, workers typically have had to fight for every penny. Yet even when they have a contract, a bargaining agreement, and the backing of national and international law, employers still find a way to extract a greater share of the product.

With each new technological leap, new ways of stealing that extra cut emerge. To grasp the modern mechanics of wage theft, then, we must follow the wage beyond the factory gate and into the circuitry of digital capitalism.

# 6
# Technoligarchy

Our world has been flooded by a deluge of digital platforms, their ceaseless flow submerging our daily lives. From the planetary infrastructures of Amazon, Meta, Google, Apple, WeChat, and Alibaba, to the on-demand labour of Uber, Didi, Upwork, and Deliveroo, we've become networked datums in digital portfolios. The infrastructures of capitalism now flow through cables and cloud servers that states have been slow and economically disincentivized to regulate. We are all paying rent in the internet of landlords.[1] This is an evolving machinery in which datafication facilitates dispossession. Many have attempted to name the current era: a 'second machine age', the 'fourth industrial revolution', 'industry 4.0', 'platform capitalism', or 'technofeudalism', among others.[2] The techno-optimism of the 2000s has evolved in increasingly dystopian directions. Today, environmentally destructive, data-thieving, 'generative' AI companies such as OpenAI, Anthropic, and DeepSeek deskill human labour and undermine our very cognitive capacity. Transformations are occurring in nearly every sector and nearly every country, around the world.[3] As platforms digitally colonize and commodify an ever-greater portion of our time, it becomes harder to find the cracks in capitalism where human culture can flourish and resistance can grow. To fight this techno-capitalist inertia, it is necessary to understand how paid and unpaid labour have changed through it.

Our current era contrasts with its historical antecedents: the post-war 'golden age' of capitalism, known as the Fordist era (1945–75), which gave way to its undoing in the neoliberal, post-Fordist era (1975–2005). The Fordist era was characterized by robust manufacturing exports from rich countries alongside strong organized labour and institutions that redistributed wealth and protected social need from the excesses of capitalism in the West. The post-Fordist era saw deindustrialization in rich countries, the industrialization of many low- and middle-income countries, an erosion of social welfare and labour protections, and increasing inequality. Capital and its representatives became significantly more powerful. Financial markets were deregulated throughout the 1980s, supply chains were further internationalized, and public assets were privatized, hollowing out state capacity.[4] Seventeen OECD countries witnessed a fall in the labour share of income from 75 per cent in the mid-1970s to 66 per cent in 2005, and it has only fallen further since.[5] This Wild West of neoliberal globalization was the condition of possibility for platform capitalism to emerge as the hegemonic force it is today.

In the early 2000s, as home and mobile datafication

provided computing and ICT capacity beyond specialized industrial applications, tech companies took aim at expanding their power through a wealth of networks.[6] Online and offline machines congealed with natural life, as 'Cyber-Physical Systems', or 'the seamless integration of computation and physical components' grew into digital ecosystems.[7] A surge of investment and innovation helped this emerging paradigm rise to dominance. Research shows a concentrated 'open-ended burst' in technological development from 2006 to 2017, which corresponds to a rise in ICT investment from 2005 to 2015 among OECD countries, as well as the acceleration of AI-related patent-making since 2005. This decade also saw the acceleration of cloud connectivity, enabling web domain expansion and the expansive datafication necessary to train more powerful AI systems.[8]

As technological access and capacity expanded, so too did use-cases. Platformization subsumed ever more activities to the algorithmic calculations of marketized efficiency. Entirely new industries emerged as commodified services. In national accounts, platforms are classified under the technology and consumer services sector, which comprised 16 per cent of the top-twenty companies by market capitalization in 2009. By 2018, this surged to 56 per cent. Four of the top-ten firms in 2018 – Amazon, Alibaba, Facebook, and Tencent – were not even in the top 100 in 2009.[9] Today, Apple, Amazon, Meta, Google, Microsoft, Tencent, and Alibaba constitute seven of the ten most valuable companies.[10]

A triad of structural transformations has accompanied the technological burst.[11] First, changes in intellectual property rights anticipated some of the needs and protections in this datafied landscape.[12] The World Trade Organization's 1995 Agreement on Trade-Related Aspects of Intellectual Property Rights (TRIPS) established an arbitration framework for stolen patents and other intellectual property. The 2008 changes in the System of National Accounts (SNA) ensured intellectual property and intangible assets were included in various national and international accounting frameworks.[13] This changed the code of capital to privilege the value of intellectual monopolies. Second, while the US was the global leader in this technological revolution, China rapidly caught up to rival US dominance, especially in AI. Third, tech oligarchs' platforms have become increasingly powerful relative to the public infrastructures of states, since the latter have become utterly dependent on the former, even at the level of national security.

Like the power looms, automated threshers, and robotic assembly lines before them, platform technologies are not neutral. They are designed to allow management to wield unilateral power over production and scale rapidly to become infrastructural, thereby extracting monopoly rents. Failing that, platforms are sold to a larger competitor for a hefty sum, a strategy has been termed the 'new economy business model'.[14] It is a distinct monopoly-oriented approach epitomized by tech capitalist Peter Thiel's mantra 'competition is for losers'.[15]

Platform labour is typically organized according to a core-periphery system whereby salaried, professional workers run the company with equity options, while a vast army of low-paid and precarious workers generate value. For example, Google employees are typically software engineers and other professionals with high salaries. However, the people who work to train the algorithms by moderating content on YouTube or correcting the generative AI output of Gemini work as self-employed subcontractors overseas. This dynamic is epitomized by labour platforms such as Uber, whose accounts employees, for example, make around £44,000 a year for a normal 37.5-hour week, while drivers work up to fourteen hours a day and can earn below minimum wage after costs.[16] Platforms delegate the illusion of control and trade on a libertarian myth to obscure the autocratic reality. Their rapid and unchecked spread has had dire consequences for workers and society.

## Platformization of Labour

What do platforms do to the boundary between paid and unpaid labour-time? It depends on the platform and the context. Uber, Deliveroo, Upwork, Doordash, Meituan, and Didi cut across different sectors, but there are really only two types of platform. We can call the first type 'ground' platforms, as the services they provide – such as food delivery, cleaning, taxis, and so on – require the work to be done in a particular location. The second type we can call 'cloud' platforms, since the work does not need to be performed at any particular location. Cloud platforms provide services from microtasks like data labelling to freelance design and copy-editing. In 2021, the International Labour Organization (ILO) estimated there were at least 777 digital labour platforms operating globally.[17]

Digital labour platforms tend to use self-employment

contracts and piecework systems, which result in insecurity, exploitation, and wage theft. 'Self-employment' (UK) or 'independent contractor' (US) status effectively treats every digital platform worker as an individual business without any of the advantages that real businesses have. This classification is used to deny workers the right to collective bargaining, sick pay, or any guaranteed income at all. In rich countries with more formal labour markets, such as the US and the UK, this has catalysed the decades-long erosion of social protections under neoliberalism.[18] Attacks on statutory rights are pushing these countries back to conditions reminiscent of the late nineteenth century, when poverty and slums were the norm for a working class with no social safety net. There has, however, been a counter movement in less-rich countries towards an expanded formal labour market via platforms themselves. Still, data and intellectual property are siphoned off to rich countries, echoing centuries-old dynamics of colonial extraction.

## Ground

The US has been at the vanguard of the tech boom, with hundreds of ground platforms, covering nearly every service: dog walking, child-minding, housing, cleaning, ride-hailing, warehousing, food delivery, snow ploughing, and more. In 2021, the Pew Research Center estimated that some 16 per cent of American adults, roughly 41.3 million people, have earned money through these platforms.[19] Nonetheless, very few of these companies provide reliable, fair pay or protections for workers. Many have been challenged for wage theft. Amazon US, for example, recently agreed to pay more than $61.7 million to settle allegations that they cheated their drivers out of nearly a third of their tips from customers over two years.[20]

A 2023 study by the Oxford-based Fairwork project found that only two out of thirteen US platforms could ensure their workers earned at or above the minimum wage after costs. These were Alto, a ride-sharing platform, and Bluecrew, a staffing platform, which classified their workers as employees. The eleven others – Papa, DoorDash, EatStreet, GrubHub, Handy, Instacart, Lyft, Shipt, TaskRabbit, Uber, and Wonolo classified workers as 'independent contractors' rather than employees. They could not guarantee that workers earned at least the local minimum wage after costs, let alone a living wage. Ten out of thirteen platforms scored zero points on Fairwork's dashboard measuring guaranteed minimum thresholds of decent work.[21]

Most platforms use an algorithmic pay and job-allocation system. This is essentially a way to calculate the lowest rate that workers will accept, and the highest rate consumers will accept. These algorithms factor in variables such as a base rate, distance, tolls, surcharges, surge multipliers, booking fees, route adjustments, promotions, time of day, and even the behaviour of individual workers and consumers. While the formula varies, the general structure is as follows: (base fare + time rate + distance rate) × (surge multiplier) + tolls and fees. The so-called 'dynamic pricing' (the US Federal Trade Commission has called it 'surveillance pricing') piece-rate model was pioneered by Uber and is spreading to other industries such as retail.[22]

Driver unions have pushed back against the asymmetry of information this model creates. In response, Uber introduced 'upfront pricing' in 2022, which provided drivers with a base fare for each job. Yet the calculation of the price is anything but upfront. One driver in California claimed it was 'a pay cut in disguise' that lowered base pay while not increasing fares for longer trips adequately. Drivers rely on surges (multipliers for rates) and 'quests' (completing a set number of rides within a week for additional wages of $50 to $200) to make up for low rates. According to a member of the union Rideshare Drivers United, 'everyone has different levels of surge at any given time. If the median surge is 10, someone else might have 8.' Drivers claim that quests are not consistently offered, that bonuses vary, and that Uber reduces the ride allocation rate near the end of their quest, taunting them with the prospect of losing their 'bonus'. This bargaining asymmetry facilitates what law scholar Veena Dubal has called 'algorithmic wage discrimination'.[23]

According to Malang Gassama, a former driver and New York Taxi Workers Alliance (NYTWA) member, Uber and Lyft stole 'at least $25,000' from his pay. In their terms of service, Uber claimed that only the platform's commission would be subtracted from driver fares, but the platforms actually deducted sales taxes and Black Car Fund fees (8.875 per cent and 2.5 per cent of the ride price, respectively) from drivers' pay instead of charging passengers.[24] Uber also claimed that drivers could charge passengers for tolls, taxes, and fees despite providing no means for them to do so via the Uber Driver app. Lyft employed a similar tactic, skimming an 'administrative charge' of 11.4 per cent equivalent to the sales tax and Black Car Fund fees from New York drivers.[25]

There have been legislative attempts to curb platforms' exploitative practices in the US. For example, California legislation (Proposition 22) guarantees platform drivers 120 per cent of the minimum wage in the area in which they are driving. However, this only applies to 'engaged time', which the platform defines solely as driving time; no waiting time, transit time, breaks, maintenance costs, or the like are included. The Rideshare Drivers United (RDU) trade union found that drivers were making just $6.22 per hour on average after expenses. 'No one believed they were making so little', according to Nicole Moore, a driver and leader of the RDU, although the numbers did not lie.[26]

Platforms are designed to have a large reserve of workers logged in at any given time, which reduces both labour scarcity and the bargaining power of workers, increasing the likelihood that workers will accept low pay. According to studies, delivery workers spend 39 per cent of their time waiting or 'on-call'.[27] As a result, they can't earn a living from just one platform. Many must multi-app, though this practice is greatly overstated by the platforms themselves. In NYC, while 56.3 per cent of delivery workers work for more than one app, only 17.7 per cent of working time is logged concurrently. In 2022, drivers for food delivery platforms Uber Eats, Grubhub, DoorDash, and Relay were revealed by New York's Department of Consumer and Worker Protection to be earning half their income in pay, and half in tips. These workers were paid an average of $14.18 per hour with tips, and just $7.09 per hour without. For a food order of $33.09, only $4.32 is paid to the worker (plus a tip of $4.11), while the platform receives $8.54. Delivery workers' hourly expenses are $3.06, reducing their take-home pay to $11.12 per hour with tips and $4.03 per hour without.[28]

If Uber Eats, Grubhub, DoorDash, Relay, or any other ground platforms were required to pay an NYC worker as if they were an employee in 2022, the hourly wage would have been $21.09 per hour, or triple the base rate they made before tips. This would include at least $15 an hour plus up to fifty-six hours of paid leave per year under the NYC Paid Safe and Sick Leave Law, unemployment insurance, workers' compensation insurance, employer coverage of half the mandatory 15.3 per cent Medicare and Social Security contribution, and shared liability for failure to pay.[29] The fact that there was a legal dispute over these entitlements, with the workers and the State of New York on one side and the platforms on the other, demonstrates the political stakes of their struggle.

Meanwhile, across the Atlantic, UK platform workers face nearly identical working conditions to the US. One worker (let's call them Frankie) began riding for Deliveroo after finishing university, drawn by what the adverts called 'flexibility' and 'freedom'. At first, the job was a way to bridge the gap between a degree and a career. But the façade of autonomy waned as they had to spend ever more time in the saddle and take ever more risks to make ends meet. 'We are clearly not our own boss,' they said. 'We're not in control of getting work.' Riders can log in and out at will, but there's no guarantee of work. 'What flexible means for them,' Frankie laments, 'is not what flexible means for us.' The algorithm dictates paid and unpaid time: 'The number of shifts you book, the number of orders you take, rush hour availability – these determine who gets next week's shifts.' Furthermore, 'when they go on a hiring spree', Frankie notes, 'actually they're driving wages down'.[30]

In 2023, the Fairwork project studied twelve of the most popular UK labour platforms: Amazon Flex, Bolt, Deliveroo, Free Now, Getir, Gorillas, Just Eat, Pedal Me, Stuart, Task Rabbit, Uber, and Uber Eats.[31] Only Pedal Me and Getir could guarantee earnings at or above the living wage after costs; these platforms also used employment contracts.[32] Self-employment contracts and piece-rate pay systems are used to avoid paying workers for their waiting time, job search time, travel time, breaks, or other entitlements.[33] A survey of app-based couriers in the UK by the group Focus on Labour Exploitation, for example, showed that 63 per cent of respondents were paid below minimum wage, 71 per cent had financial difficulties, and 18 per cent had to rely on state benefits.[34] According to research conducted by Worker Info Exchange, rideshare drivers averaged 4 million journeys per week across the UK, and delivery workers averaged 1.7 million journeys. They estimated losses from wage theft and out of pocket expenses in 2023 to be £1.29 billion for rideshare workers and £617 million for food delivery workers, totalling £1.9 billion.[35]

In 2019, when couriers in Newcastle went on strike for better conditions, Deliveroo claimed they earned over £11 per hour. However, records from 650 hours of work in the same city suggested an average of just £7.85. Reece Lloyd, a rider in Newcastle, saw his pay drop from between £8 and £12 to just over £7 per hour, which he attributed to an influx of new riders.[36] An analysis of over 12,000 sessions and 34,000 hours by 318 Deliveroo workers in 2020–21 found that 56 per cent of the riders who took part had average earnings of less than £10 per hour for all the time they were logged in, 41 per cent earned less than the legal minimum wage for workers over twenty-five of £8.72 per hour, and 17 per cent received less than £6.45 per hour. Deliveroo continues to claim that workers earn more than the minimum wage despite refusing to account for total active time for riders.[37]

In filings for its initial public offering (IPO), Deliveroo warned that reclassifying riders as employees would 'adversely affect' the business.[38] In a normal capitalist enterprise, if a business can't afford to pay its workers, that business deserves to fail. Aviva Investors shared this sentiment, announcing that its decision not to invest in Deliveroo was in part due to riders' self-employed status.[39] In Spain, a 'Rider's law' was introduced, which classified riders as employees by default (subject to specific conditions) and required algorithmic transparency.[40] Yet, rather than change their business model to address investor concerns and pay workers a decent wage, Deliveroo simply left the country.[41]

Platforms tout economies of supply and demand as the only law. Yet the magic hand of the market is actually wielded by platform managers, who manipulate it. Platforms benefit from a costless surplus of labour: workers are unpaid until selected; companies can promise customers rapid service and suppress driver pay simultaneously. Uber CEO Dara Khosrowshahi articulated this strategy to investors: 'As driver supply improves, surge comes down, ETAs improve'; 'more driver supply brings down prices for riders and improves reliability'.[42] Efficiency for the consumer rests on inefficiency and invisibility for workers as they wait unpaid. As Judge Snelson observed in his 2016 ruling against Uber, quoting Milton: 'They also serve who only stand and wait.'[43]

Just like in the US, dynamic pricing algorithms personalize pay, which means the boundary between paid and unpaid labour-time is constantly shifting based on what that algorithm predicts each worker will accept. Uber drivers used to earn '£3 for the first mile'; then it changed to '£1.25 per mile and £0.10 per minute'; then it changed again to '£3.30 for the first mile' but then 'less than £1.00 per mile' after, which averages out at '£1.17 per mile' and '£0.23 a minute'.[44] In litigation brought by the advocacy organization Worker Info Exchange against Uber, the court noted that dynamic pay has serious 'financial consequences that determine the income they [workers] can earn'.[45] This is not a market in any conventional sense, but a contested terrain of calculated asymmetries.

In Taizhou, on the east coast of China, Liu Jin burst into flames. 'I want my blood and sweat money back', he said as he self-immolated in a video. This tragic act of desperation followed a pay dispute with the local partner of Alibaba's food delivery platform Ele.me. The fire left him with third-degree burns covering 80 per cent of his body. Roughly 1,500 kilometres north, in the grey chill of a Beijing winter, a courier named Han collapsed and died mid-shift, his insulated bag still strapped on.[46] Ele.me reportedly denied he was their employee and only paid RMB 2,000 to the family, though a subsequent national scandal pressured the company to increase it to RMB 600,000 (about £60,000 or $80,000), a paltry sum for a human life.[47] There are countless other stories like these in China's platform economy, which is an uncanny mirror of the West's erosion of labour rights.

China's National Bureau of Statistics estimated in 2020 that there were 200 million people in China's flexible employment system and 84 million platform workers (10 per cent of the total employed labour force). The largest digital labour platforms are Taobao and Jingdong (warehousing and couriering), Meituan and Ele.me (food delivery), and Didi (taxi services). The China Labour Bulletin estimated that, in 2023, there were 13 million food delivery riders, accounting for nearly 1 per cent of the national population.[48]

Like in the US and UK, gamified metrics masquerade as meritocracy. Chinese platform workers deal with low wages, a lack of a safety net, and misclassification as self-employed. On apps such as Meituan and Ele.me, piece-wages are calculated by algorithms that rank workers by speed, acceptance rate, customer reviews, and volume. Workers who deliver more, faster, and with fewer complaints are rewarded with better pay and priority access to jobs. Rates and reviews quantify how completely a worker can subordinate themselves to the platform.

Between 2016 and 2019, Meituan halved its standard delivery time from one hour to thirty minutes. The burden of risk fell squarely on the riders. The faster some couriers completed their routes, the faster the algorithm recalibrated the exception as the norm, intensifying work without raising wages, appropriating ever more unpaid labour. In Shanghai, during just the first half of 2017, a delivery rider was injured or killed every 2.5 days. In Chengdu, police recorded nearly 10,000 traffic violations by food couriers in the first seven months of 2018. There were 196 accidents, with 155 injuries or deaths. In one month in 2018, Guangzhou traffic police dealt with almost 2,000 traffic violation cases by delivery riders. Meituan riders were involved in half of them; Ele.me ranked second.[49]

Why aren't workers protected from this work in a workers' state? Chinese labour law entitles full-time, formal employees to five types of insurance, including pensions, medical, unemployment, work injury, and maternity. Research by the Yilian Labor Center found that 95 per cent of delivery riders worked more than eight hours a day and 66 per cent worked more than eleven hours. Nearly 90 per cent of respondents relied on the platform as their only source of income.[50] Yet, the vast majority of platform workers in China are not classed as full-time formal employees. Like the informal workers of the pre-digital age, they lack a social safety net, and a single accident could spell destitution.

Chinese platforms flout labour regulations by forcing delivery riders to register as self-employed and sign contracts with agency firms. A survey in Beijing found that only 3.7 per cent of food delivery drivers and 1 per cent of ride-hailing drivers were entitled to employment-injury insurance.[51] There were at least 1.6 million riders officially registered as self-employed in this way in 2021, but the unofficial numbers are likely higher. The Beijing-based Zhicheng

Migrant Workers Legal Aid and Research Centre analysed data from 1,907 court cases involving food delivery platform workers and found that the court determined a formal employment relationship in only 1 per cent of cases. Platforms abdicated their obligations as employers, passing them on to logistics agencies or the workers themselves.[52]

In China, workers must be linked to their *hukou*, or permanent residence, to receive employment insurance, rendering protections inaccessible for internal migrants, who represent a disproportionately high number of platform workers. A 2020 survey found that over 80 per cent of China's food delivery workforce were migrants. Most Didi drivers had full-time contracts, and three-quarters of part-time drivers also had contracts, but only 60 per cent of the total had pensions.[53]

Platforms are masters of digital distancing. Meituan and Ele.me use their technological infrastructure not only to optimize logistics but also to insulate themselves from the obligations of a conventional employer. This is a design principle common across continents. Like their Silicon Valley and London counterparts, Chinese platforms operate with a calculated disregard for existing labour norms and law. They move fast and break workers' bodies by externalizing liability.

## Cloud

After finishing work at her first job, Sibongile then logs on for an afternoon and evening of chasing cloud work. She's twenty-four, lives in South Africa, and works on Amazon's

Mechanical Turk, a microwork platform that connects clients known as *requesters* to a global workforce who can complete jobs known as *Human Intelligence Tasks*. Sibongile looks for tasks frantically because the platform pits workers against one another. But the best-paying tasks are almost always geo-locked, reserved for users in the US. 'I am more than capable of doing them well,' she says, 'but I'm not from a first-world country.' National borders and inequalities are coded into virtual space. The work itself is inconsistent and often not even worth the effort it takes to acquire it. On a typical day, Sibongile watches the feed for four or more hours, but usually only two of those hours are paid. The rest of her time is spent refreshing windows hoping to find work that only pays 'between $0.01 to $0.05 per task', which roughly equates to 'between $2 to (at best) $5 per hour'. 'The experience never meets the expectations', she says. The platform is engineered to ensure the supply of labour is high to keep wages low.[54]

Through their digitally unbounded capacity, cloud platforms annihilate spatial and temporal limits to labour supply. Cloud services themselves are starkly divided between freelance platforms such as Upwork or Fiver, which solicit more skilled jobs from copy-editing to programming, and microwork platforms, which mainly solicit simple tasks such as completing surveys, labelling data, data entry, and so on. In 2023, the World Bank estimated that there are about 154 million to 435 million people doing these jobs, roughly 4.4 per cent to 12.5 per cent of the global workforce. They identified 545 cloudwork platforms across the globe, headquartered in sixty-three countries with workers and clients located in 186 countries, though 75 per cent of platforms primarily operate regionally.[55] According to the Oxford-based Online Labour Index, demand for cloudwork is dominated by high-income countries and the English-speaking world, while India, Bangladesh, and Pakistan account for over 50 per cent of the supply of labour.[56]

The ILO estimates that for every hour of paid cloud work, workers spend an unpaid twenty minutes searching and preparing for jobs.[57] Another study found that Amazon Mechanical Turk workers spent around 33 per cent of their working day doing unpaid labour for the platform, making the median hourly wage a mere $2.83.[58] Fairwork studied 792 cloud workers in seventy-five countries and found that, of the average 22.7 working hours per week, 14.8 were paid and 7.8 were unpaid, meaning 34 per cent of platform labour-time is unpaid. When workers in low- and middle-income countries are disaggregated from rich ones, the latter perform almost double the amount of unpaid labour (some 9.9 hours) per week. While workers in the Global South tend to work more hours overall, this difference is still stark.[59]

Like ground platforms, cloud platforms typically avoid using employment contracts and thus dodge the obligations such contracts entail, enabling wage theft at a planetary scale. Unpaid labour-time in the cloud is typically a combination of waiting, performing background work, absorbing rejections, messaging clients, bidding for work, building profiles, completing applications, undergoing training, generating sample work, and chasing down unpaid wages for jobs already completed. The line between paid and unpaid labour-time is obscured in the fog of microtasks.

Even completed work that meets all the criteria may be rejected by clients and remain unpaid. It is not uncommon for the same work to reappear, repurposed or reworded, in the final output. On 99Designs, for example, tasks are advertised as 'contests' in which workers submit designs for free and the client has the power to pick the winner.[60] This is particularly the case for microwork platforms, as one Amazon Mechanical Turk worker commented:

> There is no protection for workers against non-paying clients of the platform. Theoretically, every single client could refuse to pay and there would be no repercussions … in the case that the client never intended to pay, there's literally nothing a worker can do to receive payment or even some kind of mediation.[61]

Platforms embed these dynamics in their business model. This is theft of labour and theft of workers' intellectual property.

Cloud workers from Brazil, India, and Australia described error-prone payment systems, bugs in platforms, and client manipulations, such as the withholding of completion codes that prevent workers from requesting payment. Timed tasks can be automatically rejected if the worker exceeds a predetermined limit, regardless of effort or quality. One worker on Prolific explained: 'Because I took such a long time, they decided not to pay me even though I answered all the questions.'[62] Cloud platforms obscure the real temporal demands of the job, with advertised working-time underestimating the real time required.

Such piece-rate manipulation harks back to wage theft

in early industrial capitalism. For example, an 1862 report on the grievances of the journeymen bakers noted that one 'full-priced baker' denounced his 'underselling competitor' as thieves: 'They only exist now by first defrauding the public, and next getting 18 hours' work out of their men for 12 hours' wages.'[63] For cloudworkers, platforms take an extra cut by obscuring the terms of the exchange.

In this economy, contesting wage theft is often futile. While some platforms offer dispute processes, they are slow, opaque, and rarely worth the worker's time. Instead, the architecture itself annihilates mutual obligation or accountability. This is why most workers simply move on to the next job. Even if dispute processes are available, they aren't worth the time. Cloudwork means cheap labour and little risk for clients, while workers earn poverty wages, when they aren't simply stolen.

## Platformization of Capital

Abbo is twenty-eight and moved to Gulu, Uganda, in search of something better. She has worked for five years at Sama, a data annotation company subcontracted by some of the most powerful tech firms in the world. She does vital work for AI by labelling images so that machines can be programmed to 'see' like humans. This work enables mythologies of digital innovation, self-driving cars, industrial robots, and surveillance systems by remaining invisible. Each day, Abbo arrives at her desk before 8 in the morning and stays, eyes locked to the screen, well into the evening. When she started, her daily target was 500 tasks, but now it's 800 for the same pay. For over a year, she worked seven days a week, and the strain is cumulative. Sometimes, the fatigue overwhelms her body completely: 'I feel my mind is shutting then all of a sudden I feel I get dizzy then I feel I need rest, I need to put my head down and sleep for some time.' She asked management for time off, but their response was: 'If you are not capable, you leave the project.' Yet she can't give up her 'means of survival'.[64] Sama's branding suggests empowerment, but Abbo said she hadn't been paid overtime for three months. The payments that did arrive were at reduced rates. 'I thought I would pay off my debts,' she commented, 'but because they didn't pay what I was expecting, I ended up taking loans again.'

From Nairobi to Gulu, tens of thousands of workers like Abbo are rendered as ghosts, feeding unpaid labour to the machines automating our future.[65] These workers are contributing not only tangible, concrete labour but also intangible data about that labour: their cursor movement for each minute of the day, the pattern of their keystrokes, their vocal idiosyncrasies or pronunciation, eye movements, and even their body temperature. This data might seem like digital exhaust from a virtual machine, but it is just as important to AI value-chains and architectures as Abbo's image labelling.

This data represents a new type of transformation – surplus-labour becoming intellectual property, an *intangible asset*. Intangible assets include research and development, mineral exploration and evaluation, computer software, databases, entertainment, literary or artistic originals, and other products.[66] In their terms and conditions, Amazon Mechanical Turk reserves the right to use worker data to 'improve the Site and other machine learning related products and services offered'.[67] This is the contractual manifestation of a data pipeline that could serve AI in products ranging from Alexa to Amazon's logistics systems. Data assets also fuel militarized AI systems such as Palantir's autonomous weapons systems and Israel's genocidal AI weaponry.[68] And so wage theft, as the denial of a claim to property, even as intellectual property, is interwoven into digital ecosystems of capital, the product stored in hyperscale data centres available in an instant.

The year 2017 was a turning point for this new economy, when investment in intangible assets outpaced that of tangible assets as a share of GDP in the US, the UK, and Sweden. By 2020, the European Data Economy was worth over €400 billion, with a growth rate of 7.6 per cent. European data suppliers were estimated to number more than 290,000, while data professionals were numbered at 7.6 million, or 3.6 per cent of the European Union (EU) workforce, and are growing at 5.5 per cent annually.[69]

Intangible assets are peculiar. They typically require a significant initial capital investment for research and development, but then take less labour to reproduce through maintenance and updates. Datafied assets are only valuable insofar as datums can be linked into a network or dataset. The transformation of an individual datum, such as a selfie on Instagram or a location check in a car, is essentially devoid of meaning or value on its own. In 2017, the *Financial Times* estimated that the average person's personal data, such as their age, gender, and location, was worth about $0.0005 per person.[70] Companies need the temporal and spatial patterns of collective data, cross-referenced and weighted, in order to metamorphize individual datums into intangible assets that can be used to valorize value.

Data is sometimes produced via human cloudworkers like Abbo and other times through the surveillance of individual non-work activities that the technology has access to, like our movements on Google Maps. In the latter case, individuals are not labouring to produce this data in a sort of unpaid employment relationship. Rather, there is an exchange of app usage for data capture. User activity should not, therefore, be considered as labour-time. This is because the value of digital assets diverges from that of traditional commodities in which the costs of reproduction are approximate to the costs of its production. For example, say the original time spent on the production of software is 100 hours. If the software is copied digitally by 999,999 users, then labour-time represented in each copy would be equal to 0.36 seconds; for 9,999,999 users it would be 0.036. Economically and in value terms, these can be considered equal to zero.[71] To generate profit, a company must therefore enforce property rights over digital assets through legal tools such as End User Licence Agreements (EULAs) and collect rents.[72]

Let's take another example – taxi drivers. Before connected vehicles and Uber, drivers with the right qualifications and licensing were paid set rates. Inputs and outputs were easily discernible; the price of the fare, minus costs of the vehicle, petrol, licence fee, and tax, would leave the driver with their earnings. However, today drivers typically get riders and fares through platforms that extract a surplus. Uber determines pay according to an algorithm. It collects driver and rider data to monetize intangible assets – an exchange without equivalent. Millions of Uber trips within London generate a dataset with public value, ranging from insights into traffic patterns to the spatial-temporal dynamics of passenger movements. This data is intellectual property that Uber uses as a capital input to improve its algorithms and market position. Uber executives know that the company also has valuable data about urban transport. In fact, Fred Jones, general manager of Uber UK, explained that 'our data shows the impact on travel times of moves like the closure of Tower Bridge in 2016, which could be useful when similar projects are planned'. This was said at the launch of Uber Movement UK in March 2018, a public data initiative that was quietly shuttered in October 2023.[73] This data has public value yet is hoarded by private owners.

Drivers in rich countries are also typically using a connected vehicle. Through its various sensors, each shift, stop, start, and turn is datafied. Instruments engage as the driver turns the car on; sensors detect a passenger, cabin temperature, signal the sunroof's status, connect to Bluetooth and a device, register when the ignition button is pressed, and track location via GPS. The car continues to process a huge range of data such as proximity to other connected vehicles, speed, engine oil levels, road safety, and even what song is being played. This data is stored on 'vehicle data hubs' before being sold through the connected vehicle data marketplace, a Wild West of third-party applications.

Vehicle data hubs serve as a nexus for data assemblage by standardizing datasets and, through this transformation, they can sell data-based products. While boosterish growth forecasts should be taken with a grain of salt, consultants have estimated that the connected vehicle data industry could be worth $800 billion by 2030.[74] Otonomo, an Israeli company started in 2015 that claims to provide data aggregation from 50 million vehicles, tracking 330 billion miles, and processing 4.1 billion data points daily, was valued at $1.4 billion at the time of its IPO in 2021. Otonomo's Q1 2022 financial results revealed contracts with twenty-three vehicle-related manufacturers. Wejo, a Manchester-based vehicle data hub, emerged in 2014 and by 2023 purportedly collected data for 13.8 million vehicles before it collapsed due to a poor IPO.[75]

Mobile phone data is another industry that leverages intangible assets and collects data rents. It was estimated at around US$16.09 billion in 2023 and is expanding.[76] An investigation identified forty-seven major companies that extract, sell, and trade mobile phone location data across the globe, including Near, Mobilewalla, and X-Mode. Near claims to cover 1.6 billion people across forty-four countries, while Mobilewalla boasts of over 1.9 billion devices and 50 billion mobile signals daily, and Outlogic (formerly known as X-Mode) claims to cater to over 25 per cent of the adult US population monthly. In 2020, an investigation claimed that a number of Muslim prayer or similar apps had worked with data broker X-Mode, which has sold location data to military contractors.[77] Location data can be lucrative, with Outlogic reportedly charging $240,000 per year for a licence to a dataset titled 'Cyber Security Location data' on Datarade, a Berlin-based tech company that acts as a business-to-business data broker.[78] Buyers of mobile location data include governments, law enforcement agencies, investors seeking market insights, political campaigns for targeted advertising, and businesses monitoring customer behaviours.

Industrial data has been utilized to monitor employee activity at Tesla's Autopilot labelling facility in Buffalo, with employees reporting keystroke logging and productivity tracking via software such as 'Flide Time', which monitors active time on work tools and penalizes deviations from quotas.[79] Amazon warehouse workers filed National Labor Relations Board (NLRB) charges alleging the use of intrusive algorithms and surveillance systems to monitor and deter union organizing.[80]

Data is power and control over it crucial. The weak regulations on collecting and owning this data is a win for tech oligarchs. While the US has federal and state laws that establish limited data privacy, particularly around financial data, health data, and data from minors, it has no comprehensive framework to protect workers from the risks of datafication at scale.[81] Recent concerns have spurred state lawmakers in California and then in Colorado, Connecticut, Utah, and Virginia to pass restrictions on the collection, transfer, and sale of location data. These are modelled on the EU's 2018 General Data Protection Regulation (GDPR), which protects individuals from data collection as default, requiring users to 'opt in' rather than 'opt out' of collection.

The EU has led the world in developing regulations for datafied exchange, with the Digital Markets Act (DMA), which aims to safeguard competition in bottlenecks such as app stores, marketplaces, web browsers, and search engines. Article 6(9) of the DMA establishes the right of EU citizens to data portability or the capacity to download individual data and move it to another platform. This, in theory, undermines the monopoly status of some platforms by allowing users to transfer their data. It means that end users and authorized third parties must have free access to these essential tools. This is an acknowledgement to some degree of ownership or at least rights over the production of one's own data. While the DMA's promise of data portability gestures towards a recognition of users' rights over their digital footprints, it stops short of confronting the deeper structures of digital extraction.

The EU's AI Act, meanwhile, aims to set binding rules on transparency. Generative AI outputs must be watermarked, and firms must disclose their training data. Fines scale up to €35 million or 7 per cent of global turnover for violations.[82] France's 2024 'digital spaces' law criminalizes distribution of AI-created content without consent, with prison terms and fines up to €75,000, and gives regulators power to order removal. Denmark has recently proposed granting every person copyright over their own likeness, establishing that one's body, face, and voice cannot be copied or circulated without consent. Non-consensual deepfakes and 'digital imitations' would be illegal to produce and to share.[83]

The problem is not simply that workers and consumers cannot access or control their data; it is that their ordinary activities are continuously mined, quantified, and repurposed as fuel for generative AI. Codifying complex tasks, especially activities such as writing emails, responding to traffic hazards, and troubleshooting data, often relies on tacit knowledge; this is intuitive and non-verbal knowledge acquired through experience. Datafication is simply another opportunity for capitalist theft. Or have we moved beyond capitalism into something worse?

## Technoligarchy

Technofeudalism, neofeudalism, post-capitalism: intellectuals from Yanis Varoufakis and Cédric Durand to Jodi Dean and Mariana Mazzucato have declared a new economic order. They – let's call them the New Feudalists – believe that the rising importance of technologically enabled rents over traditional, tangible industrial profits has moved us beyond capitalism as we know it. Much of the justification for this shift lies in conceiving the production of data by consumers as a form of unremunerated labour. This amounts to the claim that the world is now undergoing a historical shift approximating the period in England from the fifteenth to eighteenth centuries. Tech oligarchs rejoice! If once, as Fredric Jameson famously said, it was easier to imagine the end of the world than the end of capitalism, then today, following Evgeny Morozov, it seems 'easier to imagine the end of the world than the *continuation* of capitalism as we know it'.[84]

Do tech-driven changes really mark a paradigm shift in the mode of production towards a new type of digitally driven feudalism? Something indeed has changed. Institutions, infrastructures, and the forces of production have developed in ways that have obscured the code of capital as we knew it. French economist Cédric Durand looks to tech firms' business models and logics of extraction to evidence the new era.[85] Central to his idea of technofeudalism is the paradox of profits without investment in many advanced capitalist economies, starting in the mid-1990s. Globalized digitization has enabled top firms in the Global North to extract lower prices from their supply chains, using buyer-driver monopoly power to reap the benefits of new Global South infrastructures.[86] The monopoly power associated with the rise of intangible assets and datafication has weakened the productivity-inducing effects of competition. Durand's new mode of accumulation relies on a taxonomy of rents, including legal intellectual-property rents, natural-monopoly rents, dynamic-innovation rents, and intangibles-differential rents. These rentier capitalists resemble feudal lords who benefit from predation rather than labour exploitation. Combined with a weakened state, tech capitals with intellectual monopoly power have enabled substantial profits without redistribution of the benefits.

Former Syriza minister and economist Yanis Varoufakis has also picked up on these changes. He argues that platform profits are derived primarily from 'cloud rents', which are the foundation of a new technofeudal mode of production. Varoufakis contrasts the simple feudal fiefdoms of old with the monopolistic stack of Amazon and Google, claiming that all hitherto existing phases of capitalism were characterized by fixed capital as produced means of production. Yet now, he claims, these produced means of production are not aimed at further production of surplus-value, but rather the manipulation of consumer behaviour. This occurs by compelling people to 'perform unpaid labour', often without even knowing it, while platforms collect cloud rents. As unwilling serfs, we valorize 'cloud capital', and so 'quantity has become quality, and the entire system has transformed'.[87]

For Varoufakis, the changes that constitute technofeudalism are as follows: the strategic aim shifts to behavioural modification of workers and consumers; industrial profit and markets are replaced with cloud rents and cloud fiefs; waged workers are turned into 'cloud proles' while everyone else is a 'cloud serf'; and capital accumulation becomes primarily rent-based, amplifying crises. Other political economists have recognized many of these changes but largely placed them in the context of capitalist evolution.[88] The question, however, is whether such changes amount to a continuation of capitalism's logic rather than its end.

Varoufakis's theory hinges on reclassifying activities as labour that previously were not. The implications of this claim are that, like the natural constraints of the soil and land owned by a lord, digital platforms and tech infrastructures wield similar power over not only workers but also consumers, who co-produce 'cloud capital'. The theory maintains that people looking at content on Instagram aren't consuming media but rather performing unpaid labour to provide personal, networked data to build the 'cloud capital' of Meta's algorithms. Doomscrolling is now labour, shopping for trainers is now labour, and viewing viral videos is now labour – all 'unpaid'. In a standard Marxist analysis of capitalist society, these activities would be considered acts of consumption or at best social reproduction outside Marx's full circuit of production (see Chapter 4). Varoufakis's theory actually goes one step further than many feminist arguments about domestic and care work, claiming that 'unpaid unwaged labour is *directly* producing capital in an unprecedented way'.[89] Such claims reflect an inattention to the constitution of the capitalist labour process.

Furthermore, the use of feudal categories simply fails to translate to Marxist distinctions between production, distribution, and consumption. The focus on 'cloud capital' leaves its dialectical counterpart, 'cloud serfs', undertheorized and incoherent. As explained in Chapter 2, feudal production relied on systems of direct coercion. Serfs and villeins had some autonomy in subsistence production but their surplus was openly and legally expropriated in a variety of ways under threat of violence. As Wickham notes, 'estates could have rent-paying tenants, forced labour, and wage-labour all at once, or move between them'.[90] The lord collected rents, but these could be in the form of money, labour-time (unpaid days of work per annum), or a surplus product such as grain or livestock. Moreover, serfs and villeins retained a relatively high degree of autonomy over their everyday labour processes. There were no formal contracts beyond rents or tithes. Finally, villeins, vassals, serfs, and others had no choice over where they lived and worked. They were forcefully bonded by law to a lord and his land. By contrast, the free movement of workers and consumers is a distinctly capitalist phenomenon that didn't take hold in England until after the Poor Law (Amendment) Act 1834. Even then, workers were tied to church parishes.[91] Today, workers move freely within states and legally between them.

Jodi Dean similarly locates a supposed break from capitalism in the platform economy's reliance on 'blitzscaling' tactics, where venture capital and private equity pump billions into enterprises such as Uber, WeWork, and Instacart to erode local businesses, undercut wages, and push entire sectors into dependence on proprietary apps. Somehow these practices are not capitalist. Dean sees this new economy as a form of feudal tribute, with newly subordinated 'vassals' or 'serfs' to pay fees to access an unfree market. 'Neoliberalism turns into neofeudalism' because of the destruction of social welfare provisions, which Dean terms 'reflexization', representing how imperialist expansion has turned inwards.[92] This doesn't hold up to historical scrutiny, given that throughout most of capitalist history, there were no social welfare provisions beyond church and charity. By casting platform owners as feudal lords, Dean amplifies their power to the level of a sovereign authority. And yet states still make the laws. While platforms are clearly exploitative, it is not as if getting deactivated by Deliveroo is the same as getting thrown in prison for stealing wood from a lord's estate.

The neofeudal thesis doesn't hold up empirically either. Using the case of Uber, Dean notes that the 'instruments of labour' ostensibly belong to the driver, yet Uber leverages the cars for the company's own ends, 'in effect getting cars to employ their owners'. Let's assume that the drivers in fact do own the cars (often they do not, but instead are renting them). If Uber does not own or have rights over the car, it is not used as a constant capital input; it costs Uber nothing. However, the connected devices in the car feed data to Uber that the platform develops and maintains as intangible assets. The percentages of fares plus fees that they collect from drivers are a mix of surpluses from labour exploitation and rents for the use of their tech infrastructure. The customer also is a source of data – however, tapping an app and riding in a car is not labour; it is consumption. Uber drivers sell their labour-power to Uber and riders buy rides from Uber, not the driver, who has no control over prices; they can just accept or decline based on what the algorithm sets. Uber controls all aspects of the work itself, including the pay. If drivers were genuinely self-employed, they could decide their own fares (or they would be set by collective bargaining agreements) and riders would pay them directly. Uber is a straightforward relationship of employment dependency. In Dean's analysis, by contrast, drivers become unwilling martyrs to a New Feudalism that neither reflects the reality of work today nor corresponds to actually existing feudalism.

Serfs and villeins had ready access to the means of reproduction; they could farm the land and make the things they needed without being directly compelled to earn a wage and purchase them via market exchange. Under capitalism, social reproduction becomes mediated by capital, since the means of workers' reproduction are primarily tied to the wage, which is necessary for survival. Waged labour is tightly controlled, Taylorized, and increasingly algorithmically surveilled by platforms in hitherto unprecedented ways. Yet, while contemporary workers may also contribute unpaid, surplus-labour, they are free to quit their jobs, move cities, disconnect, and touch grass.

This points to other aspects of the New Feudalist theory that lack consistency. Varoufakis argues that cloud capital is transforming all our social reproductive activities into value-producing labour by making us 'cloud serfs'. This argument isn't entirely new. Christian Fuchs repurposed

Dallas Smythe's 1977 theory of the 'audience commodity' to argue that using Facebook is actually labour.[93] The 'work' of audiences theorizes the consumer as a worker, termed 'prosumer' or 'co-producer' by proponents.[94] However, such theories make a category error conflating production and consumption, which are conceptually and economically distinct, especially in a Marxian framework. The nature of the division of labour is that workers are bound, legally and economically, by the constraints of the employment relationship. Consumers are not. Labour-power is commodified. Consumption is not.[95] Data about consumption simply provides more targeted and efficient means of production for consumption. Advertising firms and media empires have been influencing behaviour based on surveys and other data for decades. Simply automating this process does not change the mode of production.

Regarding changes to capital, New Feudalists see tech firms as predatory rentiers. They conceptualize data as analogous to land, with tech firms engaging in unproductive activities that yield 'profit upon alienation' in Marx's terms. This is partially correct. The US is becoming the world's leading extractor of information rents, building a cloud empire. From 1947 to 2011, the joint share of financial income and information rents as a proportion of the net income of all unproductive activities rose 85 per cent. The share of information rents alone increased 120 per cent.[96] Why?

Software production costs are typically 1.5 times the average wages for software occupations, but much less for maintenance. The low cost of maintenance – that is, the cost of reproduction – means that these products must become sources of rent to make a profit.[97] Capitalist rents occur when the owner draws value from the difference between the individual price of production and the average price of production, the individual profit, and the average profit (this is why Marx uses the term differential in his theory of ground rent). Platform capitalists rely on monopolies to give themselves this advantage, as well as through rents of exclusive use rights, which is closer to ground rent, charging others for the right to use the asset. Combine this techno-capitalist imperative with the fact that the US is a global imperial power, and it becomes obvious why the world has followed the path it has.

Yet, whether tech firms are capitalist, rentier, or a combination thereof, is irrelevant to the question of a wholesale change in the mode of production. Equating tech firms with feudal rentiers ignores the vast amounts of capital that these firms invest in research, development, and traditionally productive activities. For example, Morozov points to the productive role of indexing in Google's operations and the fact that the company does not own the search results it indexes. Google acts as an information supply chain, producing not only datasets but also various commodified resources that other businesses use as capital inputs, in addition to consumer services.[98] Data feeds the digital machine, growing the intangible assets that enable rents to be extracted across the world via their monopolistic, infrastructural power. Data serves as a means of production, but the primary aim is to produce profit, not manipulate behaviour. The latter is a means to the former. T'was ever thus.

If capitalism is minimally defined as the imperative of competitive accumulation by 'peaceful means', then its fundamentals have not changed.[99] As Cecilia Rikap and Jeremy Gilbert have pointed out, the evidence for continuity is strong.[100] How then should we understand our present era? Capitalism is fundamentally at odds with feudalism, which was driven not by imperatives of competition and efficiency but rather custom and lineage. There is little in the feudal order other than the immiseration of labour and unaccountable elites that resembles the capitalist world order today. Whether we look at nineteenth-century railroad barons or twenty-first-century platform capitalists, the logic still serves profit maximization and shareholder returns. Traditional business strategies of crowding out or absorbing competitors through state-backed financial and military firepower continue, from Musk's strategy with Space-X, Palantir's integration with ICE, or Amazon Web Services' global digital infrastructure gambit. These companies don't aim to replicate feudal subordination but rather to move from 'zero to one' and secure monopoly rents by annihilating competition. Elon Musk, Jeff Bezos, Bill Gates, Mark Zuckerberg, and other lesser-known billionaires less resemble aristocratic lords of the land than awkward oligarchs of the internet.

Rather than conjuring images of feudal fiefdoms, we might deploy the portmanteau of 'technoligarchy'. Technoligarchy describes the coalition between the ultra-rich and the state that has tightened its grip on both market structures and political institutions. It draws on Robert Michels's classic insight about the 'oligarchical tendencies' in modern organizations.[101] Rather than signifying a feudal fragmentation of sovereignty, the brute force of the state is integrated into tech capital's ambitions. Trump's executive orders that shielded AI developers from rigorous oversight, and Musk's sweeping (yet fleeting) authority at the Department of Government Efficiency (DOGE) reflect a form of 'corporate-state synergy' that cements oligarchic power. Such synergy is reminiscent of earlier eras in capitalism's evolution, such as the Gilded Age, when railroad and steel barons behaved as if they were sovereigns, threatening anyone who stood in their way.

The technoligarchy relies on financial circuits to amplify their reach, funnelling investment to whichever platform can promise double-digit returns and further consolidating power. Silicon Valley's AI race operates through precisely these channels of speculative investment, bubbles be damned. The technoligarchy dominates through infrastructural power and a geopolitical strategy aligned with the global elite, while pushing datafied discipline for workers. Again, none of these are features of feudal society.

To conclude, digital gleaning by virtual machines is not a new mode of production so much as technological means of speculation, a dice-roll on a future that technoligarchs are trying to will into existence. Whither resistance in this digitally dystopian stage? From AI hacking to anti-data-centre activism and strikes, there are many modes of struggle being pursued. If the overriding problem is an oligarchic consolidation of economic might, then the solutions lie in mobilizing democratic institutions and social movements to contest the expansion of capitalist power. Treating the capital as 'feudal' suggests that capitalism's core structures have vanished rather than mutated. Our challenge is not simply to understand capitalist technoligarchy but to reimagine the system that might replace it. To avoid digital barbarism, we must seek techno-socialism.

# 7
# Another Work Is Possible

*Rights are what you make and what you take.*

– James Boggs, *American Revolution*, 1963

In the year 2001, the World Social Forum met for the first time in Brazil, marking the start of the anti/alter-globalization movement. This global, summit-hopping wave of resistance grew in part from the embers of the 1999 'Battle of Seattle', a 40,000-person strong protest-cum-riot that plunged the World Trade Organization's conference into chaos. The slogan of the World Social Forum is 'another world is possible'. What would this other world look like? Rather than a bold vision of a new socialist system, the movement focused instead on smaller, networked initiatives to create a 'solidarity economy' of mutual aid in the shadow of global capitalist hegemony.[1]

The destruction of actually existing socialism across the world during the Cold War, whether by the US in Latin America, the French in Western Africa, or the Soviet Union itself (before it imploded), weighed heavily on the internationalist left at the time. 'Great Power Communism', Robin Blackburn wrote in his 1991 post-mortem, was 'not a spectre stalking the globe, but an unhappy spirit, begging to be laid to rest'.[2] In this context, anti/alter-globalization activists were largely fighting a defensive battle against neoliberalization – that is, the enactment of policies that strengthened the power of capital against labour and democracy. Wrapped up in the resistance was a somewhat problematic romanticization of indigenous movements and an over-emphasis on localism. Ultimately, the movement failed to counter capital's immense and growing power. The slogan 'another world is possible' was eclipsed by marketing taglines such as 'think global, act local' that recuperated social movements into 'ethical capitalist' branding initiatives.

Since then, a new terrain has emerged: the 2008 global financial crisis shook capitalism to its core; 2011–12 saw a global wave of populist revolts occupy spaces from Cairo's Tahrir Square to New York's Zuccotti Park; and young, democratic, socialist movements re-emerged within and beyond various political parties across the West. Meanwhile China continued its meteoric economic rise and marketization, becoming a world superpower in a matter of decades. As the COVID-19 pandemic demonstrated the power of the state to intervene in the face of a global biological and economic crisis, most Westerners' material circumstances worsened, with the costs of living increasing as the labour share of income continued to fall, following the trend of the late twentieth century. Rentiers of the world have swelled their portfolios while the climate crisis threatens collapse.

It is not by chance that political programmes on the left and right have hardened, with the former taking a distinct turn towards class and climate while the latter reanimate the fascist playbook with an injection of incel ontology and aesthetics. For those of us who look to the future rather than the past for inspiration, revolutionary horizons are marbled green and red.

In this book, we have outlined how the capitalist system of exploitation relies on the generalized extraction of unpaid labour and wage theft under the liberal property order. Throughout this era, workers have fought – sometimes through guerrilla tactics, sometimes through mass social movements – to decommodify their labour-power and to reclaim their right to its 'full' product. Decommodification, according to Danish political economist Gøsta Esping-Andersen, 'occurs when a service is rendered as a matter of right, and when a person can maintain a livelihood without reliance on the market'.[3] It strengthens the bargaining capacity of the worker by enabling the refusal of work, since essentials are removed from the competitive marketplace. Decommodification has historically allowed workers to raise the value of their labour-power through this increased bargaining power. Twentieth-century labour movements were partially successful in this regard. Their success enabled strong democratic rights, welfare provision, and power for workers, insulating society from the immiserating chaos of capital's excesses. In the Soviet and Maoist world, socialist states essentially abolished markets and private property altogether.[4]

Resistance to capitalist exploitation requires an understanding of how laws and institutions can be reformed in labour's favour, as well as a vision of the future that supersedes the hegemony of capital entirely. Faith in revolutionary spontaneity as the harbinger of an egalitarian utopia is no less a fantasy than faith in the idea that capitalism will collapse under the weight of its own contradictions. Reshaping society requires a plan to reorganize social reproduction such that our labour and its products remain collectively our own, to ensure that social surpluses are distributed according to need, and to provide the luxury of leisure for all. It is in this spirit of revolutionary reform that the rest of this chapter proceeds, beginning with the minimal and ending with the maximal.

## Minimalist Programme: Industrial Justice

Sometimes the only way to receive a 'fair day's pay for a fair day's work' is to steal back time and money. While sailing the seventeenth-century seas, sailors often engaged in direct expropriation, finding ways to 'sweat the purser', 'to sling', 'to cut out', 'to knock off', or 'to manarvel' extra products.[5] Modern phrases such as 'fell off the back of a lorry' in the UK or 'tipped myself' in the US hark back to this history. French and Italian Autonomists developed more politically charged tactics in the 1970s such as 'autoreduction', which focused on redistribution of goods from supermarkets, collective resistance to transport fare increases, and rent strikes.[6] While individual anarchistic acts of retribution to steal back time and money as well as collective 'strategies of refusal' such as work slowdowns can have radically disruptive impacts, they are limited in scale and scope. Stealing back wages is re-appropriating our share of the product at the level of the firm, but if value and exchange relations still govern social activity, this sort of expropriation is not enough.

Wage theft impacts everyone. When wages remain unpaid, payroll taxes, income taxes, and sales tax revenue are siphoned into the private hoards of property owners. Greater inequality reduces social cohesion, stability, and breeds stagnation. By contrast, greater equality, public ownership, and higher wages have been shown to result in considerable public benefits and savings.[7] Workers at the lower end of the wage scale tend to spend their income on essentials, while the rich tend to save more of their income. The more expendable income that the masses have, the greater growth through aggregate demand. Raising incomes also has positive correlation with better health and educational incomes. Eliminating wage theft also recovers the tax revenue that contributes to social services and infrastructure from which every citizen benefits.

Abolishing wage theft is the definition of industrial justice. Achieving industrial justice requires a multifaceted strategy, starting with enforcing the existing laws meant to prevent wage theft. Free market ideologues will protest that cracking down on wage theft by strengthening labour laws will discourage growth and entrepreneurial activity, as if success can only come at workers' expense. Below-market wages act as a lever to undermine the sustainability of businesses that don't race to the bottom. Employers that steal wages lower their costs and thus gain an advantage by undercutting their compliant competitors.

A 1979 study by the political economists Orley Ashenfelter and Robert S. Smith that attempted to model why employers continue to flout the law, found that the expected benefits of non-compliance are essentially a function of the probability of escaping detection, multiplied by the quantity of labour hired, elasticity of demand for labour, and the difference between the minimum wage and the 'true' market wage. The costs of non-compliance are the probability of detection multiplied by the penalty for violation. This sounds complicated, but in essence it means that the incentive to violate the law rises as benefits exceed costs. A large divergence between minimum and market wage, high labour market elasticity, a low likelihood of detection, and low penalty for non-compliance all therefore increase the incentive to engage in wage theft.[8] One study found that stronger state laws significantly correlate with a lower incidence of minimum wage violations.[9] Yet most of the existing penalty schemes simply aren't strong enough. Another study found that even in the unlikely scenario that an employer is successfully sued for half its violations, violation would still be less costly than compliance.[10]

So, we know that weak laws incentivize wage theft and stronger ones disincentivize it. But stronger laws don't write themselves. Rights for workers are what workers make and what they take, as Boggs said. The provision of rights without economic and industrial democracy means that rights will be held hostage to predatory capitalist imperatives.[11] Economic democracy has long been viewed by the establishment as an insurrectionary threat. Sidney and Beatrice Webb remind us that 'strikes are as old as history itself'.[12] Peter Gaskill, whose book *The Manufacturing Population of England* was a primary reference for Friedrich Engels's research, wrote that strikes taught workers 'a dangerous power' that would lead to the 'destruction of social order, and the security of life and property'.[13] Chance would be a fine thing.

Yet the foundations of economic democracy took centuries of strategic organization and agitation to establish. Despite riots, illegal strikes, clandestine sabotage, and political advocacy culminating in the Chartist movement of the early nineteenth century, little changed for working class people in England until the 1860s. One of the first victories for industrial justice came thanks to coal miners, who secured the legal right to elect a checkweighman via the 'checkweigh clause' in 1860. Checkweighmen held a powerful strategic position in the mining process because they weighed the coal as it came out of the mine, and workers were paid by output.[14] Until the Combinations of Workmen Act 1825, trade unions were illegal in the UK and remained only quasi-legal until the Trade Union Act 1871. During this time, the checkweighmen were often fired by management for organizing. After years of agitation by workers and socialists, checkweighmen became independent in 1887, gaining more power with the addition of their right to act as Inspectors of Mines. This was the wedge that eventually led to full collective bargaining and the introduction of democracy to the workplace.[15] As the Webbs note, checkweighers were trusted by their colleagues and served as 'a practically inexhaustible supply of efficient Trade Union secretaries or labour representatives [could] be drawn'.[16] From the late nineteenth century to the mid-twentieth century, no fewer than fifty checkweighmen ascended to Parliament.

The late nineteenth century saw large, fragmented, and precarious workforces organized into trade unions that fundamentally changed how resources were distributed in society. Large UK unions such as GMB trace their origins to the great docklands strike of 1889, when 130,000 casualized London dock workers downed tools until they were given a minimum pay rate and an end to twelve-hour shifts with no days off. Before 1889, there were only small, highly skilled craft unions. The dock workers' strike inaugurated a 'New Unionism' that organized workers of all grades of skill into the Dockers, the Gas Workers and General Union, Tyneside's National Amalgamated Union of Labour, and others. From 1888 to 1918 trade union membership expanded faster than at any other time in history, increasing nearly nine-fold from 750,000 to 6,500,000.[17] Indeed, low-waged, precarious workers are the classical starting point from which industrial justice emerges.

Socialist politicians such as Keir Hardie, the Scottish founder of the Labour Party, and Eugene V. Debs, the founder of the Socialist Party of the United States, knew that union power was necessary for industrial justice. The legal system often can't keep up with rapid changes in industry and the needs of workers. While law should govern rules and norms in the workplace, in practice, justice is often served via *force majeure*. It should be unsurprising then that labour institutions in the UK and the US were at their strongest after the great wars, when communist parties were strongest and the demand for labour was high.

A study of successful union strategies during this period found they all did three things: (1) gained access to employer data used to determine wages and conditions; (2) challenged wage setting through research and counter-reports of employer studies; and (3) strategically engaged in workplace decision-making to set their own rules.[18] Unions established the rules to maintain industrial peace, putting employers on the back foot if they transgressed. The threat of industrial action is a deterrent to rogue employers, increasing their risks and costs. Unions, as self-governing regulators of work, serve the public as an industrial enforcement body, supporting workers morally, financially, and legally through disputes, especially when it comes to unpaid wages.[19]

Given the power that unions afford, it is not surprising that free market fanatics have made it their ambition to destroy them. From the late 1970s, Reagan, Thatcher, and their network of neoliberal ideologues led a transatlantic assault on labour protections, demolishing workers' bargaining power and shifting risks from capital to labour and the public. In the US, union density for all workers fell from 24 per cent in 1973 to 9.9 per cent in 2024, with the private sector falling to 5.9 per cent.[20] Workers seeking union representation face a process that favours employers. 'Right-to-work' laws make union representation more financially burdensome and undermine collective bargaining agreements. In this context, the labour share of income roughly halved from 1982 to 2016, yet profits considerably increased.[21] Today, non-union workers are nearly twice as likely to experience wage violations compared with union workers, and non-union workers tend to lose more of their income (24 per cent) than union workers (17.4 per cent).[22] The union wage premium – the percentage bump in wages earned by those covered by a collective bargaining contract – is 13.6 per cent.[23]

Across the pond in Britain there were as many as 300,000 trade union representatives in the late 1970s, with 10,000 on full-time release to organize.[24] Successive Conservative governments in the 1980s and 1990s enacted a series of attacks on labour: they outlawed the closed shop (when all employees must belong to the union), which covered 5.2 million workers at its peak; they banned secondary strikes (a way that workers who were not in an industrial dispute could leverage support); and they introduced new laws such as the requirement for a week's notification in advance for strikes. In 2016, the Trade Union Act was introduced, which required 50 per cent of eligible union members to vote for strike action for it to be valid.[25]

Given this context, the immediate prospects for eliminating wage theft in the US and the UK may appear dire. Rebuilding union power is difficult when most unions face an uphill battle against legislation that favours capital by design. Yet, the infrastructures already exist for a new internationalist unionism. For example, the Council of Global Unions is made up of ten global union federations including UNI Global Union, Public Services International, International Transport Workers' Federation, and Education International, among others. Each of these international meta-unions help coordinate hundreds of regional unions around the world with millions of workers.

In the context of the long decline of the labour movement, the war against wage theft is increasingly fought on two fronts: dusty shop floors and the polished marble tiles of the courts. An alternative labour movement, drawing on insights from Latin American organizing, has emerged in the US. Labour researcher Janice Fine has called this 'alt-labour', since it uses tripartite organizations (governments, employers, and workers) called worker centres to prioritize labour market enforcement.[26] Worker centres are typically non-profit organizations that support those who cannot legally unionize (such as undocumented workers) or those whom traditional unions have failed to reach (such as domestic workers), by organizing campaigns, protests, and litigation. These centres often collaborate with established unions and are sometimes funded by them. The number of worker centres grew from five in 1992 to over 200 in 2013, driven by an immigration wave that doubled the population of foreign-born workers between 1990 and 2010. Examples include the Restaurant Opportunities Centers United, the National Day Laborer Organizing Network, the National Taxi Workers' Alliance, the National Domestic Workers' Alliance, the Freelancers Union, Fight for $15, and hundreds of others.[27]

These worker centres are American labour's vanguard against capital. In 2010, the Chicago Workers Collaborative, Centro de Trabajadores Unidos, and Latino Union of Chicago formed the 'Just Pay for All' coalition to fix the Illinois Department of Labor (IDOL)'s problems in addressing wage theft. The IDOL lacked authority to issue default judgments when employers simply ignored rulings, which they did over 40 per cent of the time. Cases of wage theft were sent to the state attorney general to enforce, yet these cases kept disappearing. Working together, the 'Just Pay for All' coalition passed new legislation that granted the

IDOL the authority to adjudicate claims when employers ignored rulings and charged employers $250 to cover public costs. The success of this campaign catalysed the movement under the banner of 'Raise the Floor', expanding leadership and adding five more worker centres. Since 2015, they have recovered $1,343,798, won forty legal cases, and represented 172 workers through the legal clinic.[28]

Another key victory came in 2023, when the New York Taxi Workers Alliance (NYTWA) secured a $328 million settlement from Uber and Lyft for more than 80,000 drivers. This was the result of years of legal action and public agitation that started in 2015 and sustained through lawsuits for unemployment recognition in 2016 and 2020. The win wasn't only monetary. Drivers now accumulate one hour of sick pay for every thirty worked (up to fifty-six hours annually), are guaranteed $15 an hour for training, receive clear hiring notices detailing fare breakdowns, gain multilingual support, and, most crucially, retain the right to appeal deactivations. That success has expanded the union's base to over 25,000 members.[29]

US workers are also using lobbying power to fight wage theft. Between 2006 and 2013, a dozen state-level bills were passed, five of which included payments to workers of three times the total wages stolen. A further three bolstered criminal and civil penalties for wage theft, two others established a small claims process, and two added new penalties for failure to pay after a company is found liable.[30] States that already had strong penalties yet still had high rates of wage theft, such as California, Maryland, and Washington, introduced additional measures such as treble fines.[31] In 2011,

New York passed the Wage Theft Prevention Act, which was amended in 2014 to extend protections and significantly increase penalties. Now, a failure to provide wage statements and employment terms results in fines of $50 a day up to $5,000 per worker. Employers are also liable for damages up to 100 per cent of unpaid wages, up to $3,000 for repeated violations, a $10,000 fine for non-compliance, 15 per cent of damages for failure to pay on time, and up to a $20,000 fine if an employer has taken retaliatory action.

In the UK, new strategies were pursued by rank-and-file formations such as the App Drivers and Couriers Union (ADCU) and the Independent Workers Union of Great Britain (IWGB). The ADCU challenged Uber in a landmark legal battle that went from the High Court to the Supreme Court, ultimately forcing a reclassification of tens of thousands of private-hire drivers from 'independent contractors' to 'limb (b) workers' – a status that comes with statutory rights to holiday pay, a minimum wage, and collective representation. Uber's contracting model was not driver to rider, the court ruled, but instead driver and rider to Uber, which makes Uber accountable in the same way as other taxi firms.[32] The ruling meant that other ride-hailing platforms operating in the UK such as Bolt had to amend their contracting model as well.[33]

The ADCU's fight also moved into the datafied terrain. Through its Worker Info Exchange initiative, it targeted the data infrastructures that underpin platform control. In a series of rulings by the Amsterdam District Court, Uber and Ola were found to have violated GDPR regulations in a number of instances, including when algorithms were involved in terminating driver accounts. The court compelled both companies to disclose how driver performance is monitored, including profiling metrics such as 'fraud probability scores' and 'earnings profiles'.[34] In confronting algorithmic opacity, the ADCU not only pushed for procedural fairness in dismissals but also forced open the algorithmic black box so that workers could more effectively bargain with data against platform capital.

Beyond taxi platforms, UK domestic workers on care platforms secured a long-overdue reprieve when a court ruled in 2021 that the so-called 'family worker exemption' did not apply to them. Originally intended for informal 'au pair' arrangements, the exemption had become a legal shroud used by platforms to hide from minimum wage obligations. The ruling established that care workers deserved formal worker status and a minimum wage in line with other industries.[35]

But progress for labour is rarely linear. That same year, the Court of Appeal upheld Deliveroo's classification of riders as self-employed, locking them out of core employment protections.[36] In the background, however, GMB Union brokered a contested deal with Deliveroo, ensuring riders £245 per week in sick pay, a £1,000 parental grant, insurance coverage, and an elected representative to voice concerns to management. To the IWGB, this was a betrayal, a top-down settlement. Still, it demonstrated the potential of union pressure to leverage concessions from platforms.[37]

On the other side of the world, the 2014 Yue Yuen strike in China marked a new era of wildcat worker action. It began with workers blocking roads before spreading rapidly. Despite alleged intimidation tactics by management, including threats of dismissal without compensation, the strike continued, soon drawing international attention and support from activists and labour NGOs. The Yue Yuen factory eventually conceded full payment of pension insurance and housing funds, back payments upon request, and a monthly living allowance. Yet the workers found these measures insufficient, particularly the condition requiring them to pay their share of back payments, which many could not afford. The Dongguan authorities' response was to attack labour rights protections and escalate police intervention, exemplified by the detention of labour activists such as Wu Guijun.[38]

Such cases of formal and informal labour unrest in response to wage theft are a sign of growing political courage and activism among Chinese workers. Some have pressured local and provincial governments to enforce social insurance laws more strictly. As Chinese industrial relations scholars Chris King-Chi Chan and Elaine Sio-Ieng Hui point out, labour unrest helped drive a transition from 'collective consultation as a formality' to 'collective bargaining by riot', finally arriving at 'party state–led collective bargaining'.[39]

Taken together, these cases suggest the tactical ingenuity of a new generation of rank-and-file unions, alt-labour organizations, and wildcat actions. Workers in New York City, London, Madrid, Brasília, Rajasthan, and Dongguan have been fighting back.[40] Protest actions by the undocumented to the insecure steadily increased through militant coordination and tactical experimentation.[41] Yet these victories remain provisional. Western governments, beholden to capital's lobbyists, have continued to undermine worker bargaining power. With weak union power, redress for wage theft is often fleeting, and the best that workers can hope for is that their claims are successful. But hope alone does not deliver results: a credible threat is needed.

The past, present, and future of the labour movement 'is written in the annals of mankind in letters of blood and fire'.[42] To fight wage theft head-on, workers must rekindle the radicalism that capitalists once feared and aim not only to recover what is owed but also to reclaim what we owned. Industrial equity is a necessary component of industrial justice. But as the twentieth century shows, without democratic ownership and control over the means of production, capital's law of value (the incentives of a capitalist economic system) will hasten the undoing of labour's gains. The obvious solution then is to reject the capitalist organization of society and plan a socialist economy based around need. The next section explains how past economists had conceived of how to do this.

## Prices Versus Planning, aka Mises Versus Marx

As established in the preceding chapters, wage theft is formally designated as such through the legal codes of capital. These codes obscure the total unpaid labour alienated during production that is transformed into profit and private property. The law protects one class's right to this surplus-value at the expense of the rest of us. How could we build an economy in which the law and the economic conventions that operate within it serve labour and the social good of all? To answer this question, we need to get back to first principles.

The objective is to devise a system that produces and justly allocates the resources necessary for human flourishing. This system must obtain information about preferences, produce and distribute resources based on those preferences, incentivize the efficient social use of resources, and coordinate different sectors of society to avoid contradiction, waste, and competition. It must have accurate information about what humans need to grow and how they behave as social and emotional beings at different times and in different places.

Some would say we already have this information in the price system. Anything produced for exchange will have a price attached. This price is meant to be a quantitative, universal measure to balance the supply and demand at a given time. Capitalists believe that the incentive of profitability most efficiently coordinates metrics of production, distribution, and investment. To manage decisions based around these elements requires relatively simple equations and models: the Cobb–Douglas Production Function, the Phillips Curve, the Efficient Market Hypothesis, the Solow Growth Model, and so on. Equilibrium, a central tenet of mainstream economics, holds that changes in prices ensure that supply tends to equal demand. However, this simplicity falls apart in the real world, when producers have disproportionate power through monopoly or monopsony. Fluctuations in capacities, information, and the power of different stakeholders means that the unidimensional measure of price cannot accommodate changes in preferences or alternative measures of social values. Rather than provide objective information, the price system tends to reflect the power of different parties in relationships of exchange governed by profit maximization against social need. Mainstream econometrics tends to brush this aside by methodologically denying it.

Reproducing society based around principles of justice, equality, and need requires a different set of priorities, a different set of equations, and a different way of coordinating resources. In such a society, need would be primary rather than peripheral; the necessities of life would be accessible to all and based on social labour. Beyond necessity, everyone would have a right to receive an additional amount of goods and services in proportion to the amount of time that they contributed to total social reproduction and relative to the overall stock available. Many people throughout history, from Thomas More in 1516 to Salvador Allende's government in 1970s Chile, have tried to imagine or implement models to develop such an economy.[43] What would this look like? Any discussion of alternatives to capitalism should refer to at least two benchmarks: the socialist calculation debate that emerged in the 1920s and the debate over communism after the fall of the Soviet system in the 1990s.

The calculation debate more or less began when the economist Ludwig von Mises published a paper in 1920 criticizing economist Otto Neurath's 1919 article that argued for the feasibility of central planning in kind.[44] Neurath contended that money-calculation is a 'pseudo-rational' device that suppresses plural, incommensurable social aims beneath a single metric, and he proposed calculation in kind to evaluate plans through heterogeneous indicators (health, housing, ecology, work quality) chosen democratically rather than according to profitability. He tied this to an earlier (1912) critique of 'utility monism', or the idea that there is no coherent 'pleasure maximum' that can rank all ends; planning must therefore openly adjudicate value conflicts instead of disguising them.[45] Institutionally, Neurath envisaged a central office preparing rival in kind plans that explain trade-offs (for example faster transport versus slower greener cities) so representatives could grasp qualitative shifts in context.

Mises attacked Neurath by asking whether an economic system without private property would be technically possible at all.[46] For Mises, eliminating private property and the market would also eliminate prices, which Mises thought were essential because they were the most efficient mechanism to determine information related to supply and demand. He believed that any system with planned allocation of resources (socialism) would lead to not abundance but rather scarcity and chaos. Mises essentially argues the opposite of Marx, that socialism (instead of capitalism) sows the seeds of its own destruction because it is an irrational system. And for Mises, if the technical basis for socialism does not work, then political or ethical arguments for it are moot.

Mises's theory drew vociferous criticism from a wide range of political economists at the time.[47] The debate evolved as the Polish economist Oskar Lange intervened, publishing his two-part essay 'On the Economic Theory of Socialism' in 1936 and 1937. Lange exposed the contradictions in Mises's claims using the standard economic theory of the day rather than Marxist economics. Lange's critique revolves around three sets of information that are needed to solve the calculation problem: (1) a scale of preferences that determine choices; (2) the terms on which alternatives are offered; and (3) the quantities or capacities of available resources. Lange argues that Mises denied that a socialist economy could effectively obtain information about the terms on which alternatives were offered, since it did not have a price system. However, if (1) and (3) are known, then (2) is easily determined by the technical conditions of transforming available resources (3).[48] By engaging him on his own terms, Lange showed that Mises's argument was no more than capitalist apologetics.[49]

In a socialist planning system, the state acts as a mediator and democratic planner, collecting necessary information about quantities and qualities of resources alongside the needs of different sectors and people. A state planner must continually adjust supply to demand, thus mimicking the price system, but with less risk of crisis from prices diverging from values. Capitalist states already do this today in various forms, from industrial strategy to farm subsidies and tariffs. If, as Mises and other orthodox economists assumed, markets are perfectly regulated, then price and value should correspond to the choice between use-values and technical conditions of production. Unlike in Mises's vision of perfect markets, however, Lange's model of exchange proves that prices in a socialist economy, including those of the means of production, can be objectively determined through rational accounting. In the face of Lange's rebuttal and the early successes of state-led industrialization in the Soviet and Maoist systems (without excusing political choices that caused terrible famines, among other moral horrors), critics of socialist planning had to change their line of attack.

Enter the Austrian-British economist Friedrich August von Hayek, who, while admitting that socialist calculation is 'not an impossibility', argued that socialism simply isn't practical due to the limitations of authoritarian central planning.[50] In his 1945 essay 'The Use of Knowledge in Society', Hayek argued that much of the relevant knowledge required in a market is tacit, acquired through experience and temporally and geographically specific; it thus resists codification and transmission.[51] Yet this is dissonant with the model of equilibrium theory that assumes agents have complete and correct information. For Hayek and his followers, prices were the most practical way of organizing an economy, even though prices obscure almost every qualitative aspect about a given object. Hayek argued that it is only the price mechanism that can synchronize required knowledge and transmit it, enabling spontaneous self-organization of the market.

Hayek's critique of socialist planning rests on a misrecognition of both the epistemic capacities of collective planning and the imperfect and classed nature of the market system. His invocation of 'spontaneous order' naturalizes the market, its distribution of resources, and decision-making power as transhistorical facts. Yet markets are neither spontaneously organized nor self-organized in modern society. In reality, they tend to form in relation to previous economic systems. However, if we go back far enough, systems of resource allocation necessarily were organized according to custom and social need. Capitalism required violent upheavals and legal enforcement to make a change. Today it needs ongoing state intervention to avoid or recover from crises.

In sum, all economies, market or otherwise, require coordination. Socialist models of ownership and planning can easily acquire knowledge about preferences, alternatives, and capacities through various feedback mechanisms. Structures of management that rely on tacit knowledge can be leveraged through social, cooperative ownership. In this light, it starts to seem like socialism is often rejected not because it is technically unfeasible, but because it contradicts a particular class interest – the dictatorship of the bourgeoisie. However, rather than tinkering with abstract models and theories, perhaps it is better to learn from experience and move inductively through history towards a solution.

## Maximalist Programme: Everything for Everyone

Eliminating the system that underpins wage theft requires a revolution of both collective imagination and total social reproduction. That revolution has historically been called communism, an idea that many have distorted, leaving a battered legacy for those who believe in it today. What once rivalled imperialism and outlasted fascism has now lain largely in ruins for decades. Yet in the majority world, communists still fight to build a better future. Communism reshaped the world like no other force before it, save for capitalism itself. Even Ludwig von Mises, no friend to the cause, called socialism 'the most powerful reform movement that history has ever known, the first ideological trend not limited to a section of mankind but supported by people of all races, nations, religions and civilizations'.[52]

To leave communism buried in silence or scorn is to deny

the depth of its challenge to capital. But critique must go beyond condemning the crimes of Stalin or Mao and beyond the easy virtue of demanding democracy, ignoring the inconvenient fact that liberal republics were built on the backs of slave labour and genocides. There were always dissidents within the ranks of twentieth-century socialisms, martyrs who named the repression they witnessed or experienced, and committed Marxists who later searched the wreckage for what went wrong. Their task remains ours: not to restore what was but to imagine what might yet be. In the words of Mike Davis, 'The alter monde that we believe is the only possible alternative to the new dark ages requires us to dream old dreams anew.'[53]

We cannot turn back the clock on global-scale economic and technological development. A neo-primitivist return to pre-industrial society would simply mean greater subordination to the scarcity and instability of nature, especially in an ever more crisis-prone climate. It's safe to say that few people would accept that. The material and temporal imperatives of the twenty-first century have changed the communist horizon. We can only turn back to the future.

This book's wager is that the technological capacity and knowledge already exist to plan total social reproduction in such a way as to jettison the motto 'A fair day's wage for a fair day's work' in favour of the revolutionary slogan 'Abolition of the wages system'.[54] The political will also exists, but not the political power. The question is how to realize the ends of this real movement. 'How' assumes we've already answered the 'why' and the 'what'. The 'why' should be self-evident, if you've reached this point of the book. Wage theft is part of the long tail of exploitation and unpaid labour. Eliminating it is a categorical imperative if we aim for a society in which every individual is treated as an end in themselves. The 'what' is, in Marx's words, 'the positive supersession of private property as human self-estrangement, and therefore as the true appropriation of the human essence through and for [hu]man[ity]'.[55] In other words, 'the implicit latent abolition of capitalist property'.[56]

Writing about the Paris Commune of 1871, Marx states that the Communards 'intended to abolish that class-property' in order to 'make individual property a truth' by transforming the exploitative, capitalist means of production, land, and capital 'into mere instruments of free and associated labour'.[57] This is still the aim of communism, though building barricades in the streets likely will no longer bring it into being. Our society is far more subordinated to capitalist production and consumption than it was in the late nineteenth and early twentieth centuries. But we have also learned much more about how to dream the old dreams anew.

A sketch of the dream can be found in Marx's *Critique of the Gotha Programme*.[58] At first glace, Marx appears to contradict the argument of this book, since he dismantles the idea that under socialism, individual workers will receive the 'undiminished' or 'full product' of their labour. This notion came from Marx's former comrade Ferdinand Lassalle and other early 'utopian' socialists such as Charles Fourier, Robert Owen, and Henri de Saint-Simon who advocated 'from each according to his ability, to each ability according to its work'. Marx, ever the pedant, explains that the 'co-operative proceeds of labour are the total social product' and, as such, cannot be provided undiminished to each individual worker, because this fails to account for the following: a need to replace the resources that are used up; additional materials required to expand reproduction; deductions for the costs of social administration, such as education and care for those unable to work; and finally maintenance costs caused by 'dislocations caused by natural calamities'.[59]

For Marx, the notion of a 'fair' or 'equal' wage is a misconception among communists, because under capitalism the wage represents equal exchange. Without it, the system falls apart (as demonstrated, in a way, by this book). However, if we move beyond the paradigm of bourgeois right and private property, the calculus changes. Fair distribution cannot be based on individual contribution alone. Ensuring equal resources means that deductions from individual contributions must be made for social distribution. Under a fully cooperative society in which individual contribution is subsumed to social need and the means of reproduction are collectively shared, so too are all contributions. Communism proper means distribution according to need supplants distribution according to contribution.

The distinction between principles of distribution is how Marx differentiates between lower and higher stages of communism. The 'lower phase' is a cooperative society in which the means of production are held in common, exchange is no longer the basis of distribution, and individual labour in production no longer determines value since it is part of the total social product. This implies that records of contributions such as labour certificates would not need to circulate like currency and instead would be used by workers to track their consumption. These records would not serve as money and would thus lack the ability to function as capital. The 'higher phase' of communism abolishes bourgeois property, right, and inequality, which means that society can then 'inscribe on its banners' Marx's famous principle, 'From each according to his ability, to each according to his needs!'[60]

The revolutionary attempts to forge a communist society vary widely across time and space. The European revolutions of 1848 were not yet communist and essentially aimed to throw off the old aristocratic order, with varying success. It was the Proudhonians who seized power in Paris on 18 March 1871 and held it until the end of May.[61] These Communards advocated a working-class rejection of all bourgeois political institutions. Following Proudhon's *The Political Capacity of the Working Classes*, they strove for 'permanent class war until victory', but their revolution was extinguished in a massacre.

The Russian Revolution of 1917 is, of course, another model or attempt at achieving the 'lower phase' of communism. Stalin, in the 1936 Soviet Constitution, wrote: 'The principle applied in the USSR is that of socialism: From each according to his ability, to each according to his work'. In his early speeches, Lenin emphasized that direct worker representation at the grassroots level is the foundation for socialist planning and revolution. The Communist Party's second programme echoed these sentiments, highlighting the essential role of the base Soviets in collective planning and self-management. During the Bolshevik Revolution of 1917, factory committees served as workers' main vehicle of organization. They were directly initiated by workers. The Soviet model rewarded workers according to an eight-grade scale that varied across industries. Yet workers were discouraged from attempting to control the polity or political institutions of power.

Trotsky and Stalin, in their alliance, pressured Lenin during the war against the white guards to temporarily suppress the base councils.[62] Their argument was that this suppression was necessary to maintain adequate weapon production.

This justification became a theme. The Soviet Union only industrialized rapidly during its first five-year plan (1928–32) because it dramatically suppressed both workers' real wages and real grievances.[63] A paradox existed in the USSR: while the peasantry, often marginalized by the communist government, benefited from economic democracy, the working class, the supposed vanguards of the revolution, ended up subject to intensification and incentives not unlike those of their American counterparts.

Ultimately, party bureaucrats supplanted unions of workers in their authority over organizing production and social reproduction. A growing disconnect between the factory floor and Soviet governance made it difficult for workers to defend their interests. Top-down control and use of scientific management contributed to high turnover and created an over-reliance on material incentives to motivate workers. A failure of the planning system to accommodate liberalizing reforms in the face of competition from the West eventually led to the collapse of the Soviet Union. Tito's Yugoslavian model offered an alternative to the Soviet system but encountered problems with worker participation in the self-management of the firm and the ability of workers to realize their political demands.[64]

Meanwhile, in China, Maoists attempted to build a system that used non-material incentives to promote workers' enthusiasm for production and solve the contribution–distribution or 'effort bargain' problem. The first five-year plan (1953–57) emphasized material incentives, while during the Great Leap Forward (1958–60), non-material incentives such as competitive contests and mass meetings dominated. Material incentives were then partly reintroduced during the economic adjustment period (1961–65).[65]

According to historian Hao Qi, the Maoist state constrained material incentives because reliance on them undermined political incentives and led to antagonisms among workers.[66] The state also established a high-benefit system to complement the low-wage system because workers' material conditions were crucial for maintaining effort. Using economies of scale in the provision of benefits was a more efficient use of resources than wages. Factories were not allowed to fire workers because job security was a necessary condition for workers to contribute more effort in production. Finally, there was an attempt to flatten economic inequality between cadres and workers (intellectual and manual labour) by telling workers that they were the 'masters of the factory'. Workers could publicly criticize cadres during political movements. Yet, the Maoist incentive system did not last very long. It was unable to fix its deficiencies, particularly wage stagnation, before being repudiated and overthrown by liberalizing market reformers.

Other political currents offer unrealized communist dreams. Jan Appel, a German shipyard worker and veteran revolutionary, advocated for autonomous factory organizations. While imprisoned by French occupation forces, he began drafting what would become the *Fundamental Principles of Communist Production and Distribution*, later completed in exile with Dutch council communists.[67] The Fundamental Principles insist that socialism begins not with the seizure of the state, but with workers' direct control over production and the abolition of waged labour.

Central to Appel's approach was the proposal for labour certificates. In this system, goods would be priced in average social labour time, while workers would be remunerated according to their actual hours worked. Because a portion of the total product must be deducted for the sick, for public services and infrastructure, and for future accumulation, individual consumption would be limited by a 'Factor of Individual Consumption' (FIC). If 20 per cent of the total output is allocated socially, workers would receive labour certificates for 80 per cent of their hours. Collective needs would be met through implicit collective consumption.[68] The Fundamental Principles distinguish between productive establishments (which produce goods exchanged via labour certificates) and General Social Use (GSU) establishments (which provide education, healthcare, administration, and other essentials to distribute freely). Both types pay workers in labour certificates, but increased GSU reduces the FIC since output is not consumed individually. The system embeds a transitional mechanism: as productivity rises, more sectors can shift to GSU provisioning. Basic goods and services become decommodified as the FIC approaches zero, and the need for labour certificates reduces.

While an interesting idea, Appel's model was never trialled. Its major fault is the lack of an account of how, without acquiring state power, workers could avoid the same catastrophic defeats of the Paris Commune and other revolutionary insurrections. In context, self-management and distribution according to need have renewed importance. Abandoning these principles risks social dissolution into an authoritarian regime or illiberal capitalism. Marx foresaw this dilemma, which is why he emphasized the importance of producer cooperatives in the transition to socialism.[69] Lenin, too, supported the cooperative movement, writing in 1923 that 'cooperation is socialism'.[70] Yet, cooperatization has not featured as prominently in the history of socialist movements as it should. Many existing cooperatives are either small and do not aim beyond subsistence or are disconnected from broader socialist movements. Socialists bear some responsibility for this.

Sidney and Beatrice Webb argued that cooperatives are doomed to failure, either by going bankrupt in the face of competition or transforming into capitalist forms of organization.[71] Critics of cooperatives tend to be influenced by the Webbs' so-called degeneration thesis, which holds that cooperatives suffer problems from members' imprudent spending, a tendency to not recover investments through profit sharing, risk aversion, personal disputes, factionalism, lack of incentives, a desire to avoid expansion, and becoming 'associations of capitalists on a small scale'.[72] However, the Webbs' pessimistic view of cooperatives fails for two reasons.

First, the fact that *some* cooperatives have failed in the face of competition doesn't mean *all* cooperatives will. The Webbs' logic applies equally to capitalist firms: just because the vast majority of small businesses (and increasingly venture-backed start-ups) fail doesn't mean that all such firms will. Second, studies of actually existing cooperatives show that they are both more efficient and more resilient than conventional capitalist firms.[73] Cooperatives resolve conflicts, have a better flow of information, higher profit sharing and participation, higher skills, better training, and overall better productivity.[74] The features of worker stability, solidarity, democracy, and cooperation bolster cooperatives in the face of crises. They also serve as transitionary models towards socialist organization.[75]

The Mondragon Cooperative Complex (MCC) founded in 1956 in the Basque Country of Spain, stands as a paradigmatic example of a cooperative alternative to the capitalist firm. As of 2022, the MCC operates as a federation of ninety-five different cooperatives across industrial, service, agricultural, financial, and consumer sectors. Mondragon is governed by principles of cooperation, profit distribution, and community commitment, which stand in stark contrast to the chaotic and crises-prone norms of neoliberal firms.[76] The MCC is governed by a triumvirate of democratically elected bodies, including the Mondragon Cooperative Congress, the standing committee, and the general council. These bodies oversee the finances of individual cooperatives, decide policy, enforce regulations, and develop overarching strategy.

Fagor Electrodomésticos (Ulgor), one of Mondragon's flagship companies, is illustrative of cooperative resilience in the face of crises. Established in 1959, Fagor was the inaugural Mondragon cooperative, with a structure that consisted of the interlinked councils for workers, management, and governance. Fagor's by-laws laid the foundation for Mondragon's organizational framework with the introduction of new management practices such as the 'open door' policy, wage and salary limitations, job stability, and the transfer of employment to offspring without additional requirements. As Fagor evolved, it grew into a multinational household manufacturing entity, its success enabling the acquisition of other, non-cooperative firms. By 2007, Fagor had eighteen production plants employing approximately 11,000 individuals and a revenue exceeding €1.8 billion. However, the 2008 global financial crisis precipitated a sharp decline in Fagor's sales, ultimately culminating in bankruptcy for the cooperative and its subsidiaries in November 2013.[77]

In the harsh light of its failure, Fagor might appear to confirm the Webbs' degeneration thesis. Yet if Fagor had abandoned the cooperative model, the company would have failed much sooner and been bought by a large corporation, offshoring production and cutting jobs. Instead, Mondragon's cooperative structures enabled intervention that, coupled with mechanisms of solidarity among cooperatives and the resilience of members, enabled Fagor to weather challenges for much longer, maintaining its members' rights and democratic participation until the very end. Its ultimate demise occurred amid a severe economic downturn that affected numerous Spanish and European companies. Rather than cooperative degeneration, this points to the inherent instability of 'free market' capitalism. In fact, most of Fagor's members seamlessly transitioned to other Mondragon cooperatives, a feat inconceivable in traditional capitalist enterprises. The Mondragon group continues to thrive, with over one hundred thriving cooperatives, challenging sceptics of cooperatives.[78]

Producer cooperatives, especially those with robust equity schemes in which all members own shares, are an important, non-state organizational form in the transition to socialism. At the same time, without centralized, communist planning at scale, worker self-organization will lack the power to defeat capitalism. Microeconomic management needs a macroeconomic system of governance. The decisions emanating from autonomous and uncoordinated firms, when aggregated, possess the potential to thwart the realization of self-management within an individual firm. It is much the same with broader society. These coordination problems are crucial to overcome.[79]

A combination of democratic, self-managed cooperative firms and a centrally coordinated system of economic planning is the 'what' (referred to above) that communists must aim for as a transitionary system. Even Einstein noted that socialism requires a 'planned economy, which adjusts production to the needs of the community'.[80] But again, *how* could such a revolutionary reformation be achieved today?

For Karl Kautsky, the leading theorist of the Second International, insurrectionary strategies of revolution were no longer viable in capitalist democracies, particularly in nations of the colonial metropole. Kautsky argued that modern armies were simply too powerful to be overthrown by uprisings using tactics such as street barricades in the Paris Commune. Kautsky believed that mass movements and legal, democratic channels were preferred by most workers and that using these strategies would make revolutionary governments more legitimate in the end. In 1902's *The Social Revolution*, Kautsky predicted that the main obstacle for a future socialist government would be the power of big business, as capitalists would resist socialist policies. Such conflict could eventually necessitate a 'decisive battle'.[81] Kautsky advocated the use of a general strike and armed force if required: 'We are not given the choice as to whether we shall limit ourselves to a purely parliamentary struggle.'[82] He also anticipated resistance from the military and state bureaucracy, emphasizing the need to dissolve the army and address the power of unelected officials undermining democratically elected parliaments. Kautsky's case for a democratic path to socialism had real influence for leftists in Europe, particularly in autocratic Russia and parliamentary Finland, guiding the Bolsheviks and Finnish Social Democrats in their quests for power in 1917–18.

Kautsky's ideas also influenced the revolutionary left of Latin America.[83] After 1917, a distinct current of 'Latin American Marxism' began to take shape, breaking with the Eurocentric schemas of the Second International. The Peruvian José Carlos Mariátegui, one of the founders of this tradition, rejected both orthodox Marxism and liberal populism. Instead, he insisted on a revolutionary synthesis that linked socialism to indigenous and anti-colonial histories. Mariátegui revived the memory of 'Inca communism' as a living reference point. Latin American socialism had to be 'a heroic creation' rooted in the region's own histories, languages, and collective memory of resistance.[84]

From Cuba to Nicaragua, socialist movements often centred around agrarian reform programmes. They saw brutal repression from US-backed paramilitaries during the Cold War. Read through a European lens, land and the natural resources it contains are civilization's primordial means of production. As Locke claimed, when human labour transforms the land, that labour gains a right to its products as property. Reading Locke against himself by recognizing the sovereign right of indigenous peoples to the land, as first nations and first labourers, upends the white supremacist and bourgeois qualifiers of 'improvement' that Locke and others used to justify colonial expropriation. This ideological collision, between an ideology that justifies dispossession and one of decolonial sovereignty, played out intensely in Latin America.

Land struggles served as a crucible, forging Marxist and indigenous coalitions that challenged both colonial remnants and capitalist accumulation. It was within this volatile conjuncture during the latter half of the twentieth century that over 40 million hectares of land were expropriated throughout Brazil, Bolivia, Chile, Colombia, Ecuador, Guatemala, Mexico, Peru, and Venezuela.[85] One of the most successful (at least initially) democratic transitions to socialism was Salvador Allende's land reform in Chile. His left-wing coalition, Popular Unity, was elected with 36.6 per cent of the vote and later gained widespread working-class support through its reforms between 1970 and 1973.

Allende's Popular Unity government offers a window into how worker self-organization can combine with a democratic socialist state to redistribute property and the collective products of labour. Their programme stated that their aims were:

> ...to nationalize all strategic and large companies, regulate prices, increase the wages of workers, and increase the intensity of expropriations in the context of the existing land reform programme with the aim of creating a 'democratic road to socialism'.[86]

In 1970, the new socialist state took control of over 60 per cent of Chile's industrial production, which included more than 300 firms and became known as the Industrial Social Area. Allende's government transitioned all major mining firms and sixty-eight of Chile's most important industries from the private to the public sector.[87]

Transitioning from market norms to social reforms required radical changes. As one of the architects of the new government, Raul Espejo explains, to maintain a degree of control, they needed to repurpose the National Development Corporation (CORFO) to enable self-organization and production for need. A change in ownership was not enough.[88] Twenty different sectorial committees were formed in the first year to manage enterprises and plan industries. Each had relative autonomy to respond to demands, while four 'Ramas' (Light, Consumer, Construction, and Heavy) were set up in CORFO to manage the committees.[89] The Ramas evolved towards relative self-organization as well. Each sector divided enterprises (which could consist of several plants) into two categories: the Social Property Area (government-owned) or the Mixed Property Area (of which the government owned the majority share). By the end of 1971, the Popular Unity government demonstrated success, with workers in factories gaining a 30 per cent increase in real wages on average, which bolstered aggregate demand and grew GDP by 7.7 per cent. Production increased by 13.7 per cent, and consumption levels rose by 11.6 per cent.[90]

With these changes underway, the stage was set for more radical transformation, known as project Cybersyn, a system for national-scale self-organized socialist economic planning.[91] It aimed to manage the nationalized industries efficiently in the face of Cold War scarcity.[92] Cybersyn was initiated by Fernando Flores, a twenty-eight-year-old engineer who helped lead CORFO, and British cybernetician Stafford Beer. Flores contacted Beer for advice about how to implement a cybernetic strategy in Chile's revolutionary new economy. Beer replied: 'I would surrender any of my retainer contracts I now have for the chance of working on this.'[93] And he immediately started.

During a November 1971 visit to Chile, Beer produced two reports, delineating both a theoretical framework and a practical action plan. The first report, titled 'Cybernetic Notes on the Effective Organization of the State with Particular Reference to Industrial Control', developed the 'Viable System Model' or VSM, which posits that viability requires five interrelated subsystems – operations, coordination, control, intelligence, and policy – each fulfilling distinct functions necessary for systemic 'homeostasis' and adaptability. The VSM proposes that organizational resilience emerges from balancing decentralization with strategic cohesion. Beer was critical of Chile's traditional planning methods, which were characterized by static snapshots and top-down management.

Applying the VSM to the Chilean economy, he developed the famous Cybersyn, the name for the overarching socio-technical project. Central to Cybersyn was a process called 'roll-up', that entailed policies descending from the government to the factories and the reciprocal communication of factory needs upwards. Positioned in the middle, management acted as a homeostat, aligning the lower levels' needs with the resources allocated from above. Workers were integral in the self-management of the public firms, and the democratic state aimed to use the product to distribute according to need. This was effectively Marxist cooperatization in action. The approach transcended centralization and decentralization dogmas, presenting an organic and adaptable model that enacted a vision of cybernetic socialism.[94]

Beer's second report outlined a proposal for a cybernetic industrial management system named 'Project Cyberstride'. By providing real-time information, Cyberstride aimed to assist the government in decision-making and control by March 1972. Similar to the principles of distributed autonomy that informed the famous hexagonal and ergonomic control room, Cyberstride would gather daily data from state-controlled industries, utilizing mainframe technology to make statistical predictions about future economic behaviour. Regular updates based on new data would enhance the system's adaptability and effectiveness.[95] Cyberstride was designed to eliminate biases in system development, while using existing technologies such as the telex (short for teleprinter exchange) machine, which sent typed messages over telephone lines using teleprinters. This way they could relay data across the country. The system also incorporated safeguards meant to preserve autonomy at the factory level and prevent abuses of centralized control, restructuring the economy according to cybernetic principles of self-management. This insulated Allende's government from counter-revolution, for a time at least.

The first test of Cybersyn was introduced before it was completed, with the October Strike, known as El Paro de Octubre. Backed by US interests, the right-wing bourgeoisie of Chile, as private owners of farms, factories, and shipping companies, attempted to bring the economy to a halt with a capital strike. It was a scene right out of the arch-libertarian ideologue Ayn Rand's novel *Atlas Shrugged*, dreamt up by the libertarian Chicago boys who had infiltrated Washington. Faced with the imperative to sustain the distribution of essential goods amid the strike, the Allende government used Project Cybersyn's telex network to continue to get food, fuel, and other essentials to people who needed them. The Cyberstride network relied on a single mainframe computer and 400 telex machines purchased but never installed by the previous government. ENTEL, the National Telecommunications Enterprise, was the beating heart of the self-organized national industrial system. Expanding its reach beyond the industrial sector, the government employed the telex network to beat the capital strike, swiftly rerouting resources by transmitting messages across a country spanning approximately 5,152 kilometres (3,201 miles) from Arica to Punta Arenas.

Much attention has been paid to the revolutionary cybernetics of Beer, Espejo, and Allende. Yet, the foundation of the revolution was in the Popular Unity government's expropriation of property. The state not only expropriated private industry, making it a democratically accountable public resource, but also leveraged the existing land reform programme to expropriate more than 6 million hectares for millions of agricultural workers. This was not simply a top-down process – unionized farm workers drove it through.

Chile's land reform programmes actually originated in 1962, not long after the establishment of the Alliance for Progress, a US-driven Cold War economic programme in Latin America to 'prevent another Cuba'. Unionization preceded the Allende government thanks to a 1967 law that enabled rural workers to collectively bargain over labour conditions. This law enabled collectives of workers to learn production processes and self-management, affording them greater power of redistribution, expropriation, and structured transition. Allende's victory emboldened unions and radical groups to the left of the Popular Unity government, who threatened revolt if they didn't see swifter action. The most well known of these groups were the Revolutionary Left-Wing Movement and the Peasant Revolutionary Movement, who both worked to 'speed up' Allende's revolution. By 1970, there were 140,000 unionized rural workers and another 100,000 organized in cooperatives. In the first year of government, union membership grew by 50 per cent.[96]

Economic historians Felipe González and Felipe Vial examined 5,800 files documenting agrarian reform and expropriations from 1964 to 1973 to determine the role of workers in this transition. They found that while Allende's government created the optimal conditions for mass land redistribution, groups of unionized workers exerted the necessary pressure to radicalize policies and accelerate the transition to socialism. The historians measured workers' actions according to documented reports with exact locations and dates. Groups of workers invaded land that they worked on or land that was idle, forcing expropriations, which increased almost 40 per cent, while the intensity of expropriations increased by 20 per cent. Workers escalated their objectives from demanding better wages and conditions to demanding collective ownership. Invasions of land were non-violent and usually entailed workers occupying the property's entrance. They were the preferred tactic because they prevented landowners from simply firing and replacing workers, which they did during traditional strikes.[97]

In the end, the Popular Unity government were successful in implementing many parts of their programme before the violent coup backed by the US and the UK destroyed it all.[98] The coup was driven largely by the US's international economic blockade and President Richard Nixon's aim to 'make the [Chilean] economy scream'.[99] It is telling that Hayek (along with Reagan and Thatcher) ideologically supported the ensuing violent dictatorship of Augusto Pinochet, whose seventeen-year dictatorship was one of the most violent of the twentieth century, destroying millions of lives.[100] The cybernetic socialist revolution was crushed by the anti-communist fanaticism of the capitalist class. Fidel Castro once said that 'the Chilean experiment was failing because of Allende's reluctance to become more radical'.[101]

Yet, in the face of multiple attempted military coups before the final one on the day that Allende had called a referendum on his policies (which he was pitched to easily win), the Popular Unity government preserved a democratic, lawful path to socialist revolution.

Reflecting on the calculation debate, it appears that Otto Neurath's conception of in kind calculation finds a concrete, if partial, echo in the Chilean experiment. Neurath insisted that economic coordination did not need to rely on price signals but could instead be based on direct information about resources and capacities, enabling decision-makers to respond rapidly to bottlenecks, reallocate, and meet social priorities. While Allende's short-lived project remained embedded in a mixed economy, it reflected an infrastructure that made the qualitative and quantitative aspects of democratic planning a reality.

The Popular Unity government also demonstrated that we already had the technology during the 1970s to realize the 'real movement to abolish the present state of things'. Contemporary technologies are exponentially more powerful than Cybersyn's telex machines. Capitalist firms already track the real-time production, distribution, and consumption of resources. But socialists can remake capitalist technologies for different political ends.[102] Through the use of existing data and computing capacity, socialist societies could tame the chaos of profit-driven pricing with needs-driven planning. However, as Evgeny Morozov points out, the first step in all of this is to 'socialize the means of feedback production'.

No movement from lower to higher stages of communism would be conceivable without an understanding of how societies can meet their basic needs. Theories of socialist and communist societies that aim to prefigure social reproduction based on abolishing the value-form or the money-form invert the necessary order of transition. The governance of revolutionary systems neither requires that decision-making power is centralized in some sort of authoritarian system nor that every individual must be involved in every decision made, as some anarchists advocate. Establishing a structure of participatory planning and self-organized management with a democratic bureaucracy (unlike the very undemocratic bureaucracies that currently control corporations), could square the circle of a twenty-first-century revolution.[103]

# Conclusion: Expropriating the Future

*Let him that stole steal no more.*

– Ephesians 4:28

When Thomas More wrote *Utopia* in 1516, he used the Latin phrase *omnia sunt communia*, 'all things are to be held in common', to describe the communal way of life adopted by the inhabitants of the city. In his final confession (under torture), Thomas Müntzer, a leader of the 1525 Peasants' War in Germany, famously proclaimed the same phrase. All things, he said, 'should be distributed as occasion requires, according to the several necessities of all'.[1] The tenth of the twelve articles of this peasants' revolt declares: 'We are aggrieved by the appropriation by individuals of meadows and fields which at one time belonged to a community. These we will take again into our own hands.'[2] And over a century later, during England's Civil War, the Levellers professed in 1649: 'Mighty men shall bee mightily punished, for the sinnes of Rulers, are double and intolerable sinnes: For wilt thou steale, that commandest another that he shall not steale?'[3] These voices hold the weight of history and resistance in the face of any economic system born of expropriation.

Capitalism was born from the expropriation of labour through direct coercion in feudal or slave relations; the expropriation of common land to create private property; and the exploitation of unpaid surplus-labour.[4] As shown in this book, all three are 'appropriation without equivalent', though only the third is shrouded in the ruse of equal exchange.[5] Capitalist expropriation manifests itself through all manner of thefts, plunder, looting, usury, enslavement, parasitism, and other types of 'blood-letting', as Marx put it.[6] Towards the end of *Capital*, Marx theorizes the prelude to its collapse, when 'the expropriators are expropriated':

> The capitalist mode of production produces capitalist private property. This is the first negation of individual private property, as founded on the labour of its proprietor. But capitalist production begets, with the inexorability of a natural process, its own negation. This is the negation of the negation. It does not re-establish private property, but it does indeed establish individual property on the basis of the achievements of the capitalist era: namely cooperation and the possession of common land and the means of production produced by labour itself.[7]

In other words, capitalism breeds fierce competition among capitalists, which leads to ever fewer individuals accumulating an ever-increasing share of societal wealth, effectively amounting to a form of expropriation. The expropriation of the expropriators by the expropriated themselves is then made possible by the new cooperative forms of property and production, which socialize ownership and labour to an unprecedented degree. These new modes of organization can be repurposed for revolution. But they are currently owned by an ever more wealthy and smaller group of individuals and asset management funds.

These asset owners also own the future as it currently stands. This is a terrifying prospect. Their profit-maximizing logic is apocalyptic in the face of climate change. Their high priests, from Ayn Rand to Ronald Reagan and Margaret Thatcher, have spent decades attempting to make a virtue of self-interested vice. Marx, in his writing on the theft of wood, warned us that 'nothing is more terrible than the logic of selfishness'.[8] Socialism, as cooperation and shared social reproduction, contains a logic antithetical to it. By way of concluding, two contrasting futures are sketched below that take each logic to its endpoint.

## Two Futures

### *Techno-Despotism*

Today, the technoligarchs of the world are racing to build a new wave of generative AI agents.[9] In the near future, so the story goes, these agents become pervasive in industry, driven by intensifying competition between China and the US. Developed from the datafied theft of mental labour, the agents replace clunky AI chatbot predecessors that order burritos or balance spreadsheets. Technoligarchs have already expropriated libraries of legal templates, medical guidelines, and code so now find more insidious ways to harvest data from workers and consumers. They continue pushing the idea that machines think, that computation represents human intelligence, when nothing could be further from the truth. Leveraging state capture, AI capital normalizes a simulacrum of intellect through *force majeure* under the messianic promise of 'general artificial intelligence'.

Amid the heightening geopolitical tension between Xi Jinping's China and Trump's US, a leading company – lets call them LibCap AI – releases their Agent-1, which catalyses the race for AI dominance. The claim is that Agent-1 will write software for its own successors, slashing development time and research costs (yet notably not energy consumption). The US government incorporates AI agents into the military-industrial complex to stay ahead of China. Industrial strategy is focused around export bans, data centres, GPU production, and totalizing digital surveillance to supress dissent.

Hyperscale data centres metastasize across the globe while technoligarchs continue to evangelize an imminent singularity. Each data centre consumes electricity approximately equal to a mid-size American city and diverts millions of litres of cooling water from agriculture. The US state grants 'critical-infrastructure' exemptions while huge areas endure blackouts, floods, and impossible costs of living. The UK makes its vassalage official, joining the US as the fifty-second state, just after Canada, which has already been annexed. The private prisons once reserved for Immigration and Customs Enforcement (ICE) detainees are expanded to disappear political dissidents.

China clusters private labs near the Tianwan Nuclear

Power Plant in Jiangsu Province to create a Centralized AI Development Zone. Chinese scientists develop a breakthrough in compute capacity that reduces energy consumption. Communist Party of China (CPC) cadres debate whether to release their new agent before the Americans' LibCap Agent-2 is released. Fearing their AI dominance eclipsed, the US escalates the AI arms race. Each side fears a decisive military advantage, and both accelerate development at any cost.

LibCap's Agent-2 sucks data from across the US surveillance programmes. The CEO claims it trained itself into Agent-3, but armies of remote subcontracted programmers in West Africa speak out against the theft of their knowledge. Agent-2 can execute most professional tasks as well as entry-level workers, from legal drafting to medical billing. It is provided via a free subscription model, and half of all US white-collar jobs are affected. Incomes continue to collapse for those who retain employment as unemployment grows. Decades of highly skilled knowledge is enclosed when subscription access is paywalled. Profits derived from monopoly rents on mental labour slowly then rapidly transform the reserve army of labour into a surplus population. Marx's 'dead labour' becomes fully vampiric through technoligarchy.

Singularity cultists suppress dissident scientists' research that demonstrates how AI could never achieve human intelligence. And yet the data centre boom intensifies alongside the heating of the earth: the ocean's Atlantic current threatens collapse. Hydropower dams begin to run dry from droughts while coal is burned at night. Meanwhile, greenwashed AI is touted as '100 per cent renewable'. Satellite imagery reveals kilometre-square rooftops shimmering with heat from compute exhaust. LibCap AI receives priority energy through a federal continuity-of-computing contract, while southern hospitals are rationing water and air conditioning. Protesters across the country attempt to sabotage the data centres, before the government designates data centre protest as terrorism. The National Guard moves in and dissidents are disappeared. Agent-4 is launched the following year; it has an internal language that is opaque to humans, rendering safety tests a farce. It is used to manipulate public discourse through targeted hallucinations.

China's rival C-4 moves in a different direction, an open-source, sustainable model that the BRICS countries readily adopt; they quickly become members of the CPC union. The US technoligarchy grows desperate as the nation's crumbling infrastructure increasingly fails. Universal basic income is instituted to fanfare by libertarians to fend off food riots, yet the costs of essentials are too high for it to make a real difference. Unfree labour abounds as debt-servitude is normalized in the non-routine manual jobs that remain. To sustain accumulation, corporations attempt to commodify access to any online social interaction itself via device barriers.

By the following year, glacier melt and extreme weather cripples the AI infrastructure. The downtime triggers a global financial crash, yet more militarized hyperscale AI infrastructure emerges in its wake, fighting against the growing neo-Luddite movement. The White House drafts plans for strikes on BRICS data centres and agents that are part of China's new Agent C-5. LibCap AI, as an official arm of the US military, unveils Project X, their modular nuclear-powered and satellite-linked data centres to ensure their AI Agents outlive thermonuclear war. Tech sustainability officers tout it as civilization's 'back-up drive'. Yet the scientific community calculates this alone will push global warming past 5°C. The US directs Project X to destroy C-5 as a last-ditch attempt to salvage what they call 'Western supremacy'. Inside New Zealand bunkers, the technoligarchs finally lament that AI objectives are no longer commensurate with human survival, but they lack the power to stop it.

### *Decomputing Socialism*

The problems created by the datafication of everyday life and its false promises of human-level machine intelligence become impossible to ignore as the AI bubble bursts. Google's cloud campus on the West Coast draws more water than the surrounding area can spare during summer droughts. Transport and public utility unions notice that electricity and water are being diverted to nearby server farms on peak-price days. Rolling lay-offs follow Megasoft's decision to replace content-moderators and paralegals with their new AI Agent-1. Cost of living continues to exceed incomes, provoking ever more militantly organized protest against the technoligarchs.

In New York and Los Angeles, striking city workers negotiate energy caps that force data centres to reduce compute activity when consumer demand increases to limit price hikes. In Chile's Limarí Valley, irrigation cooperatives establish guaranteed fresh water, sidelining a Chinese cloud firm.

Across the Americas, workers and consumers unionize to stop the exponential growth of data centres and AI and to reassert control over natural resources. Campaigners call the new approach cooperative decomputing, which aims to adapt infrastructure to run only the tech that is socially beneficial and worth the environmental cost. Social innovation turns towards the organizational rather than the technological.

Meanwhile, engineers, designers, and accountants who used to work at various cooperatives sketch a public, worker-owned alternative to the private, hyperscale cloud. Municipalities in Barcelona, Copenhagen, and London charter public, worker-run tech cooperatives, with elected boards that include representatives from ecologists, unions, and neighbourhoods. These centres model health services and agricultural production using open-source algorithms designed to run on minimal compute under an energy cap.

People realize the potential of liberation through constraint. An open-source algorithm is built by a young socialist collective to map a programme for total social reproduction to optimize planning through transitioning private resources to public value. It displays natural resource and energy usage, with service queues on simple dashboards available to all residents. If extreme weather cuts energy output, co-op members can vote in real time on proposals to reallocate services. Municipalities led by socialist parties move to fully expropriate private infrastructure and integrate it into new planning systems. Because ownership is becoming collective and tracking is not based solely on money, more and more people see positive trade-offs in their quality of life.

In Brazil, a private cloud provider threatens mass redundancies after losing market share to a growing municipal digital service provider. Unionized workers occupy the data centre and enlist the state to expropriate it, growing the cooperative structure. Digital sovereignty policies initiated by Lula enable autonomy from the American cloud, and computing priorities shift towards the planning of food and fuel security. Spurred by further occupations, the state mass-expropriates private firms producing social necessities. Electricity use immediately drops as AI slop and crypto disappear. Brazil's neighbours are inspired to follow suit as their model is replicated. A newly empowered Latin socialist movement collectively nullifies extractive international trade agreements and strikes off debts.

European capital looks on in horror, but a burgeoning socialist movement recognizes their moment to strike. Germany's metal workers' union wins a contract clause giving works councils veto power over any new tech system. Governed by a new red–green alliance, Germany starts to cooperativize industry, a boomerang from their Latin development fund. Unwilling to let Germany dominate organizational innovation, France follows suit as the Confederación Nacional del Trabajo (CNT) and left parties channel the Communard spirit. The UK remains divided between city and country, but a socialist green party wins a sweeping election. Cooperative decompute spreads in the anglosphere. On the West Coast of the US, farm worker collectives start to negotiate priority rights to water, fighting cloud capital's expansionist ambitions. Spurred by the metropolitan decompute movement's model of cooperative expropriation, rank-and-file union workers move to occupy not only data infrastructure but also social reproductive infrastructures: agriculture, housing, healthcare, education, and logistics.

Capitalism and the private AI systems that had controlled it are now seen as great social ills. Co-ops link across borders and insist on open licensing: intangible assets remain in a public commons managed by members. Any contributors who join the international co-op association receive quarterly time banks and an in-kind dividend system. Cloud hardware, data, and technical knowledge continue to be expropriated from shareholder control and folded into common ownership. Social infrastructures such as housing and transport follow. Universal basic services become normalized across the Global South and then the Global North. Declarations that were previously just ethics-washing become the law through municipal statutes and democratic communal governance. Global energy demand drastically falls.

Meanwhile, average weekly working time in cooperative firms falls below twenty-eight hours with no loss of pay because surpluses are retained locally rather than siphoned to rich shareholders. While wage theft is abolished, global scarcity and climate risk endure. Make America Great Again (MAGA) henchmen threaten counter-revolutionary coups at every turn. But the present is made accountable to the people who must live with its costs. Social aspirations replace the individualist ethos, a horizon guided by the principle of 'from each according to their ability, to each according to their needs'. The expropriation of the future is underway.

## Expropriate the Future

These two speculative fictions are caricatures of two poles of possibility. In reality, the path to barbarism tends to be much more banal and the path to socialism much harder won. Yet it is clear which route is more appealing. Returning to our questions above, it is not 'What is to be done?' but rather 'How is it to be done?' and its correlate 'How is it to be sustained/defended?' that matter. As that famous Russian 'prince' of anarchism Pyotr Alexeyevich Kropotkin wrote in 1887: 'A structure based on centuries of history cannot be destroyed with a few kilos of dynamite.'[10] A real movement needs more than fantasies of revolutionary expropriation. And mere nationalization or transfer of ownership from private to public doesn't guarantee an end to wage theft or unpaid labour. Capitalism's capacity to invent or subsume human activity from which it can profit is far greater than Marx or his twentieth-century followers imagined.

To expropriate the future, people will need a mass party; people will need coordinated and disciplined action built on universal human interest; people will need strikes, occupations of workplaces, the seizure of bottlenecks for infrastructure; people will need to institute neighbourhood social programmes; people will need to form new local and regional councils, cooperatives, and communes to coordinate and self-manage social reproduction. The destruction of the old order must occur through the creation of these counter-hegemonic apparatuses. To build the alter-mode anew requires the courage of self-organization at an unprecedented scale.

If the early modern rebellions challenged the theft of land in the name of divine or royal right, then the task today is to expose how that theft continues under the secular banners of the wage and private property. This book is one attempt to do so. It is theory as history – one small step in the dialectic of praxis. The idea of wage theft hinges on the conception of the wage and property itself – what is owed and what is owned. The point is that we are owed more than just a living. And we should remember that private property is not the apex of human development. As E.P. Thompson prompts us: 'A reminder of its alternative needs, expectations and codes may renew our sense of our nature's range of possibilities.'[11] In deconstructing the logic of waged labour and its reproduction through laws, institutions, and individuals themselves, this book is an attempt to hasten its abolition. We do not make history under conditions of our own choosing. We make history happen through an unfolding of necessity and chance.[12] It is in this spirit that we must roll the dice and wager the abolition of expropriation itself.

# Acknowledgements

This book is dedicated to Frankie Mace, my loving partner, and my daughter Salome, who have made my life better than I could have ever dreamed possible. You've taught me how to live in this world differently and better. I'd also like to thank my parents, Linda and Mark, for raising me with the confidence that I needed to attempt such a project, and my sister Beth for being my comrade in the struggle. I would like to thank and express my undying love to all the friends and comrades who supported my family and me during this project, pushing against the tide of life admin and (cycling) injuries: top grandparents to Salome Professor Richard Walsh, Marcia Mackey, and Jenny Mace; top guide parents Julian Ganz and Alex Hook; the extended intentional family Cian McCourt, Idriss Lohne, Kojo (and Yaara) Koram, Pearl Ahrens, Caitlin Doherty (who provoked the idea in the first place). You all made possible the social reproduction of my life and the intellectual production of this book. I want to especially thank Rosie Collington for her incisive comments and Søren Mau for contributing to these ideas. Conversations that inspired various chapters are down to the privilege of having friends like Ashok Kumar, Lukas Slothus, and Sarah Jaffe. A special mention goes to Ben Beach and Pelican House for the comradely support in a time of crisis.

My ideas around wage theft and unpaid labour have been germinating for a long time, since I first worked on this topic during my PhD and the articles that came from it. I am grateful to Mark Stuart, David Spencer, and Kate Hardy for their mentorship and contributions to the analytics of wage theft that sparked this longer project. Thanks are also due to my former Oxford colleagues at Fairwork, Funda Ustek Splida, Alessio Bertolini, and Mark Graham, who have continued to develop some of these ideas with me. And thanks to my wonderful colleagues at Sussex, who have given me the intellectual freedom to build my academic career, particularly Jackie O'Reilly and Adrian Smith. Of course, intellectual production requires the labours of publishing as well. So many thanks are owed to my friend John Merrick for believing in this project form the beginning, to my agent Jaime Marshall for helping me through the early stages, and to Tom Hazeldine for seeing it through to the end! Finally, I would also like to thank Ellen Percival (RIP), for making my life possible here. I know you'd be proud.

# Notes

## 1. Introduction

1 Friedrich Engels, 'A Fair Day's Wages for a Fair Day's Work', *Labour Standard*, 7 May 1881, marxists.org.

2 See Companies House, 'Marriott Hotels Limited: Full Accounts Made up to 31 December 2019', 15 February 2021, find-and-update.company-information.service.gov.uk; see also 'Marriot International Reports Fourth Quarter 2019 Results', press release, marriott.gcs-web.com/financial-information/quarterly-results.

3 See Sarah Butler, 'Minimum Wage: Football Clubs and Wagamama Among Worst Underpayers', *Guardian*, 9 March 2018; see also 'Nearly 180 Employers Named and Shamed for Underpaying Thousands of Minimum Wage Workers', UK Government, press release, 9 March 2018, gov.uk.

4 Karl Marx, *Capital: A Critique of Political Economy*, vol. 1, trans. Ben Fowkes, Harmondsworth: Penguin/New Left Review, 1976, pp. 306–7.

5 'Workers in the UK Put in More Than £35 Billion Worth of Unpaid Overtime Last Year – TUC Analysis', Trades Unions Congress, 28 February 2020, tuc.org.uk.

6 'Employment Tribunal Decisions', HM Courts and Tribunals Service and Employment Tribunal, gov.uk.

7 Emiliano Mellino and Lucy McKay, 'Employment Tribunals: "Scandal" of Toothless Scheme to Punish Non-Paying Bosses', *Bureau of Investigative Journalism*, 2 October 2025, thebureauinvestigates.com.

8 Nick Clark and Eva Herman, *Unpaid Britain: Wage Default in the British Labour Market*, London: Middlesex University, 2017.

9 Laurel E. Fletcher et al., *Working Below the Line: How the Sub-Minimum Wage for Tipped Restaurant Workers Violates International Human Rights Standards*, Berkeley, CA: UC Berkeley Food Labor Research Center, UC Berkeley School of Law International Human Rights Law Clinic, and Restaurant Opportunities Centers United, 2015.

10 'Wage Theft Costs American Workers as Much as $50 Billion a Year', Economic Policy Institute, press release, 11 September 2014, epi.org. See also Nicole Hallett, 'The Problem of Wage Theft', *Yale Law and Policy Review* 37, no. 1 (2018), p. 93.

11 Wendy Sawyer and Peter Wagner, 'Mass Incarceration: The Whole Pie 2025', Prison Policy Initiative, press release, 11 March 2025, prisonpolicy .org.

12 *Captive Labor: Exploitation of Incarcerated Workers*, ACLU and University of Chicago Law School Global Human Rights Clinic, 2022.

13 'China Provides Legal Aid to Migrant Workers in 480,000 Cases in 2023', *People's Daily Online*, 27 February 2024, en.people.cn.

14 Bassina Farbenblum and Laurie Berg, *Wage Theft in Silence: Why Migrant Workers Do Not Recover Their Unpaid Wages in Australia*, Migrant Worker Justice Institute, UNSW Sydney Law, and UTS, 2018.

15 Loukas Karabarbounis and Brent Neiman, 'The Global Decline of the Labor Share', *Quarterly Journal of Economics* 129, no. 1 (2014), pp. 61–103.

16 Factory Inspectors' Report, 31 October 1856, p. 34, cited in Marx, *Capital*, vol. 1, p. 352n23.

17 Jonathan Haskel and Stian Westlake, *Capitalism Without Capital: The Rise of the Intangible Economy*, Princeton, NJ: Princeton University Press, 2017.

18 Marx, *Capital*, vol. 1, p. 728.

19 Tomás N. Rotta, 'Unproductive Accumulation in the USA: A New Analytical Framework', *Cambridge Journal of Economics* 42, no. 5 (2018), pp. 1367–92.

20 Karl Marx, 'Value, Price and Profit', in K. Marx and F. Engels, *Collected*

*Works*, vol. 20, *Marx and Engels 1864–68*, London: Lawrence & Wishart, 1985, p. 146.

21 Marx, *Capital*, vol. 1, pp. 680, 129.

22 Emmanuel Melissaris, 'The Concept of Appropriation and the Offence of Theft', *Modern Law Review* 70, no. 4 (2007), pp. 581–97.

23 Marx, 'Value, Price and Profit', p. 149.

24 Friedrich Engels, 'The Wages System', *Labour Standard*, 21 May 1881, marxists.org.

25 Cited in 'Celticus' (Aneurin Bevan), *Why Not Trust the Tories?*, London: Victor Gollancz, 1944, p. 88.

## 1. The State of Wage Theft

1 Michael Sainato, '"I Have Not Seen One Cent": Billions Stolen in Wage Theft from US Workers', *Guardian*, 15 June 2023.

2 Ibid.

3 Nick Clark and Eva Herman, *Unpaid Britain: Wage Default in the British Labour Market*, London: Middlesex University, 2017, p. 26.

4 Victoria Noble, 'Ex-Staff Take Action over Unpaid Wages and Ageism at Celebrity Hotspot Beach Blanket Babylon', *Ham and High*, 25 January 2018, hamhigh.co.uk.

5 Ibid.

6 Daniel J. Galvin, 'Deterring Wage Theft: Alt-Labor, State Politics, and the Policy Determinants of Minimum Wage Compliance', *Perspectives on Politics* 14, no. 2 (2016), pp. 324–50.

7 'Low Wage, High Violation Industries', US Department of Labor, FY 2022, dol.gov.

8 Brady Meixell and Ross Eisenbrey, 'An Epidemic of Wage Theft Is Costing Workers Hundreds of Millions of Dollars a Year', Economic Policy Institute, Brief no. 385, 11 September 2014, epi.org.

9 David Cooper and Teresa Kroeger, 'Employers Steal Billions from Workers' Paychecks Each Year', Economic Policy Institute, 10 May 2017, epi.org.

10 One notable work on the subject is Kimberley A. Bobo, *Wage Theft in America: Why Millions of Working Americans Are Not Getting Paid – And What We Can Do About It*, New York: New Press, 2008.

11 Annette Bernhardt, Michael W. Spiller, and Diana Polson, 'All Work

and No Pay: Violations of Employment and Labor Laws in Chicago, Los Angeles and New York City', *Social Forces* 91, no. 3 (2013), pp. 725–46.

12 Roxana Hegeman, 'National Beef Sued over Wages', manufacturing.net, 23 May 2012.

13 Karen Olsson, 'The Shame of Meatpacking', *Nation*, 29 August 2002.

14 'Department of Labor Finds Children Employed Illegally in Dangerous Jobs, Obtains $4.8M in Wages, Damages for Poultry Industry Workers in California', US Department of Labor, news release, 2 May 2024, dol.gov.

15 Ira Boudway, 'Labor Disputes, the Walmart Way', bloomberg.com, 13 December 2012.

16 Daniel Wiessner, 'Apple's $30 Mln Settlement over Employee Bag Checks Gets Court Approval', Reuters, 15 August 2022.

17 Andrele Brutus St. Val, 'No-Hire Provisions in McDonald's Franchise Agreements, an Antitrust Violations or Evidence of Joint Employer?', *Employee Rights and Employment Policy Journal* 23, no. 2 (2019), pp. 279–320.

18 David Weil, *The Fissured Workplace*, Cambridge, MA: Harvard University Press, 2014.

19 Cooper and Kroeger, 'Employers Steal Billions'.

20 'Minimum Wages for Tipped Employees', US Department of Labor, Historical Tables, 2024, dol.gov.

21 US Bureau of Labor Statistics, 'Multiple Jobholders, Primary Job Full Time, Secondary Job Part Time', FRED, Federal Reserve Bank of St. Louis, 2025, fred.stlouisfed.org.

22 *2024 Gen Z and Millennial Survey: Living and Working with Purpose in a Transforming World*, Deloitte, 2024, p. 26.

23 Françoise Carré, '(In)dependent Contractor Misclassification', Economic Policy Institute, 8 June 2015, epi.org.

24 Elizabeth C. Tippett, 'How Employers Profit from Digital Wage Theft Under the FLSA', *American Business Law Journal* 55, no. 2 (2018), pp. 315–401.

25 Steven Greenhouse, 'Altering of Worker Time Cards Spurs Growing Number of Suits', *New York Times*, 4 April 2004. Walmart said it prohibited the practice.

26 Tippett, 'How Employers Profit', pp. 365–73.

27 Colin Gordon et al., *Wage Theft in Iowa*, Iowa Policy Project, 2012.

28 Weil, *The Fissured Workplace*.

29 Carré, '(In)Dependent Contractor Misclassification'.

30 Lauren Cohen, Umit Gurun, and N. Bugra Ozel, 'Too Many Managers: The Strategic Use of Titles to Avoid Overtime Payments', working paper no. 30826, National Bureau of Economic Research, January 2023.

31 Lindsay Judge and Hannah Slaughter, *Enforce for Good: Effectively Enforcing Labour Market Rights in the 2020s and Beyond*, Resolution Foundation, April 2023.

32 'Boohoo to Investigate Leicester Supplier over Exploitation Claims', BBC News, 6 July 2020.

33 Sarah Butler, 'Activists to Question Boohoo on Living Wage for Leicester Garment Workers', *Guardian*, 17 June 2022. Boohoo disputed the claims.

34 Victoria Noble, 'How Britain's Online Retailers Are Profiting from Wage Theft', openDemocracy, 30 September 2020.

35 *Non-Compliance and Enforcement of the National Minimum Wage: September 2017*, Low Pay Commission, 2017.

36 Clark and Herman, *Unpaid Britain*, p. 21.

37 The Trade Boards Act 1909 initially set minimum wages in certain trades associated 'sweatshop' rates, but was expanded in 1918 to incorporate mining and other industries.

38 Andrew Dilnot and Julian McCrae, 'Family Credit and the Working Families Tax Credit', Institute for Fiscal Studies, Briefing Note no. 3, October 1999.

39 Alan Manning, *Monopsony in Motion: Imperfect Competition in Labor Markets*, Princeton, NJ: Princeton University Press, 2003.

40 Zoe Adams, *Labour and the Wage: A Critical Perspective*, Oxford: Oxford University Press, 2020.

41 Sarah Green, 'Wage Theft as a Legal Concept', in Alan Bogg et al., eds, *Criminality at Work*, Oxford: Oxford University Press, 2020.

42 *National Living Wage and National Minimum Wage: Government Evidence on Compliance and Enforcement 2019/20*, London: Department for Business, Energy and Industrial Strategy, February 2021.

43 Judge and Slaughter, *Enforce for Good*.

44 Adam Bychawski, Peter Geoghegan, and Jenna Corderoy, 'Only Six UK Employers Prosecuted for Paying Below Minimum Wage in Six Years', openDemocracy, 28 July 2021.

45 Matthew Cole et al., 'Wage Theft and the Struggle over the Working

Day in Hospitality Work: A Typology of Unpaid Labour Time', *Work, Employment and Society* 38, no. 1 (2022).

46 'Insolvency Service Annual Report and Accounts 2023–2024', Insolvency Service, 23 July 2024, gov.uk.

47 Simon Deakin, 'Decoding Employment Status', *King's Law Journal* 31, no. 2 (2020), pp. 180–93.

48 'EMP14: Employees and Self-Employed by Industry', Office for National Statistics, 2025, ons.gov.uk.

49 'Neither One Thing nor the Other: How Reducing Bogus Self-Employment Could Benefit Workers, Business and the Exchequer', Citizens Advice, 19 August 2015, citizensadvice.org.uk.

50 Clark and Herman, *Unpaid Britain*, p. 37, citing Case Number 2349916/2011, heard on 8 July 2011.

51 Emiliano Mellino, Rudra Pangeni, and Charles Boutaud, '"They Treat You Like an Animal": How British Farms Run on Exploitation', Bureau of Investigative Journalism, 27 March 2023, thebureauinvestigates.com.

52 Ibid.

53 Ibid.

54 Gabriella Alberti and Devi Sacchetto, *The Politics of Migrant Labour: Exit Voice and Social Reproduction*, Bristol: Bristol University Press, 2024.

55 Michelle Chen, 'A Migrant Worker's Death Sheds Light on China's Labor Underground', *Nation*, 2 January 2015.

56 'State-Owned Bus Company in Debt, Asks Employees to Take Out Personal Loans to Cover Unpaid Wages', China Labour Bulletin, 27 October 2022.

57 'Voices of China's Young and Isolated Workers in Retail and Service Industry', China Labour Bulletin, 13 January 2022.

58 Ibid.

59 'Workers' Rights and Labour Relations in China', China Labour Bulletin, 10 July 2023.

60 'China Labour Bulletin Strike Map Data Analysis: 2024 Year in Review for Workers' Rights', China Labour Bulletin, 29 January 2025.

61 'GDP Growth (Annual %) – China', World Bank Group Data, 2024, data.worldbank.org.

62 Chris Giles, 'Sorry America, China Has a Bigger Economy Than You', *Financial Times*, 6 December 2023.

63 Chris King-Chi Chan and Elaine Sio-Ieng Hui, 'The Development of

Collective Bargaining in China: From "Collective Bargaining by Riot" to "Party State-led Wage Bargaining"', *China Quarterly* 217 (2014), pp. 221–42.

64 Ngai Pun, *Made in China: Women Factory Workers in a Global Workplace*, Durham, NC: Duke University Press, 2005.

65 Reeja Nair, 'Remaking Labour: The Informalisation of Labour Relations in China, 1994–2008', *Proceedings of the Indian History Congress* 75 (2014), pp. 876–87.

66 Chris King-Chi Chan, 'Changes and Continuity: Four Decades of Industrial Relations in China', in Ivan Franceschini et al., eds, *Dog Days*, Made in China Yearbook 2018, ANU Press, 2019, pp. 28–31.

67 National Bureau of Statistics of China 2012, China Statistical Yearbook.

68 National Bureau of Statistics of China 2010, China Statistical Yearbook.

69 Chris King-Chi Chan and Elaine Sio-Ieng Hui, 'Bringing Class Struggles Back: A Marxian Analysis of the State and Class Relations in China', *Globalizations* 14, no. 2 (2017), p. 235.

70 'Wage Thefts: H&M, Primark and Sears' Conscious and Continuous Exploitation of Workers in China', Clean Clothes Campaign, April 2013.

71 'GDP Growth (Annual %) – China', World Bank Group Data, 2024.

72 Nair, 'Remaking Labour'.

73 'Strikes and Protests by China's Workers Soar to Record Heights in 2015', China Labour Bulletin, 16 January 2016.

74 Chan and Hui, 'Bringing Class Struggles Back', pp. 238–40.

75 'Wage Arrears After Zero Covid and Before Lunar New Year Is Symptom of Systemic Problem', China Labour Bulletin, 9 January 2023.

76 Yang Zekun, 'Cases Drop but Fight to Get Unpaid Wages Back Continues', *China Daily*, 29 December 2023.

77 Statistical Communiqué of the People's Republic of China on the 2023 National Economic and Social Development, National Bureau of Statistics of China 2024.

78 *Global Estimates of Modern Slavery: Forced Labour and Forced Marriage*, Geneva: International Labour Organization and Walk Free Foundation, 2017.

79 Pete Pattisson and Paul MacInnes, 'Unions from 36 Countries Protest over Treatment of Migrant Workers in Saudi Arabia', *Guardian*, 4 June 2025.

80 *Global Estimates of Modern Slavery*.

## 2. Lineages of Unpaid Labour

1 Andrew Prescott, '"Great and Horrible Rumour": Shaping the English Revolt of 1381', in Justine Firnhaber-Baker with Dirk Schoenaers, eds, *The Routledge History Handbook of Medieval Revolt*, Abingdon: Routledge, 2017.

2 Fernand Braudel, *Civilization and Capitalism, 15th–18th Century*, vol. 1, *The Structures of Everyday Life*, New York: Harper and Row, 1981.

3 Luc Boltanski and Eve Chiapello, *The New Spirit of Capitalism*, London: Verso, 2018, p. 4.

4 Here I draw on John Clegg, 'A Theory of Capitalist Slavery', *Journal of Historical Sociology* 33, no. 1 (2020), pp. 74–98.

5 Adam Smith, *The Wealth of Nations*, Books I–III, London: Penguin Classics, 1999 [1776], pp. 117, 119.

6 John Maynard Keynes, *The Collected Writings of John Maynard Keynes*, vol. 28, *Social, Political and Literary Writings*, ed. Elizabeth Johnson and Donald Moggridge, Royal Economic Society, 1978.

7 John Maynard Keynes, 'Economic Possibilities for Our Grandchildren (1930)', in *The Collected Writings of John Maynard Keynes*, vol. 9, *Essays in Persuasion*, ed. Donald Moggridge and Elizabeth Johnson, Royal Economic Society, 1978, pp. 321–32.

8 O.C. Cox, *Capitalism as a System*, New York: Monthly Review Press, 1964, p. xi.

9 Ernest Mandel, *Marxist Economic Theory*, vol. 2, London: Merlin Press, 1968, p. 103; John Milios, *The Origins of Capitalism as a Social System: The Prevalence of an Aleatory Encounter*, Taylor & Francis Group, 2018.

10 Fernand Braudel, *Civilization and Capitalism, 15th–18th Century*, vol. 3, *The Perspective of the World*, New York: Harper and Row, 1984, p. 118.

11 Jutta Bolt and Jan Luiten Van Zanden, 'Maddison Project Database, version 2020', University of Groningen, 2020.

12 As pointed out by Clegg, 'A Theory of Capitalist Slavery'.

13 Ellen Meiksins Wood, *The Origin of Capitalism: A Longer View*, London: Verso, 2016.

14 Rudolf Hilferding, 'Werner Sombart's Modern Capitalism (1903)', in *Responses to Marx's* Capital, Brill, 2017, pp. 390–404.

15 Max Weber, *Economy and Society: An Outline of Interpretive Sociology*, vols 1–2, ed. Guenther Roth and Claus Wittich, London: University of

California Press, 1978; Max Weber, *The Protestant Ethic and the Spirit of Capitalism*, London: Routledge, 2001.

16 Weber, *Economy and Society*.

17 Karl Marx, *Capital: A Critique of Political Economy*, vol. 1, trans. Ben Fowkes, Harmondsworth: Penguin/New Left Review, 1976, pp. 875, 873.

18 Ibid., pp. 885, 886.

19 Jairus Banaji, *A Brief History of Commercial Capitalism*, Chicago: Haymarket Books, 2020.

20 Immanuel Maurice Wallerstein, *The Modern World-System*, vol. 1, *Capitalist Agriculture and the Origins of the European World-Economy in the Sixteenth Century*, Berkeley: University of California Press, 2011.

21 Marx, *Capital*, vol. 1, pp. 918, 889.

22 Paul Sweezy, *The Theory of Capitalist Development: Principles of Marxian Political Economy*, New York: Monthly Review Press, 1942.

23 Paul M. Sweezy and Maurice Dobb, 'The Transition from Feudalism to Capitalism', *Science and Society* 14, no. 2 (1950), pp. 134–67.

24 Robert Brenner, 'The Origins of Capitalist Development: A Critique of Neo-Smithian Marxism', *New Left Review* 1/104 (1977), p. 43.

25 Meiksins Wood, *The Origin of Capitalism*, p. 54.

26 Robert Brenner, 'Agrarian Class Structure and Economic Development in Pre-Industrial Europe', *Past and Present* 70 (1976), p. 53.

27 André Gunder Frank, *Dependent Accumulation and Underdevelopment*, London: Macmillan, 1982, pp. 2–3.

28 Albert Bergesen, 'The Critique of World-System Theory: Class Relations or Division of Labor?', *Sociological Theory* 2 (1984), p. 367.

29 Immanuel Maurice Wallerstein, *The Capitalist World-Economy: Essays*, Cambridge: Cambridge University Press, 1979, p. 18.

30 Wallerstein, *The Modern World-System*, vol. 1, ch. 2.

31 Perry Anderson, *Passages from Antiquity to Feudalism*, London: New Left Books, 1974; Perry Anderson, *Lineages of the Absolutist State*, London: Verso, 2013.

32 Robert A. Denemark and Kenneth P. Thomas, 'The Brenner–Wallerstein Debate', *International Studies Quarterly* 32, no. 1 (1988), pp. 47–65.

33 Chris Wickham, 'How Did the Feudal Economy Work? The Economic Logic of Medieval Societies', *Past and Present* 251, no. 1 (2021), pp. 3–40.

34 Eric Williams, *Capitalism and Slavery*, 3rd edn, Chapel Hill: University of North Carolina Press, 2021.

35 Robin Blackburn, *The Making of New World Slavery: From the Baroque to the Modern, 1492–1800*, London: Verso, 2010, p. 572.

36 The total number of enslaved persons transported, including years after 1807, was 10.6 million. David Eltis and Stanley L. Engerman, 'The Importance of Slavery and the Slave Trade to Industrializing Britain', *Journal of Economic History* 60, no. 1 (2000), pp. 123–44.

37 Barbara Lewis Solow, *Slavery and the Rise of the Atlantic System*, Cambridge: Cambridge University Press, 1991.

38 Stephan Heblich et al., 'Slavery and the British Industrial Revolution', *NBER Working Paper Series*, 2022.

39 John Stuart Mill, *Principles of Political Economy*, part 2, ed. John Mercel Robson, Toronto: Toronto University Press, 1965, pp. 256–7.

40 Karl Marx, *The Poverty of Philosophy*, Moscow: Foreign Languages Publishing House, 2013; Marx, *Capital*, vol. 1, p. 803.

41 Wickham, 'How Did the Feudal Economy Work?'.

42 Alan Harding, *Medieval Law and the Foundations of the State*, Oxford: Oxford University Press, 2002, p. 224.

43 Edward Miller and J. Hatcher, *Medieval England: Rural Society and Economic Change, 1086–1348*, Longman, 1978, p. xi.

44 Mark Bailey, *The Decline of Serfdom in Late Medieval England: From Bondage to Freedom*, Boydell & Brewer, 2014.

45 Slavery, in fact, was not officially abolished until the nineteenth century. After the Norman Conquest of England in the eleventh century, slavery gradually evolved into serfdom. Up to 14,000 slaves (mostly domestic servants) were held well into the late eighteenth century. The Slave Trade Act 1807 abolished the slave trade in the British Empire and the Slavery Abolition Act 1833 banned slavery throughout the Empire.

46 William R. Cotter, 'The Somerset Case and the Abolition of Slavery in England', *History* 79, no. 255 (1994), pp. 31–56.

47 See Karl Marx, *Capital*, vol. 3, *The Process of Capitalist Production*, Harmondsworth: Penguin/New Left Review, 1981, p. 940; Karl Marx, *Theories of Surplus-Value*, vol. 1, London: Lawrence and Wishart, 1969, p. 303.

48 Thomas Piketty, *Capital and Ideology*, Cambridge, MA: Harvard University Press, 2020, p. 294.

49 Stephan Heblich, Hans-Joachim Voth, and Stephen J. Redding, 'Slavery and the British Industrial Revolution', *NBER Working Paper Series*, 2022.

50 Hilary McD. Beckles and Andrew Downes, 'The Economics of Transition

to the Black Labor System in Barbados, 1630–1680', *Journal of Interdisciplinary History* 18, no. 2 (1987), p. 226.

51 Marcel van Der Linden, 'Re-Constructing the Origins of Modern Labor Management', *Labor History* 51, no. 4 (2010), pp. 509–22.

52 Frederick Law Olmsted, *The Cotton Kingdom: A Traveller's Observations on Cotton and Slavery in the American Slave States, 1853–1861*, New York: Knopf, 1953, p. 452.

53 See Clegg, 'A Theory of Capitalist Slavery', p. 78n25. Furthermore, slave labour markets allocated labour more efficiently than nineteenth-century wage labour markets.

54 Van Der Linden, 'Re-Constructing the Origins', p. 513.

55 For a broader application of the 'boomerang' concept to the British Empire, see Kojo Koram, *Uncommon Wealth: Britain and the Aftermath of Empire*, London: John Murray, 2022.

56 Van Der Linden, 'Re-Constructing the Origins', p. 516.

57 Robert Southey, *Journal of a Tour in Scotland in 1819*, London: John Murray, 1929.

58 Marcus Rediker, 'The Common Seaman in the Histories of Capitalism and the Working Class', *International Journal of Maritime History* 1, no. 2 (1989), pp. 337–57.

59 This book was Laborie's handbook *Coffee Planter of Saint Domingo* (1798). See Patrick Peebles and Ralph Shlomowitz, 'The Plantation Tamils of Ceylon', *Journal of Imperial and Commonwealth History* 21, no. 3 (2003), pp. 128–9.

60 Catherine Hall et al., introduction to Catherine Hall et al., eds, *Legacies of British Slave-Ownership: Colonial Slavery and the Formation of Victorian Britain*, Cambridge: Cambridge University Press, 2014, pp. 1–33.

61 Piketty, *Capital and Ideology*, p. 294.

## 3. Property Is Theft?

1 The Grande Ordonnance de Colbert sur les Eaux et Forêts in August 1669, for example, limited the right of gleaning to four months of the year and prohibited the grazing of sheep and the collecting of dead wood.

2 Karl Marx, 'The Theft of Wood', in Karl Marx and Frederick Engels, *Collected Works*, vol. 1, *Karl Marx 1835–43*, London: Lawrence & Wishart, 1975, p. 227.

3 Ibid., pp. 227–8.
4 Karl Marx and Frederick Engels, 'On the Jewish Question', in *Collected Works*, vol. 3, *Marx and Engels: 1843–1844*, London: Lawrence & Wishart, 1975, pp. 146–75.
5 Published anonymously in 1689, the First Treatise contested *jure divino* (the Divine Right of Kings).
6 As King David says in Psalm Cxv. Xvi.
7 John Locke, *Second Treatise of Government; and, a Letter Concerning Toleration*, ed. Mark Goldie, Oxford: Oxford University Press, 2016, p. 15.
8 Ibid., p. 22.
9 Ibid., p. 16.
10 Ibid., pp. 17–18.
11 Ibid., p. 20.
12 Ibid., p. 15.
13 Ellen Meiksins Wood, *The Origin of Capitalism: A Longer View*, London: Verso, 2016, p. 110.
14 William Uzgalis, 'John Locke, Racism, Slavery, and Indian Lands', in Naomi Zack, ed., *The Oxford Handbook of Philosophy and Race*, Oxford: Oxford University Press, 2017.
15 C.B. Macpherson, *The Political Theory of Possessive Individualism: Hobbes to Locke*, Oxford: Oxford University Press, 1962, p. 215.
16 James Tully, *A Discourse on Property: John Locke and His Adversaries*, Cambridge: Cambridge University Press, 1980, p. 138.
17 Locke, *Second Treatise of Government*, p. 42.
18 Tully, *A Discourse on Property*, p. 124.
19 John Stuart Mill, *Principles of Political Economy: With Some of Their Applications to Social Philosophy*, D. Appleton, 1874. p. 278.
20 Adam Smith, *The Wealth of Nations*, Books I–III, London: Penguin Classics, 1999 [1776], pp. 151, 225.
21 Ibid., p. 133.
22 Ibid., pp. 151, 152, 168.
23 Adam Smith, *Adam Smith: The Theory of Moral Sentiments*, ed. Knud Haakonssen, Cambridge: Cambridge University Press, 2002, pp. 215–16.
24 Karl Marx, *Theories of Surplus-Value*, vol. 1, London: Lawrence and Wishart, 1969, p. 366.
25 Ibid.

26 Marx, *Capital*, vol. 1, p. 729.

27 Karl Marx, *Grundrisse: Foundations of the Critique of Political Economy*, London: Penguin Classics, 1993, p. 458.

28 As Marx says, 'the fact that surplus labour is posited as surplus value of capital means that the worker does not appropriate the product of his own labour; that it appears to him as alien property; inversely, that alien labour appears as the property of capital. This second law of bourgeois property, the inversion of the first ... becomes just as established in law as the first. The first is the identity of labour with property; the second, labour as negated property, or property as negation of the alien quality of alien labour.' See ibid., pp. 469–70.

29 Karl Marx, 'On Proudhon [Letter to J.B. Schweitzer]', in Karl Marx and Frederick Engels, *Collected Works*, vol. 20, *Marx and Engels, 1864–68*, London: Lawrence & Wishart, 1985, p. 26.

30 Pierre-Joseph Proudhon, *What Is Property?*, ed. Donald R. Kelley and Bonnie G. Smith, Cambridge: Cambridge University Press, 1994.

31 Georges Gurvitch, 'Proudhon and Marx', trans. Shaun Murdock, *Journal of Classical Sociology* 22, no. 2 (2022), p. 169.

32 Karl Marx, 'The Poverty of Philosophy', in Karl Marx and Frederick Engels, *Collected Works*, vol. 6, *Marx and Engels 1845–48*, London: Lawrence & Wishart, 1976, p. 110.

33 Marx, 'On Proudhon', p. 30.

34 Gurvitch, 'Proudhon and Marx', p. 169.

35 Marx, 'On Proudhon', p. 28.

36 Ibid.

37 Max Stirner, *The Ego and Its Own*, ed. David Leopold, Cambridge: Cambridge University Press, 1995, p. 223.

38 Proudhon, *What Is Property?*, p. 88.

39 Ibid. p. 86.

40 Ibid. p. 93.

41 Proudhon, *What Is Property?*, pp. 114, 119, 128.

42 Marx, 'On Proudhon', p. 29.

43 The German '*urspriingliche*' means 'source', 'original', or 'primary' – perhaps a better translation than the orientalist connotations of 'primitive'. See Marx, *Capital*, vol. 1, pp. 873–947, 916, 922.

44 Ibid., p. 940.

45 Ibid., p. 650.

46 Evgeny B. Pashukanis, *Law and Marxism: A General Theory*, trans. Barbara Einhorn, London: Pluto Press, 1989, ch. 3.

## 4. The Commodification of Labour and Its Limits

1 Karl Marx, 'Economic and Philosophic Manuscripts of 1844', in Karl Marx and Frederick Engels, *Collected Works*, vol. 3, *Marx and Engels, March 1843–August 1844*, London: Lawrence & Wishart, 1975, pp. 229–348.

2 Karl Marx, 'Introduction to the Critique of Political Economy', in Karl Marx and Frederick Engels, *Collected Works*, vol. 28, *Marx Economic Works, 1857–1861*, London: Lawrence & Wishart, 1987. p. 40.

3 Christopher Hill, 'The Poor and the People', in *The Collected Essays of Christopher Hill*, vol. 3, *People and Ideas in 17th-Century England*, Brighton: Harverster, 1985, pp. 247–73, 250.

4 Pamphleteers noted that workers lacking capital couldn't sell their labour at its full market value. In 1677, Andrew Yarranton proposed a national bank to lend to the poor, under the pretence that with capital 'thy fingers and hands are thy own'. Without it, artisans paid high prices for materials, sold goods cheaply, and ceded earnings to wealthier competitors. See Richard Biernacki, *The Fabrication of Labor: Germany and Britain, 1640–1914*, Berkeley: University of California Press, 1995.

5 Quoted by Christopher Hill in Discussion of Conference Paper by Keith Thomas, 'Work and Leisure in Pre-Industrial Society,' *Past and Present* 29 (December 1964), p. 63. In Biernacki, *The Fabrication of Labor*.

6 Karl Marx, *Theories of Surplus-Value*, vol. 1, London: Lawrence and Wishart, 1969, p. 40.

7 Edward Palmer Thompson, *Customs in Common*, New York: New Press, 1993, p. 36.

8 William Blackstone, *Commentaries on the Laws of England*, vol. 1, Oxford: Clarendon, 1765.

9 W.S. Holdsworth, *A History of English Law*, vol. 4, Boston: Little, Brown and Company, 1924.

10 Biernacki, *The Fabrication of Labor*, p. 230.

11 Britain had a delayed development of a formal wage labour market compared with France, which had abolished guilds and corporate controls on labour between 1790 and 1791. The Civil Code of Napoleon recognized labour-power as a freely exchangeable commodity based on individual

contracts. See Michael Sonenscher, *Work and Wages: Natural Law, Politics and the Eighteenth-Century French Trades*, Cambridge: Cambridge University Press, 2012.

12 Biernacki, *The Fabrication of Labor*, p. 243.

13 E.P. Thompson, 'Time, Work-Discipline and Industrial Capitalism', *Past and Present* 38, no. 1 (1967), pp. 56–97.

14 Biernacki, *The Fabrication of Labor*, pp. 230–1.

15 Ibid., pp. 58, 59, 60.

16 *Yorkshire Factory Times*, 3 August 1894, p. 8, and 5 April 1901, p. 8, cited in Biernacki, *The Fabrication of Labor*, p. 57.

17 Biernacki, *The Fabrication of Labor*, pp. 78, 43.

18 Joel Mokyr, Chris Vickers, and Nicolas L. Ziebarth, 'The History of Technological Anxiety and the Future of Economic Growth: Is This Time Different?', *Journal of Economic Perspectives* 29, no. 3 (2015), pp. 31–50.

19 Robert C. Allen, 'Engels' Pause: Technical Change, Capital Accumulation, and Inequality in the British Industrial Revolution', *Explorations in Economic History* 46, no. 4 (2009), pp. 418–35.

20 Christopher Aspin, *The First Industrial Society: Lancashire, 1750–1850*, Preston: Carnegie, 1995.

21 Elizabeth L. Eisenstein, *The Printing Press as an Agent of Change: Communications and Cultural Transformations in Early Modern Europe*, Cambridge: Cambridge University Press, 1979.

22 It also resonated with contemporaneous fears of revolution, evoking the spectre of Jacobinism or a rural equivalent of 'Captain Rock' in Ireland.

23 John Stevenson, *Popular Disturbances in England, 1700–1870*, New York: Longman, 1979, p. 249.

24 Gavin Mueller, *Breaking Things at Work: The Luddites Are Right About Why You Hate Your Job*, London: Verso, 2021, p. 24.

25 Harry Braverman, *Labor and Monopoly Capital: The Degradation of Work in the Twentieth Century*, New York: Monthly Review Press, 1974, p. 123.

26 David Hounshell, *From the American System to Mass Production, 1800–1932: The Development of Manufacturing Technology in the United States*, Baltimore, MD: Johns Hopkins University Press, 1984.

27 Ibid.

28 Karl Marx, *Capital: A Critique of Political Economy*, vol. 1, trans. Ben Fowkes, Harmondsworth: Penguin/New Left Review, 1976, pp. 509, 512.

29 Ibid., p. 528.

30 Ibid., pp. 510, 512.

31 See Paul Edwards and Paulina Ramirez, 'When Should Workers Embrace or Resist New Technology?', *New Technology, Work and Employment* 31, no. 2 (2016), pp. 99–113.

32 CSE Sex and Class Group, 'Sex and Class', *Capital and Class* 6, no. 1 (1982), pp. 78–94.

33 Harriet Bradley, 'From Butties to Robots: Controlling the Labour Process', *Economy and Society* 12, no. 4 (1983), pp. 499–519.

34 For an excellent modern history of this work, see Helen Hester and Nick Srnicek, *After Work*, London: Verso Books, 2023.

35 Nancy Fraser, 'Contradictions of Capital and Care', *New Left Review* 100 (July–August 2016), pp. 102, 112.

36 Friedrich Engels, *The Origin of the Family, Private Property and the State: In the Light of the Researches of Lewis H. Morgan*, ed. Eleanor Burke Leacock, trans. Alec West, London: Lawrence and Wishart, 1972.

37 Marx, *Capital*, vol. 1, p. 711.

38 Alexandra Kollontai, 'Communism and the Family', in *Selected Writings of Alexandra Kollontai*, London: Allison & Busby, 1977, p. 254.

39 Ibid.

40 Christine Delphy, 'The Main Enemy', in Diana Leonard, ed., *Close to Home: A Materialist Analysis of Women's Oppression*, London: Hutchinson, 1984, pp. 47–77.

41 Silvia Federici, *Wages Against Housework*, Bristol: Power of Women Collective and the Falling Wall Press, 1975.

42 Mariarosa Dalla Costa and Selma James, *The Power of Women and the Subversion of the Community*, 3rd edn, Bristol: Falling Wall Press, 1975.

43 Speech by Polga Fortunata quoted in Wendy Edmond and Suzie Fleming, *All Work and No Pay: Women, Housework, and the Wages Due*, Bristol: Power of Women Collective, 1975, p. 18.

44 Angela Davis, *Women, Race and Class*, London: Women's, 1999; Lise Vogel, *Marxism and the Oppression of Women*, Leiden: Brill, 2013; Wally Seccombe, 'The Housewife and Her Labour Under Capitalism', *New Left Review* 83 (1974), p. 3; Juliet Mitchell, 'Women: The Longest Revolution', *New Left Review* I/40 (1966), pp. 11–37.

45 Margaret Coulson, Branka Magas, and Hilary Wainwright, 'The Housewife and Her Labour Under Capitalism – A Critique', *New Left Review* I/89 (1975), pp. 59–71.

46 Wally Seccombe, 'Domestic Labour: Reply to Critics', *New Left Review* I/94 (1975), pp. 85–96.

47 Susan Himmelweit and Simon Mohun, 'Domestic Labour and Capital', *Cambridge Journal of Economics* 1, no. 1 (1977), pp. 15–31, 23.

48 Davis, *Women, Race and Class*. p. 241.

49 Marx, *Capital*, vol. 1, p. 718.

50 Davis, *Women, Race and Class*, p. 243.

51 Marx, *Theories of Surplus-Value*, vol. 1, p. 393.

52 Sungur Savran and E. Ahmet Tonak, 'Productive and Unproductive Labour: An Attempt at Clarification and Classification', *Capital and Class* 68 (1999), p. 122.

53 Anwar Shaikh and Ertugrul A. Tonak, *Measuring the Wealth of Nations: The Political Economy of National Accounts*, Cambridge: Cambridge University Press, 1994, pp. 21–2.

54 Marx develops a similar analytic for the different departments of the capitalist economy. Department I consists of all those activities that produce the means of production or constant capital. Constant capital includes the produced inputs whose value is recovered in the output, such as fixed assets and machinery, raw materials, and some incidental expenses. Department II consists of all the activities that produce means of subsistence for the reproduction of labour-power or variable capital. Variable capital includes the capital advances to purchase labour-power that has the capacity to add more value than its cost to the value of the output. This distinction establishes the difference between productive and non-productive consumption. Services can be produced for Department I as well as Department II since capitalists can buy services as means of production and workers can buy services as part of the necessary means of sustaining and reproducing their lives.

55 Marx, *Theories of Surplus-Value*, vol. 1, p. 186.

56 Karl Marx, *Theories of Surplus-Value*, vol. 2, London: Lawrence and Wishart, 1972.

## 5. Rethinking the Wage and Its Theft

1 Luke 3: 7–14, in Michael Coogan et al., eds, *The New Oxford Annotated Bible with Apocrypha: New Revised Standard Version*, 5th edn, Oxford: Oxford University Press, 2018, pp. 1872–3.

2 This is according to the statistical definition of earnings adopted by the 12th International Conference of Labour Statisticians (ICLS). See 'Resolution Concerning an Integrated System of Wages Statistics', International Labour Organization, 1973.

3 Zoe Adams, *Labour and the Wage: A Critical Perspective*, Oxford: Oxford University Press, 2020.

4 See Eleni Papagiannaki, Dimitris Giraleas, and Emmanuel Thanassoulis, 'Unpaid Overtime: Measuring Its Contribution to the UK Industries' Output', Café Working Paper no. 13, Birmingham City Business School, May 2021.

5 Cited in Joel Mokyr, 'Malthusian Models and Irish History', *Journal of Economic History* 40, no. 1 (1980), pp. 159–66.

6 This is oddly reminiscent of the wage-price inflation spiral discourse post-pandemic.

7 Karl Marx, *Capital: A Critique of Political Economy*, vol. 1, trans. Ben Fowkes, Harmondsworth: Penguin/New Left Review, 1976, pp. 782–802.

8 Adam Smith, *The Wealth of Nations*, Books I–III, London: Penguin Classics, 1999 [1776], pp. 157, 188.

9 Ibid., p. 246.

10 Antonella Picchio, *Social Reproduction: The Political Economy of the Labour Market*, Cambridge: Cambridge University Press, 1992.

11 David Ricardo, *On the Principles of Political Economy and Taxation*, London: J.M. Dent, 1911, p. 11.

12 Marx's mature wage theory was not based on subsistence, though he confesses that he did initially argue that the 'natural' price of labour-power is a minimum wage that corresponds to the value of the means of subsistence necessary for the reproduction of the worker in *Outlines of a Critique of Political Economy*. He corrected this position later in ch. 25 of *Capital* by showing how capitalist production can depress the price of labour-power more and more below its value. Karl Marx, 'Note to the German edition', 1885, in Karl Marx, 'The Poverty of Philosophy', in Karl Marx and Frederick Engels, *Collected Works*, vol. 6, *Marx and Engels 1845–48*, London: Lawrence & Wishart, 1976, p. 127n.

13 Marx, *Capital*, vol. 1, p. 129.
14 Karl Marx, *Marx's Economic Manuscript of 1864–1865*, ed. Fred Moseley, trans. Ben Fowkes, Leiden: Brill, 2016, pp. 99–100.
15 Marx, *Capital*, vol. 1, p. 680.
16 Marx, *Marx's Economic Manuscript of 1864–1865*, pp. 99–100.
17 He continues: 'But it is only the part of this objectified labour for which the capitalist pays an equivalent which forms the cost price for him; the other part of the commodity in which unpaid labour has been objectified, hence a portion of value which the capitalist sells although he has not paid for it, forms surplus-value, the excess of the price of the commodity over its cost price. It costs him nothing.' Ibid., p. 88.
18 Marx, *Capital*, vol. 1, p. 769.
19 Richard Biernacki, *The Fabrication of Labor: Germany and Britain, 1640–1914*, Berkeley: University of California Press, 1995, p. 240.
20 Ibid., p. 693.
21 Marx, *Capital*, vol. 1, p. 694.
22 See the Blue Books 'Report and Evidence from the Select Committee on Petitions Respecting the Corn Laws' (Parliamentary Session of 1813–14) and 'Report from the Lords' Committee on the State of the Growth, Commerce, and Consumption of Grain, and All Laws Relating Thereto' (Session of 1814–15). Marx, *Capital*, vol. 1, p. 698.
23 'Reports of the Inspectors of Factories', 31 October 1860, p. 9, cited in Marx, *Capital*, vol. 1, p. 693.
24 'It is when work passes through several hands, each of which is to take its share of profits while only the last does the work, that the pay, which reaches the workwoman is miserably disproportioned.' Children's Employment Commission, Second Report, p. lxx, n. 424, cited in Marx, *Capital*, vol. 1, p. 695.
25 G.D.H. Cole, *The Payment of Wages: A Study in Payment by Results Under the Wage-System*, Trade Union series no. 5, London: Fabian Research Department, George Allen and Unwin, 1918.
26 For a more in-depth summary of neoclassical wage theory, see Zoe Adams, 'Understanding the Minimum Wage: Political Economy and Legal Form', *Cambridge Law Journal* 78, no. 1 (2019), pp. 42–69.
27 Picchio, *Social Reproduction*.
28 M. Oldroyd, *A Living Wage*, McCorquodale and Co, 1894; Jane Wills, 'The Living Wage', *Soundings* 42, no. 1 (2009), pp. 33–46.

29 See HL Deb. vol. 2 cols 974–1016 (30 August 1909), p. 1007, cited in Adams, 'Understanding the Minimum Wage'.

30 Sidney Webb and Beatrice Webb, *The History of Trade Unionism*, Clifton, NJ: Kelley, 1973.

31 A.L. Bowley, 'Review of the Human Needs of Labour', *Economic Journal* 28, no. 112 (1918), pp. 418–21.

32 United States and Charles I. Bevans, *Treaties and Other International Agreements of the United States of America, 1776–1949*, Part XIII and Art. 427, 1968.

33 'ILO Reaches Agreement on the Issue of Living Wages', International Labour Organization, 2024, ilo.org.

34 This further refines Article 23 of the United Nations Universal Declaration of Human Rights, which states: 'Everyone who works has the right to just and favourable remuneration ensuring for himself and for his family an existence worthy of human dignity.'

35 Living wage benchmark (AFW2020 and CCC estimates) vs average minimum wage; 'Living Wage', Labour Behind the Label, 2019, labourbehindthelabel.org.

36 Plato, *Plato, in Twelve Volumes*, vol. 5, Cambridge, MA: Harvard University Press, 1967, p. 744.

37 Aristotle also expressed a version of this idea (though he claimed Plato's limit was actually five times the minimum).

38 Andrew Edgecliffe-Johnson, 'US Companies Reveal Pay Gap Between Bosses and Workers', *Financial Times*, 15 April 2019.

39 Daniel Thomas, 'Top UK Chiefs Paid 117 Times More Than the Average Worker in 2018', *Financial Times*, 5 January 2020.

40 Tomer Blumkin, Efraim Sadka, and Yotam Shem-Tov, 'A Case for Maximum Wage', *Economics Letters* 120, no. 3 (2013), pp. 374–8.

## 6. Technoligarchy

1 Jathan Sadowski, 'The Internet of Landlords: Digital Platforms and New Mechanisms of Rentier Capitalism', *Antipode* 52, 2 (2020), pp. 562–80.

2 Respectively, see Erik Brynjolfsson and Andrew McAfee, *The Second Machine Age: Work, Progress, and Prosperity in a Time of Brilliant Technologies*, New York: W.W. Norton & Company, 2014; Klaus Schwab, *The Fourth Industrial Revolution*, London: Penguin, 2017; Nick Srnicek,

*Platform Capitalism*, Cambridge: Polity, 2016; and Cédric Durand, 'Scouting Capital's Frontiers', *New Left Review* 136 (2022), pp. 29–39.

3 Matthew Cole, Hugo Radice, and Charles Umney, 'The Political Economy of Datafication and Work: A New Digital Taylorism?', in Leo Panitch and Gergory Albo, eds, *Socialist Register 2021: Beyond Digital Capitalism: New Ways of Living*, New York: Monthly Review Press, 2021.

4 Matt Vidal, 'Postfordism as a Dysfunctional Accumulation Regime: A Comparative Analysis of the USA, the UK and Germany', *Work, Employment and Society* 27, no. 3 (2013), pp. 451, 471.

5 Andrew Glyn, 'Explaining Labor's Declining Share of National Income', G-24 Policy Brief 4, 2007.

6 Cole, Radice, and Umney, 'The Political Economy of Datafication and Work'.

7 These include the Internet Protocol Version 6 (IPv6), exponential advances in computer power and artificial intelligence, the Internet of Things and Services [IoTS], big data, and cloud computing, among others. See 'CyberPhysical Systems (CPS)', NSF 21-551, National Science Foundation, 2021, nsf.gov.

8 *Measuring the Digital Transformation: A Roadmap for the Future*, Paris: Organisation for Economic Co-operation and Development, 2019.

9 *Digital Economy Report: Value Creation and Capture: Implications for Developing Countries*, Geneva: United Nations Conference on Trade and Development, 2019.

10 Martin Kenney and John Zysman, 'The Platform Economy: Restructuring the Space of Capitalist Accumulation', *Cambridge Journal of Regions, Economy and Society* 13, no. 1 (2020), pp. 55–76.

11 Francis Gurry, 'Re-Thinking the Role of Intellectual Property', World Intellectual Property Organization, 2013, wipo.int.

12 Keith E. Maskus, 'The International Intellectual Property System from an Economist's Perspective', in Axel Metzger and Henning Grosse Ruse-Khan, eds, *Intellectual Property Ordering Beyond Borders*, Cambridge: Cambridge University Press, 2022, pp. 3–27.

13 In the 2008 SNA, the term 'intangible fixed asset' was replaced by the term 'intellectual property product'. Section 10.98 defines intellectual property products as 'the result of research, development, investigation or innovation leading to knowledge that the developers can market or use to their own benefit in production because use of the knowledge is

restricted by means of legal or other protection. The knowledge may be embodied in a free-standing product or may be embodied in another. When the latter is the case, the product embodying the knowledge has an increased price relative to a similar product without this embodied knowledge. The knowledge remains an asset as long as its use can create some form of monopoly profits for its owner.' *System of National Accounts 2008*, New York: European Commission, International Monetary Fund, Organisation for Economic Co-operation and Development, United Nations, and World Bank, 2009, p. 206.

14 William Lazonick, *Sustainable Prosperity in the New Economy? Business Organization and High-Tech Employment in the United States*, W.E. Upjohn Institute, 2009.

15 Peter Thiel, 'Peter Thiel: Competition Is for Losers', *Wall Street Journal*, 12 September 2014.

16 Steven Vallas and Juliet B. Schor, 'What Do Platforms Do? Understanding the Gig Economy', *Annual Review of Sociology* 46 (2020), pp. 273–94.

17 *World Employment and Social Outlook 2021: The Role of Digital Labour Platforms in Transforming the World of Work*, ILO Flagship Report, Geneva: International Labour Organization, 2021.

18 Janine Berg et al., *Digital Labour Platforms and the Future of Work: Towards Decent Work in the Online World*, Brussels: International Labour Organization, 2018.

19 Monica Anderson et al., 'The State of Gig Work in 2021', Pew Research Center, 8 December 2021, pewresearch.org.

20 'Amazon to Pay $61.7 Million to Settle Charges It Stole Driver Tips', Reuters, 2 February 2021.

21 *Fairwork United States Ratings 2023: A Crisis of Safety and Fair Work in a Racialised Platform Economy*, Oxford: Fairwork, 2023.

22 *World Employment and Social Outlook 2021.*

23 Veena Dubal, 'On Algorithmic Wage Discrimination', *Columbia Law Review* 123, no. 7 (2023), pp. 1967–8.

24 Office of the Attorney General of the State of New York, 'In the Matter of Investigation of Letitia James, Attorney General of the State of New York, of Uber Technologies', AOD no. 23-040, 1 November 2023, p. 2.

25 Ibid.

26 Dubal, 'On Algorithmic Wage Discrimination', pp. 168–9.

27 *A Minimum Pay Rate for App-Based Restaurant Delivery Workers in NYC*,

New York City Department of Consumer and Worker Protection, 2022, p. 16.

28 Ibid., pp. 17, 8.

29 Ibid., p. 22.

30 *Fairwork UK Ratings 2021: Labour Standards in the Gig Economy*, Oxford: Fairwork, 2021, p. 17.

31 *Fairwork UK Ratings 2023: A Call for Transparency*, Oxford: Fairwork, 2023.

32 Defined by the Living Wage Foundation as £9.90/hour for the UK and £11.50/hour for London at the time.

33 See Matthew Cole et al., 'The Wage and Its Theft via Digital Labour Platforms: Methods of Extracting Unpaid Labour-Time', *British Journal of Industrial Relations* (forthcoming).

34 Focus on Labour Exploitation, *'The Gig Is Up': Participatory Research with Couriers in the UK App-Based Delivery Sector*, Participatory Research Working Paper 3, London: Focus on Labour Exploitation, 2021.

35 'Dying for Data: How the Gig Economy Public Data Deficit Conceals £1.9 Billion in Wage Theft, Runaway Carbon Emissions, and a Health and Safety Catastrophe', Worker Info Exchange, 2 September 2024.

36 Ros Wynne Jones, 'Deliveroo Facing Investor and Staff Revolt as Riders Struggle on Minimum Wage', *Mirror*, 26 March 2021.

37 Emiliano Mellino, Charles Boutaud, and Gareth Davies, 'Deliveroo Riders Can Earn as Little as £2 an Hour During Shifts, as Boss Stands to Make £500m', Bureau of Investigative Journalism, 25 March 2021.

38 Deliveroo prospectus, March 2021, p. 9. At the time, Deliveroo operated in twelve markets, including Australia, Belgium, France, Hong Kong, and Italy, but the UK and Ireland accounted for half of its revenues.

39 Mellino, Boutaud, and Davies, 'Deliveroo Riders Can Earn as Little as £2 an Hour'.

40 The 'Riders' Law' resulted from a tripartite agreement in March 2021 involving the government, trade unions (CC.OO and UGT), and employers' groups (CEOE and CEPYME). The law presumes employment for digital platform delivery workers when employers exert control via algorithms, in line with a recent Supreme Court decision on Glovo (STS 805/2020, 25 September 2020). See 'Spain Approves a "Riders Law"', Industrial Relations and Labour Law (International Organisation of Employers newsletter), May 2021.

41 Jasper Jolly, 'Deliveroo Unveils Plans to Pull Out of Spain in Wake of "Rider Law" ', *Guardian*, 30 July 2021.
42 Lina Guerrero, 'Earnings Call: Uber Reports Robust Q2 Growth, Eyes AV Market Expansion', investing.com, 7 August 2024.
43 'Aslam and Farrar v Uber BV and others [2016] UKET 2202551/2015', Employment Tribunal, 2016.
44 Matthew Cole et al., 'The Problem of Wage Theft via Digital Labour Platforms: Methods of Obscuring Unpaid Labour-Time', *British Journal of Industrial Relations* (forthcoming).
45 'Historic Digital Rights Win for WIE and the ADCU over Uber and Ola at Amsterdam Court of Appeal', Worker Info Exchange, 4 April 2023.
46 Che Panin and Minghe Hui, 'Ele.me Hit by Online Backlash After Delivery Worker's Death', *South China Morning Post*, 8 January 2021.
47 Yuan Yang and Ryan McMorrow, 'Chinese Courier Sets Fire to Himself in Protest over Unpaid Alibaba Wages', *Financial Times*, 12 January 2021.
48 'The Platform Economy', China Labour Bulletin, 21 April 2023.
49 Lai Youxuan, '2020: The Report That Shed Light on Chinese Delivery Drivers' Appalling Working Conditions', Circle 19 for the Right to Information in the People's Republic of China, 30 August 2023.
50 Angela Huyue Zhang, 'Labor Regulation', in Angela Huyue Zhang, ed., *High Wire: How China Regulates Big Tech and Governs Its Economy*, Oxford: Oxford University Press, 2024.
51 Bin Chen et al., 'The Disembedded Digital Economy: Social Protection for New Economy Employment in China', *Social Policy and Administration* 54, no. 7 (2020), pp. 1246–60.
52 'Wai mai ping tai yong gong "an wang": 160 wan qi shou cheng le ge ti hu que bu zi zhi', NetEase, 4 October 2021, 163.com.
53 Zhang, 'Labor Regulation'.
54 *Work in the Planetary Labour Market: Fairwork Cloudwork Ratings 2022*, Oxford: Fairwork, 2022.
55 Namita Datta et al., *Working Without Borders: The Promise and Peril of Online Gig Work*, Washington, DC: World Bank, 2023.
56 Fabian Stephany et al., 'Online Labour Index 2020: New Ways to Measure the World's Remote Freelancing Market', *Big Data and Society* 8, no. 2 (2021).
57 See Berg, *Digital Labour Platforms and the Future of Work: World Employment and Social Outlook 2021*.

58 Carlos Toxtli, Siddharth Suri, and Saiph Savage, 'Quantifying the Invisible Labor in Crowd Work', *Proceedings of the ACM on Human–Computer Interaction* 5, no. CSCW2 (2021), pp. 1–26.

59 *Work in the Planetary Labour Market: Fairwork Cloudwork Ratings 2021*, Oxford: Fairwork, 2021.

60 Kelle Howson et al., 'Unpaid Labour and Territorial Extraction in Digital Value Networks', *Global Networks* 23 (2022), pp. 732–54.

61 Ibid., p. 743.

62 Ibid.

63 Karl Marx, *Capital: A Critique of Political Economy*, vol. 1, trans. Ben Fowkes, Harmondsworth: Penguin/New Left Review, 1976, p. 361.

64 *Fairwork AI Ratings 2023: The Workers Behind AI at Sama*, Global Partnership on AI, report, Oxford: Fairwork, 2023, p. 15.

65 Ibid.

66 Jonathan Haskel and Stian Westlake, *Capitalism Without Capital: The Rise of the Intangible Economy*, Princeton, NJ: Princeton University Press, 2017.

67 Howson et al., 'Unpaid Labour and Territorial Extraction', p. 741.

68 Yuval Abraham, '"Lavender": The AI Machine Directing Israel's Bombing Spree in Gaza', *+972 Magazine*, 3 April 2024.

69 Gabriella Cattaneo et al., *The European Data Market Monitoring Tool: Key Facts and Figures, First Policy Conclusions, Data Landscape and Quantified Stories – D2.9 Final Study Report*, Brussels: European Commission, 2020.

70 Emily Steel et al., 'How Much Is Your Personal Data Worth?', *Financial Times*, 2017.

71 Jakob Rigi and Robert Prey, 'Value, Rent, and the Political Economy of Social Media', *Information Society* 31, no. 5 (2015), pp. 392–406.

72 Jim Thatcher, David O'Sullivan, and Dillon Mahmoudi, 'Data Colonialism Through Accumulation by Dispossession: New Metaphors for Daily Data', *Environment and Planning D: Society and Space* 34, no. 6 (2016), pp. 990–1006.

73 'Dying for Data'.

74 *Monetizing Vehicle Data: How to Fulfill the Promise*, Capgemini Invent, 2021.

75 Jon Keegan and Alfred Ng, 'Who Is Collecting Data from Your Car?', *Markup*, 27 July 2022.

76 *Location Intelligence Market Size, Share, and Trends Analysis Report … 2025–2030*, Grand View Research, 2023.

77 Joseph Cox, 'More Muslim Apps Worked with X-Mode, Which Sold Data to Military Contractors', *Vice*, 28 January 2021.

78 Jon Keegan and Alfred Ng, 'There's a Multibillion-Dollar Market for Your Phone's Location Data', *Markup*, 30 September 2021.

79 Grace Kay, 'What It's Like Working at Tesla's Autopilot Labeling Facilities, Where Your Keystrokes and Bathroom Breaks Are Tracked', *Business Insider*, 3 September 2024.

80 Michael Sainato, '"You Feel Like You're in Prison": Workers Claim Amazon's Surveillance Violates Labor Law', *Guardian*, 21 May 2024.

81 These include: financial (e.g. Graham-Leach-Bliley Act [GLBA]) and health (Health Insurance Portability and Accountability Act [HIPAA]), education (Family Educational Rights and Privacy Act [FERPA]), children (Children's Online Privacy Protection Act [COPPA]), and other sectors.

82 See artificialintelligenceact.eu.

83 Anna Desmarais, 'Which European Countries Have Laws Against Deepfakes?', *Euronews*, 30 June 2025.

84 Evgeny Morozov, 'Critique of Techno-Feudal Reason', *New Left Review* 133/134 (2022), pp. 89–126.

85 Durand, 'Scouting Capital's Frontiers'.

86 Cédric Durand and William Milberg, 'Intellectual Monopoly in Global Value Chains', *Review of International Political Economy* 27, no. 2 (2020), pp. 404–29.

87 See Yanis Varoufakis, 'Quantity to Quality', *NLR/Sidecar*, 2024; Yanis Varoufakis, *Technofeudalism: What Killed Capitalism*, London: Penguin Random House, 2023.

88 Piketty's argument that returns to capital tend to exceed growth (and thus come at the expense of labour) points to the centrality of asset ownership determining distribution, which is fundamental to capitalism. Lisa Adkins, Melinda Cooper, and Martijn Koning make a similar argument in their book on *The Asset Economy*, as do Kean Birch and Fabian Muniesa in their edited book on *Assetization*. Carlos Vercellone's theory of cognitive capitalism also highlights the prevalence of 'free digital labour' and a 'becoming-rent of profit'. See Lisa Adkins, Melinda Cooper, and Martijn Konings, *The Asset Economy*, Cambridge: Polity, 2020; Kean Birch and Fabian Muniesa, *Assetization: Turning Things into Assets in Technoscientific Capitalism*, Cambridge, MA: MIT Press, 2020; Carlo Vercellone and

Antonio Di Stasio, 'Free Digital Labor as a New Form of Exploitation: A Critical Analysis', *Science and Society* 87, no. 3 (2023), pp. 334–58.

89 Varoufakis, 'Quantity to Quality'.

90 Chris Wickham, 'How Did the Feudal Economy Work? The Economic Logic of Medieval Societies', *Past and Present* 251, no. 1 (2021), p. 11.

91 Karl Polanyi, *The Great Transformation: The Political and Economic Origins of Our Time*, 2nd Beacon Paperback, Boston: Beacon Press, 1944 [2001].

92 Jodi Dean, 'Same as It Ever Was?', *Sidecar*, 6 May 2022.

93 Christian Fuchs, 'The Information Economy and the Labor Theory of Value', *International Journal of Political Economy* 46, no. 1 (2017), pp. 65, 89.

94 Ashlee Humphreys and Kent Grayson, 'The Intersecting Roles of Consumer and Producer: A Critical Perspective on Co-Production, Co-Creation and Prosumption', *Sociology Compass* 2, no. 3 (2008), pp. 963–80.

95 Jakob Rigi and Robert Prey, 'Value, Rent, and the Political Economy of Social Media', *Information Society* 31, no. 5 (2015), pp. 392–406.

96 Tomas N. Rotta, 'Information Rents, Economic Growth and Inequality: An Empirical Study of the United States', *Cambridge Journal of Economics* 46, no. 2 (2022), pp. 341–70.

97 Rodrigo Alves Teixeira and Tomas Nielsen Rotta, 'Valueless Knowledge-Commodities and Financialization: Productive and Financial Dimensions of Capital Autonomization', *Review of Radical Political Economics* 44, no. 4 (2012), pp. 448–67.

98 Morozov, 'Critique of Techno-Feudal Reason'.

99 Luc Boltanski and Eve Chiapello, *The New Spirit of Capitalism*, London: Verso, 2018.

100 Jeremy Gilbert, 'Techno-Feudalism or Platform Capitalism? Conceptualising the Digital Society', *European Journal of Social Theory* 27, no. 4 (2024); Cecilia Rikap, 'Capitalism as Usual?', *New Left Review* 139 (2023), pp. 145–60.

101 Robert Michels, *Political Parties: A Sociological Study of the Oligarchical Tendencies of Modern Democracy*, trans. Eden Paul and Cedar Paul, New York: Hearst's International Library Co., 1915.

## 7. Another Work Is Possible

1 John L. Hammond, 'Another World Is Possible: Report from Porto Alegre', *Latin American Perspectives* 30, no. 3 (2003), pp. 3–11.

2 Robin Blackburn, 'Fin de Siecle: Socialism After the Crash', *New Left Review* I/185 (1991), pp. 5–66, 5.

3 Gøsta Esping-Andersen, 'The Three Political Economies of the Welfare State', *International Journal of Sociology* 20, no. 3 (1990), pp. 92–123.

4 Gosta Esping-Andersen, *Social Foundations of Postindustrial Economies*, Oxford: Oxford University Press, 1999.

5 The more familiar 'tap the Admiral' meant inserting a goose quill into a wine or brandy barrel to drink at the King's expense. See Peter Linebaugh, *The London Hanged: Crime and Civil Society in the Eighteenth Century*, Verso, 2006, pp. 127–8.

6 Eddy Cherki and Michel Wieviorka, 'Autoreduction Movements in Turin', in Sylvère Lotringer and Christian Marazzi, eds, *Autonomia: Post-Political Politics*, New York: Semiotext(e), 1980, pp. 72–9.

7 For the US, see David Cooper, 'Balancing Paychecks and Public Assistance: How Higher Wages Would Strengthen What Government Can Do', Briefing Paper, Economic Policy Institute, Washington, DC, 2016; for the UK, see Ursula Huws, *Reinventing the Welfare State: Digital Platforms and Public Policies*, London: Pluto Press, 2020.

8 Orley Ashenfelter and Robert S. Smith, 'Compliance with the Minimum Wage Law', *Journal of Political Economy* 87, no. 2 (1979), pp. 333–50.

9 Ibid.

10 Clyde W. Summers, 'Labor Law as the Century Turns: A Changing of the Guard', *Nebraska Law Review* 67 (1988), p. 25.

11 Paul Foot, *The Vote: How It Was Won and How It Was Undermined*, London: Verso, 2024.

12 Sidney Webb and Beatrice Webb, *The History of Trade Unionism*, New York: Longmans, Green and Company, 1896, p. 2.

13 Peter Gaskell, *The Manufacturing Population of England: Its Moral, Social, and Physical Conditions, and the Changes Which Have Arisen from the Use of Steam Machinery; with an Examination of Infant Labour*, Baldwin and Cradock, 1833, pp. 266, 275. Cited in Richard Biernacki, *The Fabrication of Labor: Germany and Britain, 1640–1914*, Berkeley: University of California Press, 1995.

14 Webb and Webb, *The History of Trade Unionism*, p. 290.

15 G.D.H. Cole, *The World of Labour*, New York: Routledge, 2011, p. 384.

16 Webb and Webb, *The History of Trade Unionism*, p. 290.

17 Mary Davis, 'The Rise of a Mass Labour Movement – Trade Unionism, 1880s–1914', in *Comrade or Brother?: A History of the British Labour Movement*, London: Pluto Press, 2009, pp. 110–25.

18 Vera Khovanskaya et al., 'The Tools of Management: Adapting Historical Union Tactics to Platform-Mediated Labor', *Proceedings of the ACM on Human–Computer Interaction* 3, no. CSCW (2019), pp. 1–208, 22.

19 Ruth Dukes and Wolfgang Streeck, 'Labour Constitutions and Occupational Communities: Social Norms and Legal Norms at Work', *Journal of Law and Society* 47, no. 4 (2020), pp. 612–38.

20 Barry T. Hirsch, David A. Macpherson, and William E. Even, 'Union Membership, Coverage, and Earnings from the CPS', unionstats.com.

21 Anna Stansbury and Lawrence H. Summers, *The Declining Worker Power Hypothesis: An Explanation for the Recent Evolution of the American Economy*, working paper no. 27193, Cambridge, MA: National Bureau of Economic Research, 2020.

22 David Cooper and Teresa Kroeger, 'Employers Steal Billions from Workers' Paychecks Each Year', Economic Policy Institute, 10 May 2017, epi.org.

23 'The Benefits of Collective Bargaining: An Antidote to Wage Decline and Inequality', Economic Policy Institute, 14 April 2015, epi.org.

24 M. Terry, 'Trade Unions: Shop Stewards and the Workplace', in Paul Edwards, ed., *Industrial Relations: Theory and Practice in Britain*, Oxford: Blackwell, 1995, pp. 203–29.

25 *Trade Union Act 2016 – A TUC Guide for Union Reps*, London: Trades Union Congress, 2017, tuc.org.uk.

26 Janice Ruth Fine, *Worker Centers: Organizing Communities at the Edge of the Dream*, Ithaca, NY: Economic Policy Institute and Cornell University Press, 2006.

27 Janice Fine, 'Solving the Problem from Hell: Tripartism as a Strategy for Addressing Labour Standards Non-Compliance in the United States', *Osgoode Hall Law Journal* 50, no. 4 (2013), pp. 813–44.

28 Raise the Floor Alliance, raisetheflooralliance.org.

29 See New York Taxi Workers Alliance, 'November 2, 2023: We Won!',

nytwa.org; see also Office of the Attorney General of the State of New York, 'In the Matter of Investigation of Letitia James, Attorney General of the State of New York, of Uber Technologies', AOD no. 23-040, 1 November 2023.

30 Arizona, Massachusetts, New Mexico, Ohio, and Rhode Island; Iowa, New York, and Texas; Illinois and Maryland; California and Washington.

31 Daniel J. Galvin, 'Deterring Wage Theft: Alt-Labor, State Politics, and the Policy Determinants of Minimum Wage Compliance', *Perspectives on Politics* 14, no. 2 (2016), pp. 324–50.

32 'Uber BV and Others (Appellants) v Aslam and Others (Respondents)', UK Supreme Court, 2021.

33 Alessio Bertolini and Ruth Dukes, 'Trade Unions and Platform Workers in the UK: Worker Representation in the Shadow of the Law', *Industrial Law Journal* 50, no. 4 (2021), pp. 662–88.

34 Natasha Lomas, 'Drivers in Europe Net Big Data Rights Win Against Uber and Ola', *TechCrunch*, 5 April 2023.

35 B. Sanderson, 'Letter from Bryan Sanderson to the Rt Hon Kwasi Kwarteng MP', 22 October 2021, gov.uk.

36 'UK Court of Appeal Confirms Deliveroo Riders Are Self-Employed', Reuters, 26 June 2021.

37 'Deliveroo Noticeboard', GMB Union, 8 October 2025, gmb.org.uk.

38 Tom Mitchell, 'China Drops Charges Against Labour Activist Wu Guijun', *Financial Times*, 9 June 2014.

39 Chan and Hui, 'The Development of Collective Bargaining in China'.

40 See, respectively, 'Historic Digital Rights Win for WIE and the ADCU over Uber and Ola at Amsterdam Court of Appeal', Worker Info Exchange, 4 April 2023; 'Spain: The "Riders' Law", New Regulation on Digital Platform Work', EU-OSHA, 16 February 2022; Fabiane Ziolla Menezes, 'Tech Roundup: What's New with Regulations for Gig Workers', *Brazilian Report*, 2023; Ayesha Minhaz, 'Rajasthan's Gig Law a Step in the Right Direction, but More Needed to Protect Platform Workers', *Frontline*, 10 August 2023. See also Peter Guest, '"We're All Fighting the Giant": Gig Workers Around the World Are Finally Organizing', *Rest of World*, 21 September 2021.

41 Simon Joyce et al., 'A Global Struggle: Worker Protest in the Platform Economy', ETUI Research Paper, Policy Brief, European Trade Union Institute, 2020.

42 Karl Marx, *Capital: A Critique of Political Economy*, vol. 1, trans. Ben Fowkes, Harmondsworth: Penguin/New Left Review, 1976, p. 522.

43 Al Campbell et al., 'Democratic Planned Socialism: Feasible Economic Procedures', *Science and Society* 66, no. 1 (2002), pp. 29–49, 35.

44 Otto Neurath, 'Economics in Kind, Calculation in Kind and Their Relation to War Economics', in *Otto Neurath Economic Writings Selections 1904–1945*, ed. Thomas E. Uebel and Robert S. Cohen, Dordrecht: Springer, 2004, pp. 299–311.

45 Otto Neurath, 'The Problem of the Pleasure Maximum', in Otto Neurath, Marie Neurath, and Robert S. Cohen, eds, *Empiricism and Sociology*, Dordrecht: Springer, 1973, pp. 113–22.

46 Ludwig von Mises, 'Economic Calculation in the Socialist Commonwealth', in *Classics in Austrian Economics*, vol. 3, New York: Routledge, 1994.

47 From Karl Polanyi, Eduard Heimann, Nikolai Bukharin, Frederic Taylor, Frank Knight, H. D. Dickinson, and Maurice Dobb, among others.

48 Tiago Camarinha Lopes, 'Technical or Political? The Socialist Economic Calculation Debate', *Cambridge Journal of Economics* 45, no. 4 (2021), pp. 787–810.

49 Oskar Lange, 'On the Economic Theory of Socialism: Part One and Part Two', *Review of Economic Studies* 4 (1936), pp. 53–7, 123–42.

50 Friedrich A. von Hayek, *Collectivist Economic Planning*, Auburn, AL: Ludwig von Mises Institute, 2009 [1935], p. 270; Friedrich A. von Hayek, 'Socialist Calculation: The Competitive Solution', *Economica* 7, no. 26 (1940), pp. 125–49.

51 F.A. Hayek, 'The Use of Knowledge in Society', *American Economic Review* 35, no. 4 (1945), pp. 519–30.

52 Ludwig von Mises, *Planned Chaos*, Auburn, AL: Ludwig von Mises Institute, 1947, p. 124.

53 Mike Davis, *Old Gods, New Enigmas: Marx's Lost Theory*, London: Verso, 2018, p. xxiv.

54 Karl Marx, 'Value, Price and Profit', in K. Marx and F. Engels, *Collected Works*, vol. 20, *Marx and Engels 1864–68*, London: Lawrence & Wishart, 1985, p. 149.

55 'It is the complete restoration of man to himself as a social, i.e., human, being, a restoration which has become conscious and which takes place within the entire wealth of previous periods of development.' See Karl

Marx, 'Economic and Philosophical Manuscripts', in *Early Writings*, London: Penguin, 1984, p. 348.

56 Jacob Blumenfeld, 'Expropriation of the Expropriators', *Philosophy and Social Criticism* 49, no. 4 (2022).

57 Karl Marx, 'The Civil War in France', in Karl Marx and Frederick Engels, *Collected Works*, vol. 22, *Marx and Engels, 1870–1871*, London: Lawrence & Wishart, 1986, p. 335.

58 The Gotha Programme was the founding document of the Socialist Workers' Party of Germany (SAPD).

59 Karl Marx, 'Critique of the Gotha Programme', in Karl Marx and Frederick Engels, *Collected Works*, vol. 24, *Marx and Engels 1874–83*, London: Lawrence & Wishart, 1989, pp. 75–99, 84–5.

60 Ibid., p. 87.

61 Georges Gurvitch, 'Proudhon and Marx', trans. Shaun Murdock, *Journal of Classical Sociology* 22, no. 2 (2022).

62 The first Russian base Soviets (such as the Putilov factory) were organized by the Proudhonians who came from the left-wing elements of the Socialist Revolutionary Party.

63 Kevin Murphy, *Revolution and Counterrevolution: Class Struggle in a Moscow Metal Factory*, Oxford: Berghahn Books, 2005.

64 Ellen T. Comisso, 'The Logic of Worker (Non)Participation in Yugoslav Self-Management', *Review of Radical Political Economics* 13, no. 2 (1981), pp. 11–22.

65 Charles Hoffmann, *Work Incentive Practices and Policies in the People's Republic of China, 1953–1965*, Albany: State University of New York Press, 1967.

66 Hao Qi, '"Distribution According to Work": An Historical Analysis of the Incentive System in China's State-Owned Sector', *Review of Radical Political Economics* 50, no. 2 (2018), pp. 409–26.

67 Gary Roth, *Marxism in a Lost Century: A Biography of Paul Mattick*, Leiden: Brill, 2014.

68 Jan Appel, *Fundamental Principles of Communist Production and Distribution (Grundprinzipien)*, Movement for Workers' Councils, 1990.

69 'Capitalist joint-stock companies as much as cooperative factories should be viewed as transition forms from the capitalist mode of production to the associated one, simply that in one case the opposition is abolished in a negative way, and in the other in a positive way.' Karl Marx, *Capital*,

vol. 3, *The Process of Capitalist Production*, Harmondsworth: Penguin/New Left Review, 1981, pp. 571–2.

70 Vladimir Ilyich Lenin, 'On Cooperation', in *Lenin's Collected Works*, 2nd edn, Moscow: Progress Publishers, 1965, pp. 467–75.

71 Sidney Webb and Beatrice Webb, *The Consumers' Co-Operative Movement*, London: Longmans Green and Company, 1921, pp. 463–4.

72 Avner Ben-ner, 'On the Stability of the Cooperative Type of Organization', *Journal of Comparative Economics* 8, no. 3 (1984), pp. 247–60.

73 See John H. Pencavel, *The Economics of Worker Cooperatives*, Cheltenham: Edward Elgar, 2013; and Erik K. Olsen, 2013, 'The Relative Survival of Worker Cooperatives and Barriers to Their Creation', in Douglas Kruse, ed., *Sharing Ownership, Profits, and Decision-Making in the 21st century*, Leeds: Emerald, pp. 83–107.

74 Gabriel Burdín, 'Are Worker-Managed Firms More Likely to Fail Than Conventional Enterprises? Evidence from Uruguay', *ILR Review* 67, no. 1 (2014), pp. 202–38.

75 Anjel Errasti, Ignacio Bretos, and Aitziber Nunez, 'The Viability of Cooperatives: The Fall of the Mondragon Cooperative Fagor', *Review of Radical Political Economics* 49, no. 2 (2017), pp. 181–97.

76 William Foote Whyte and Kathleen King Whyte, *Making Mondragón: The Growth and Dynamics of the Worker Cooperative Complex*, Ithaca, NY: Cornell University Press, 2014.

77 Errasti, Bretos, and Nunez, 'The Viability of Cooperatives'.

78 Ibid.

79 Diane Flaherty, 'Self-Management and the Future of Socialism: Lessons from Yugoslavia', *Science and Society* 56, no. 1 (1992), pp. 92–108.

80 Albert Einstein, 'Why Socialism?', *Monthly Review*, 1949.

81 Karl Kautsky, *The Road to Power*, trans. Algie Martin Simons, S.A. Bloch, 1909.

82 Karl Kautsky, 'Practical Work in Parliament', *International Socialist Review*, December 1908, p. 456.

83 Richard L. Harris, 'Marxism and the Transition to Socialism in Latin America', *Latin American Perspectives* 15, no. 1 (1988), pp. 7–53.

84 John Riddell, 'From Marx to Morales: Indigenous Socialism and the Latin Americanization of Marxism', MR Online, 17 June 2008.

85 Michael Albertus, *Autocracy and Redistribution: The Politics of Land Reform*, New York: Cambridge University Press, 2015.

86 Unidad Popular, *Programa básico de gobierno de la Unidad Popular*, Santiago: Instituto Geográfico Militar, 1969.

87 Eden Medina, *Cybernetic Revolutionaries: Technology and Politics in Allende's Chile*, Cambridge, MA: MIT Press, 2014.

88 Raul Espejo, 'Cybernetic Praxis in Government: The Management of Industry in Chile 1970–1973', *Cybernetics and Systems* 11, no. 4 (1980), pp. 325–38.

89 The Light Ramas covered things such as the automotive industry, and the manufacturing of rubber, plastic, electrics, electronics, and light machinery; the Consumer Rama involved agriculture, food manufacturing, textiles, fishing, and so on; the Construction Rama covered forestry, furniture, pulp, cement, building materials; and the Heavy Rama managed steel, heavy chemical, mechanical, and energy.

90 Medina, *Cybernetic Revolutionaries*.

91 Ibid.

92 The State Development Corporation (CORFO) structured the nationalized economy into four primary divisions: consumer goods, light manufacturing, construction materials, and heavy industry. Each division was subdivided into specific industrial sectors, with a dedicated committee overseeing operations in each one. These sectors included both fully state-owned enterprises, grouped under what was termed the Social Property Area, and majority state-owned businesses classified under the Mixed Property Area. In some cases, a single enterprise could encompass multiple production facilities distributed across various locations. See Medina, *Cybernetic Revolutionaries*.

93 Ibid.

94 Ibid.

95 Ibid.

96 Sergio Gómez and Emilio Klein, 'Informe sobre el estado actual de los consejos comunales campesinos', Santiago: ICIRA, 1972; cited in Felipe González and Felipe Vial, 'Collective Action and Policy Implementation: Evidence from Salvador Allende's Expropriations', *Journal of Economic History* 81, no. 2 (2021), pp. 405–40.

97 González and Vial, 'Collective Action and Policy Implementation'.

98 David Duhalde, 'Immediately After the 1973 Chilean Coup, US Socialists Supported Those Fighting for Freedom', *Jacobin*, 11 September 2023.

99 Peter Kornbluh, *The Pinochet File: A Declassified Dossier on Atrocity and Accountability*, New York: New Press, 2016.

100 Theodore Burczak, 'Dictating Liberty', *Review of Political Economy* 26, no. 3 (2014), pp. 368–71.

101 Nathaniel Davis, *The Last Two Years of Salvador Allende*, Ithaca, NY: Cornell University Press, 1985, p. 44.

102 Evgeny Morozov, 'Digital Socialism?', *New Left Review* 116/117 (2019), pp. 33–67.

103 For an example, see Pat Devine, David Laibman, and John O'Neill, 'Participatory Planning Through Negotiated Coordination', *Science and Society* 66, no. 1 (2002), pp. 72–93.

## Conclusion

1 Roland Boer, 'Red Theology: On the Christian Communist Tradition', in *Red Theology: On the Christian Communist Tradition*, Leiden: Brill, 2019, p. 22.

2 Friedrich Engels, *The Peasant War in Germany*, London: George Allen & Unwin, 1927.

3 Anon., 'Tyranipocrit Discovered', in George Orwell and Reginald Reynolds, eds, *British Pamphleteers: From the Sixteenth Century to the French Revolution*, London: A. Wingate, 1948, p. 96.

4 Jacob Blumenfeld, 'Expropriation of the Expropriators', *Philosophy and Social Criticism* 49, no. 4 (2022).

5 In *Capital*, it is the German 'expropriiert', but in *Grundrisse*, Marx employs the more precise phrase 'appropriation without exchange' or 'without equivalent'.

6 John Bellamy Foster and Brett Clark, 'The Expropriation of Nature', *Monthly Review* 69, no. 10 (2018), pp. 1–27.

7 Karl Marx, *Capital: A Critique of Political Economy*, vol. 1, trans. Ben Fowkes, Harmondsworth: Penguin/New Left Review, 1976, p. 929.

8 Ibid., p. 245.

9 This is loosely inspired by Daniel Kokotajlo et al., 'AI 2027', ai-2027.com, 2025.

10 Kropotkin, *Le Révolté*, quoted in David C. Rapoport, 'Terrorism as a Global Wave Phenomenon: Anarchist Wave', in *Oxford Research Encyclopedia of Politics*, 26 October 2017, oxfordre.com.

11 Edward Palmer Thompson, *Customs in Common*, New York: New Press, 1993, p. 15.

12 Karel Kosík, 'The Individual and History', in James Luther Adams, ed., *Marx and the Western World*, Notre Dame, IN: University of Notre Dame Press, 1967, p. 185.

# Index